Gender in African Women's Writing

JULIANA MAKUCHI
NFAH-ABBENYI

Gender in African Women's Writing

Identity, Sexuality, and Difference

INDIANA UNIVERSITY PRESS

Bloomington and Indianapolis

The paper used in this publication meets the minimum requirements of American National Standard
for Information Sciences—Permanence of Paper for Printed Library Materials, ANSI Z39.48–1984

Manufactured in the United States of America

Library of Congress Cataloging-in-Publication Data

Nfah-Abbenyi, Juliana Makuchi, date
   Gender in African women's writing : identity, sexuality, and
difference / Juliana Makuchi Nfah-Abbenyi.
      p.   cm.
   Includes bibliographical references and index.
   ISBN 0-253-33344-X (alk. paper). — ISBN 0-253-21149-2 (pbk. :
alk. paper)
    1. African literature—Women authors—History and criticism.
    2. African literature—20th century—History and criticism.
    3. Women in literature.   4. Women and literature—Africa—
History—20th century.   I. Title.
PL8010.N467   1997
809'.89287'096—dc21   97–13083

1 2 3 4 5   02 01 00 99 98 97

In Loving Memory of My Mother

To you
Ngonda Patricia
The grassroots feminist
I dedicate this work

You never lived past your prime
But your songs and stories
Mold, shape, influence
More than I can tell

But then you always *knew*
You know and bear witness

Contents

Preface

I can trace when the seeds were sown for the writing of this book to as far back as when I attended an all-girl Catholic boarding secondary school, in my native Cameroon. I was in either Form One or Form Two at the time. That year, we were supposed to read Chinua Achebe's *Things Fall Apart*, among other books. Our textbooks had been ordered (as they usually were then) from England, but the books were still at sea when the first term began in September. So one morning, during the literature period, the Reverend Sister brought an LP record and a record player to the classroom. We watched in silence as she proceeded to play the record for us. That was my first encounter with contemporary African written literature. I can still hear the voice, a deep, throaty, male voice that filled our silent classroom, vibrating through the walls: *Okonkwo had just blown out the palm-oil lamp and lain down on his bamboo bed when he heard the* ogene *of the town-crier piercing the still night air.* I was mesmerized by the words, by the voice. I can still remember thinking to myself, literature, African literature was coming to us *from a record.* Certainly, I could not have known then that Chaucer and Shakespeare were beginning to have rivals. I remember vividly how much I had hoped that I would one day write a story and instead of hearing this faceless voice reading it to me, I imagined my mother, though "illiterate" according to Western categorization, reading my story, propelling me into dreamland the same way I felt on that day. She is dead now. She died in the prime of her life, at the youthful age of forty-six, on August 15, 1984.

When I completed Our Lady of Lourdes Secondary School and C.C.A.S.T. Bambili and proceeded to the University of Yaounde, the courses were flooded with male authors, mostly Western, some African/non-Western. Where were the women? I often wondered. Were there any women? besides the Brontës? the Austens? More seeds were thus planted at the University of Yaounde, and their roots grew deeper. I did my graduate research at Yaounde on orature, with emphasis on the representation of women in folktales. While a good majority of my classmates were furiously researching Soyinka, wa Thiong'o, Mongo Beti, I took a short leave of written literature and immersed myself in oral traditions, going to my home village of Beba, recording, transcribing, and translating folktales and lyrics. I was enjoying myself doing something different. Then I went to McGill University in Montreal and I could not pass up the chance to write another dissertation on women, but, this time, in written literature. I knew exactly what I had to do. I had a debt to pay, I had a score to settle with/ for myself. I finally had the chance to let my late mother speak to my work, speak about my work and about herself. She was "illiterate," a devout Catholic; but she was also witty, intelligent, pragmatic, courageous, raised ten children, was an activist, a "feminist" who in many ways grounded and shaped my feminism.

I have over the years tried to figure out what feminism means for me (that will be another book), but I know that in working on this book, some aspects of my African mothers' and my own feminism find themselves written within the text. How else would I as a Beba, Cameroonian, African, "Third World" cum post-colonial woman-as-subject join in this dialogue with feminist literary criticism and the other Western theories that weigh down on our work? This book is, for me, the first in a series of dialogues that I hope to continue to have with Western theoretical perspectives. "Third World" scholars cannot and should not continue to be seen or placed at the consumption end of theory. We must be part of the production of theory as well. That is the main objective of all the many voices that will speak within the pages of this book.

I have chosen to include both Anglophone and Francophone women writers in this book and have decided to read them as a complementary whole without necessarily presenting them as belonging to a distinctive literary tradition because of their linguistic affiliations. This is because I refuse to maintain a dichotomy or promote the splintering of African literature into linguistic camps reinforcing the false notion that these literatures are inherently different, for a number of reasons. My being Cameroonian has a lot to do with it, given our triple (colonial) domination: German, British, French. English and French are Cameroon's official languages. I am of the minority Anglophone population, but our lives are partly grounded in the politics of a dominant Francophone majority population. Although my education is fundamentally Anglo-Saxon (I wrote the London University General Certificate of Education, known as the G.C.E., Ordinary and Advanced Levels), I also attended the University of Yaounde, where the grading system was French (using coefficients as opposed to credits) and degrees were issued in French. When I studied at McGill, the linguistic roles were reversed: I found myself in a bastion of Anglo-Saxon education niched in a Francophone province seeking to define itself as a distinct society from the dominant Anglophone majority. Either way, whether in Cameroon or in Canada, the language barrier did not matter, though the multiple levels of my minority status always did. These two languages and the cultures that they promote have come together so often in my lived experiences that I can comfortably place writers from both traditions in one study without seeking to treat them as two distinct categories.

Even at McGill, I realized that if/when African literature (the literatures of an entire continent) is taught, in most North American universities, it is often subsumed under what is called "Third World Literature," or what the MLA persistently calls "English Literatures Other than British and American," or—more fashionably, these days—under what is known as post-colonial literature. Needless to say, African women writers are often left in the shadows of their male counterparts. It is true that a number of books have been published on African women's writing. A few are on a single author, but the rest are edited collections of critical essays either on one author or on a number of authors. The final impulse that drove my writing of this book, therefore, was the need to do something different. I wanted, as an African woman/literary critic, to do a full-length book on various African women writers, from various linguistic/(post)colonial traditions. I selected authors, some whose work has received a lot of critical attention (Emecheta, Head); and some whose work, comparatively, has not, though interest has been/is growing (Liking, Beyala, Tlali, Zanga Tsogo, Dangarembga). Even with well-known authors like Bâ and Aidoo, I chose from among their novels that have received the least attention. Consequently, I have sometimes been very generous with my quotations, not only because they make the points I want to emphasize but also because by letting these women's words speak eloquently for themselves, I am fulfilling one of my goals in writing this book.

Acknowledgments

I have had to overcome multiple hurdles as I worked on this project. I could not have done it without the help of many people who knowingly or unknowingly contributed to the writing of my manuscript. I cannot thank everyone on these pages, but I wish to offer my profound gratitude to the following:

My parents, John Nfah Nkanah and Patricia Ngonda Afuba, and my nine brothers and sisters: Jude Nkontemur, Sulpitius Ndeh, Mary Baba, Ezekiel Takumberh, Marcellus Ndoh, Eustace Mbaka, Sylvester Nsemelah, Timothy Afuobne, and Gertrude Ngwemeti.

My husband, Amos Sam-Abbenyi, for all his love, support, encouragement, and the sacrifices he has had to make to enable me to pursue my dreams. For always making me see the speck in my eye that I took for a log. For taking care of the kids all these years and doing an excellent job. To him, and my children, Patricia Ekwe, Adeline Tito, and Abbenyi wa Abbenyi, I am most grateful for the letters, the giggles, the tears, the laughter, the love, and the friendship.

All my mothers and fathers (aunts and uncles) and cousins back home, who pour libation for my safety and well-being in distant lands.

For all their friendship, encouragement, and unending support, I wish to thank Eloïse Brière, Carrol Coates, Sarah Westphal, and Rosemarie Schade.

Special thanks go to my brother, Jude Nfah, and the anonymous reviewers, for reading my manuscript and sharing valuable comments.

Gender in African Women's Writing

Introduction

In October of 1985, Michigan State University sponsored a conference, "The Black Woman Writer and the Diaspora." A selection of the presentations made at this conference were published in a special issue of *The Black Scholar*.[1] In her editorial introducing this issue, Gloria T. Hull writes:

> One of the most dramatic changes in the literary world over the last decade has been the blossoming of a large corps of female writers, poets, critics. It is not that black women writers did not exist prior to this period, but the black literary scene had historically been predominantly a male preserve. On the one hand, a white, male-dominated publishing industry hadn't seen fit to publish the works of black women writers; on the other hand, even among the black intelligentsia, only the male articulation of the black experience had been viewed as worthy of literary expression. In conjunction with the growth of a movement for women's liberation, however, this situation has dramatically been reversed in recent years. . . . In the process black women are currently making a valuable contribution to the U.S. literary landscape, bringing their own experiences as women to life in the form of exciting female characters who confront not only a racist world but a sexist one.

The changes alluded to by Hull did not occur on their own. Black women/feminists in America who had embraced the women's movement were soon to raise their voices in protest against what they considered to be the politics of exclusion, bigotry, and homophobia of a predominantly white, middle-class feminist movement.[2]

These black women/feminists sought to speak out and bring their own (her)stories to the forefront, to express their points of view on (black) women's culture, on (black) women's silence. They rejected the hegemonic and totalizing conceptualizations of "Woman" by Anglo-American feminists, as well as those presented by African American men, who always claimed to speak for all Negroes and in so doing subsumed or erased the black woman's voice.[3] Black feminists defined and redefined the marginal position of black women as one characterized by double jeopardy,[4] multiple jeopardy, and multiple consciousness.[5] They called for the uplift of black people by rejecting and combating the existent stereotypes of black women, as well as the privileges enjoyed by black male authors within an androcentric African American literary tradition. They also suggested that black women bring to their work a critical self-consciousness about their position as defined by race, class, and ideology.[6] They rightly noted the exclusion of black women writers by white feminist critics both in publications and in the classroom, insisting that not only should black women writers be read and taught, but that they must be studied from a feminist perspective. By so doing, these women articulated the need for critics to value black women's writing as an identifiable literary tradition.[7] African American women's writing has thus gained a lot of ground in academia and within (feminist) literary studies.

The Neglect of African Women's Writing

African women writers have had to endure these same kinds of exclusions and contempt from a male-oriented African literary scene. The study of African literature has long been the preserve of male writers, and despite the enviable position women have occupied as oral artists African women writers were not given the attention they deserved; even after the advent of the feminist movement, the male voice continued to be the dominant one.[8] Lloyd Brown best expresses this dilemma in his *Women Writers in Black Africa*, published in 1981:

> [I]nterest in African literature continues to grow, and there is every reason to believe that the African writer will be heard and studied for a long time to come, as artist, social analyst, and literary critic. But in all of this, African literature has to be understood as a literature by African men, for interest in African literature has, with very rare exceptions, excluded women writers. The women writers of Africa are the other voices, the unheard voices, rarely discussed and seldom accorded space in the repetitive anthologies and the predictably male-oriented studies in the field. Relatively few literary magazines and scholarly journals, in the West and in Africa itself, have found significant space or time for African women writers. The ignoring of African women writers on the continent has become a tradition, implicit, rather than formally stated, but a tradition nonetheless—and a rather unfortunate one at that. (3)

A number of reasons have been offered to justify why African women writers have generally been ignored, excluded, and/or forgotten. It has been suggested that African women's late arrival on the African (written) literary scene is one of the major reasons. Other reasons include African family systems, marriage customs, and the system of formal education that for a long time was the preserve of men.[9] Men were the first to be educated and the first to write, while fewer women were sent to school or obtained the university educations that have "traditionally been prerequisites for the writing of African literature in European languages" (Brown 4). Nonetheless, although marriage, family organization, and the paucity of women's education significantly hampered women's written literary expression, these reasons cannot explain why those who did write were simply ignored. After all, Ama Ata Aidoo's play *The Dilemma of a Ghost* was published in 1965; Flora Nwapa's first novel, *Efuru*, in 1966; Thérèse Kuoh Moukouri's *Rencontres essentielles*, in 1969. A good number of women have been published since. What happened more often than not was that men—male writers, male critics—promoted their work and the ideas of other men such that even those images of women that were fostered systematically excluded images of women by women.[10]

Ama Ata Aidoo cogently described the problems that the African woman writer has faced, and still continues to deal with, at the Second African Writers' Conference held in Stockholm in 1986. Here she presented a paper, "To Be an African Woman Writer—An Overview and a Detail,"[11] in which she acknowledged gender discrimination and the traditional roles assigned to women within patriarchal society as some of the drawbacks to African women's writing:

> It is definite that anything that had to do with African women was, of all vital pieces of information, the most unknown (or rather unsought), the most ignored of all concerns, the most unseen of all the visibles, and we might as well face it, of everything to do with humanity, the most despised. This had nothing to do with anything that African women did or failed to do. It had to do with the politics of sex and the politics of the wealthy of this earth who grabbed it and who held it (156–57).

Aidoo also criticized the attitudes of publishers and other elements of the book industry. She especially decried the blatant exclusionary practices and lack of attention from the world of (predominantly male) critics, both African and non-African:

> In March of 1985, Professor Dieter Riemenschneider came to Harare to give a lecture on some regional approach to African literature. The lecture lasted at least two hours. In all that time, Professor Riemenschneider did not find it possible to mention a single African woman writer. When this was pointed out to him later, he said he was sorry, but it had been 'so natural'. I could have died. It had been natural to forget that quite a bit of modern African literature was produced by women?

> Why should it be 'natural' to forget that some African women had been writing and publishing for as long as some African men writers? (159)

Aidoo noted that though critical material on women writers has appeared sporadically—either in a few special-topic books or in so-called "special issues" of a few critical journals[12]—even then the criticism undermines women's writing, as it is "often absent-minded at the best, and at the worst, full of ridicule and resentment. When commentary on African women in literature is none of the above, it is certain to be disorganized (or rather unorganized) and choked full of condescension" (165). Aidoo maintains that as writers, African women have the right to be treated as equals, to expect that "critics try harder to give [their] work some of their best in time and attention, as well as the full weight of their intelligence, just like they do for the work of their male counterparts" (168).

Given what these women writers have had to endure, one can understand Aidoo's bitterness. Nevertheless, the plight of the African woman writer has begun to change drastically, partly because of growing interest toward African women and their writing, coupled with the explosion in the mid-1980s of scholarly inquiries on, by, and about women.[13] Although the space that is allocated to the writings of African women in university curricula is still minimal, some progress has been made. Scholars of African literature in Europe and North America are increasingly feeling the need to include at least one African woman writer in their course material. The spirit is also catching on in African universities, given that the curricula of these institutions have traditionally been Eurocentric and/or male-oriented.[14] What this means is that more work is being done on African women writers. Africans and critics are slowly coming to grips with a distinctive and diverse literary tradition that demands to be given as much attention as and/or treated differently from the dominant male literary tradition.

One facet of this male tradition that has come increasingly under attack has been the subservient image that the African male writer has given of African women.[15] They are portrayed as passive, as always prepared to do the bidding of their husbands and family, as having no status of their own and therefore completely dependent on their husbands. Such representation has promoted what Deidre LaPin has suggested is the "classic and inescapable image of wife-mother at the core of the feminine literary persona."[16] These men have been criticized for providing few images of African women as heroic characters, or as self-determined subjects with agency.[17]

The central themes about women that were broached by the poets of the Négritude movement or those who wrote in the Négritude tradition were the first to be severely censured.[18] Foremost was the idealization of precolonial Africa and the concomitant romanticization of the African woman, who is described by Senghor (for example) in his poetry as the symbol of the Earth, of the Nation, as Mother Africa.[19] Senghor went as far as to state that "the African woman does not need to be liberated. She has been free for many thousands of years."[20] This idealization of the African woman that posits her status as transcendental symbol found itself duplicated in African literature with a parallel stress on the supremacy of motherhood, of the fertile mother, of fecundity. This emphasis had the adverse effect of reaffirming women's subordinate roles, given that in the writing and thinking of these male authors, African women were virtually silent observers who simply fulfilled their destiny without questioning it or the structures that sanctioned the roles they were made to assume.

Furthermore, the Mother Africa trope was sometimes converted into the prostitute metaphor, which, as Florence Stratton has argued, is not only ubiquitous to the African male written tradition, its embodiments "are one of its *defining* features."[21] Stratton contends that even though the conflated symbol of mother and whore was sometimes revised by employing woman as the symbol of change within post-independence African nations, the trope ultimately worked against the interests of women.

> Whether she is elevated to the status of a goddess or reduced to the level
> of a prostitute, the designation is degrading, for he does the naming,
> whereas her experience as a woman is trivialized and distorted. Meta-
> phorically, she is of the highest importance; practically she is nothing.
> She has no autonomy, no status as a character, for her person and her
> story are shaped to meet the requirements of his vision. One of these re-
> quirements is that she provide attractive packaging. She is thus con-
> structed as beauty, eroticism, fecundity—the qualities the male Self val-
> ues most in the female Other. (123)

The African woman was thus spoken for; she herself was no speaking subject. She was, as Christopher Miller has pointed out, "a woman who exists on paper." Miller makes these illuminating points in his reading of Senghor's classic poem "Femme noire" [Black Woman]:

> Her mouth is not for speaking directly; it is a condition of *his* lyricism.
> Her voice, which says nothing, is only the organ of a love-object, the
> Loved one. The concluding gesture places the poet in a godlike position
> of promoting the woman to eternal status while at the same time reduc-
> ing her to fertilizer for future generations of poets. While the status of
> 'woman' here is full of ambiguity (she is elevated and debased at the
> same time), there is no doubt about the fundamental inequality of the

sexes. . . . In the days of colonialism and anticolonialism, it was thought that certain forms of liberation had to precede others: first racial liberation, then, eventually, perhaps, gender liberation. Rarely stated explicitly, but highly influential, this thesis is often at work within the history of African literature.[22]

The African woman was not only silent as depicted in print, but was ignored when she herself spoke, when she broke that silence. Brown has rightly stated that "the neglect of the woman as writer in Africa has been an unfortunate omission because she offers self-images, patterns of self-analysis, and general insights into the woman's situation which are ignored by, or are inaccessible to, the male writer" ("African Woman," 495). He goes on to stress the fact (as have other critics)[23] that "these self-descriptions provide us with useful contexts within which to assess the frequently uniform generalizations about African womanhood." Women in their writing have therefore posited the African woman as speaking subject, making their "self-descriptions" the nucleus to challenging "uniform generalizations" by many male authors.

African Women (Writers) and the Issue of Feminism

African critics now generally agree that African women writers offer more dynamic representations of women than the images of subordination often presented by their male counterparts. Although some of the women in these works are still inscribed in traditional or secondary roles centered around motherhood and the family, these same roles have also been sharply problematized by some of the women writers. They have sought to "subvert and demythologise indigenous male writings and traditions which seek to label [them],"[24] and by so doing have claimed the right not only to name themselves but also to "define themselves from the point of view of what they *have* and *do* with their lives, rather than the point of view of what they lack or must not do."[25] They have therefore inscribed in literary discourse an invaluable "generational and cultural continuity" of and for African women.[26] Such dynamism is attributable to the fact that women are now writing about women and bringing not only their points of view but lived experiences as women to their writing.

The works of these women have been hailed as feminist or stemming from a feminist consciousness. But it is worth noting that some male critics have condemned these women writers for the same reasons.[27] According to Femi Ojo-Ade, for instance, feminism breeds the hate and bitterness that underlies women writers' complaints about male chauvinism; as such, "extremism" becomes the "hallmark" of their feminism. It is "the veneer of the progressive striving to become a man" (84). Nancy Bazin articulates a different point of view (and a more acceptable one, I might add). She notes that, "[t]he works of [Emecheta, Nwapa, Head, and Bâ] belie the myth that feminist issues are not important to African women, that African women already have sufficient power, that women choose to support polygamy because they like it, and whatever misery African women suffer can be blamed on the introduction of Western cultures into Africa."[28]

However, some African women/writers are themselves not terribly pleased with being defined as feminist for very personal and political reasons. Consider the following questions and answers:

> Q: You have been identified as a feminist writer. How do you feel about this label?
> A: I am a feminist with a small "f." I love men and good men are the salt of the earth. But to tell me that we should abolish marriage like the capital "F" (Feminist) woman who says women should live together and all that, I say NO! Personally I'd like to see the ideal, happy marriage. But if it doesn't work, for goodness sake, call it off. (Buchi Emecheta in a 1980 interview)
> I write about the little happenings of everyday life. Being a woman, and African born, I see things through an African woman's eyes. I chronicle the little happenings in the lives of the African women I know. I did not know that by doing so I was going to be called a feminist. But if I am now a feminist then I am an African feminist with a small f. (Buchi Emecheta, at the 1986 Stockholm Second African Writers' Conference)
> Q: Why do you refuse to be called a feminist?
> A: I will not be called a feminist here, because it is European. It is as simple as that. I just resent that . . . I don't like being defined by them . . . It is just that it comes from outside and I don't like people dictating to me. I do believe in the African type of feminism. They call it womanism, because, you see, you Europeans don't worry about water, you don't worry about schooling, you are so well off. Now, I buy land, and I say, 'Okay, I can't build on it, I have no money, so I give it to some women to start planting.' That is my brand of feminism. (Buchi Emecheta in a 1989 interview)
> Q: What impact has the women's movement had on you as an African woman writer?
> A: The women's movement has definitely reinforced one's conviction about the need for us to push in whatever way we can for the develop-

ment of women. But I don't think that one woke up one morning and found that they were talking about the development of women, and one should also join the bandwagon—no. What it has done is that it has actually confirmed one's belief and one's conviction. Our people say that if you take up a drum to beat and nobody joins then you just became a fool. The women's movement has helped in that it is like other people taking up the drum and beating along with you. (Ama Ata Aidoo in a 1986 interview)

Q: In this period of "isms" and deconstructed canons, what label would you like for yourself?

A: I identify myself as a black woman writer. In South Africa we live under a pyramid of power, so I regard myself as the voice of the African woman who is oppressed politically, socially and culturally. There is not enough emphasis given to the plight of the South African woman. I insist on this in my collection of short stories called *Soweto Stories*. . . . In that book, I show the terrible predicament of the South African woman. She is oppressed by her man, by the white woman and of course by the system. . . . African women have no voice, no platform and nobody cares. Winnie Mandela has made a difference on the political agenda, but she usually does not speak on women's issues, these issues are not emphasized, they are not considered important. Therefore, I feel that I must address them in my writing. (Miriam Tlali in a 1990 interview)

Q: Are you pleased to learn that publishers are now falling over themselves to secure translation rights [of *Une si longue lettre*] . . . ?

A: Naturally, because this book that has so often been described as a 'cry from the heart', this cry is coming from the heart of *all women everywhere*. It is first a cry from the heart of the Senegalese women, because it talks about the problems of Senegalese women, of Muslim women, of the woman with the constraints of religion which weigh on her as well as other social constraints. But it is also a cry which can symbolize the cry of the woman everywhere. . . . [T]here is everywhere a cry, everywhere in the world, a woman's cry is being uttered. The cry might be different, but there is still a certain unity. There is the social fact of physiology. The fact that she is the bearer of the children. And from the fact of this responsibility, is also the fact of a partner, a man. A man who has not always been loyal to her. I am happy, however, that if this book is translated, there will be many countries who will be able to hear our cry, our own cry. The cry that they utter, the women from these other countries, their cry will not be exactly the same as ours—we have not all got the same problems—but there is a fundamental unity in all of our sufferings and in our desire for liberation and in our desire to cut off the chains which date from antiquity. (Mariama Bâ in a 1980 interview)

I have quoted these women at length so as to let their thoughts and voices speak to this issue of feminism, and also because what they say directly puts into perspective the objectives of this study. What these women writers say underlines the complex nature of feminism for all women and for themselves as African women. They raise a number of issues. They disapprove of, or simply eschew, the word "feminist" (Emecheta, Tlali), because of the implications that they suspect are inherent in such identification. Tsitsi Dangarembga has also stated in an interview that "The white Western feminism does not meet my experiences at a certain point, the issues of me as a black woman. The black American female writers touch more of me than the white ones."[29] Emecheta questions the very context from which the word "feminist" originates—one that is European, Western, literate, developed and affluent. By refusing to be dictated to and/or defined by Western women, Emecheta is alluding to the fact that some African women tend to see feminism as a form of imperialism with a woman's face, an imperialism that has come to impose or dictate its views and visions on African or "Third World" women. It is therefore the neo-colonial tendencies that these women see as intrinsic to feminism that they are actively rejecting. Such neo-colonialism is aptly discussed by Madhu Kishwar in her essay "Why I Do Not Call Myself a Feminist." She examines the situation of women's struggles in India and is alarmed by the fact that

> the general flow of ideas and of labels is one way—from west to east, in the overall context of a highly imbalanced power relation, feminism, as appropriated and defined by the west, has too often become a tool of cultural imperialism. The definitions, the terminology, the assumptions, even the issues, the forms of struggle and institutions are exported from west to east, and too often we are expected to be the echo of what are assumed to be more advanced women's movements in the west.[30]

An example of this, says Kishwar, is the fact that countless Western feminists in the last decade have asked Indian women whether they have "battered women's homes" in India? Underlying this question is the assumption that "not to have such homes is to be at a lower stage of development in the struggle against violence on women, and that such homes will be one inevitable outcome of the movement's development" (5). Aihwa Ong elucidates this point further when she argues that

Western standards and goals—rationality and individualism—are . . . used to evaluate the cultures of non-Western societies. . . . [W]hen Western feminists look overseas, they frequently seek to establish *their* authority on the backs of non-Western women, determining for them the meanings and goals of their lives. If, from the feminist perspective there can be no shared experience with persons who stand for the Other, the claim to a common kinship with non-Western women is at best, tenuous, at worst, non-existent.[31]

These women are also suspicious of a feminism that lays claim to radical separatist tendencies. They claim men as part of their struggle, affirming their heterosexuality without necessarily idealizing this sexual preference or the men with/by whom they define and experience their sexuality (Bâ, Emecheta). They posit the anteriority of an "African feminism" (Aidoo), an unlabeled feminism, and endorse the feminist movement as that which confirms their actions, providing both political and theoretical grounding for the issues that African women have been concerned with for millennia. At the Stockholm Writers' Conference, Aidoo rightly rejected Taban lo Liyong's accusation that African women writers were not keeping the "African house-hold intact" by "going off and joining in dances in lapland which concern only the people of Lapland." As Aidoo responds:

African women struggling both on behalf of themselves and on behalf of the wider community is very much a part of our heritage. *It is not new and I really refuse to be told I am learning feminism from abroad, from Lapland.* Africa has produced a much more concrete tradition of strong women fighters than most other societies. So when we say that we are refusing to be overlooked we are only acting today as daughters and grand-daughters of women who always refused to keep quiet. We haven't learnt this from anybody abroad. (183, emphasis added)

What this means is that before feminism became a movement with a global political agenda, African women both "theorized" and practiced what for them was crucial to the development of women, although no terminology was used to describe what these women were actively doing, and are still practicing, on a day-to-day basis. (It is this fact—that African women were "theorizing" in an empirical, ad hoc way through daily lived experience long before the advent of feminism—that grounds my contention, further discussed in the next chapter, that African theory is embedded in the texts we will consider). In this way the women translate their "cry" or "drumbeat" into a universal war-cry, while at the same time stressing the particularities and/or complex and multiple levels of their own oppression. They believe this oppression cannot be identified by a separatist Western feminism that needs to move beyond an essentialist "physiology" by simultaneously problematizing both the universal and particular nature(s) of women's oppression. As Emecheta convincingly points out, (most) Western women do not have to bother about water or education, this is a given for the latter; meanwhile, for African women, water and education are basic needs. They are a point from which to begin, those very essential needs that are uppermost on their list of requirements for daily survival, those that ground their own feminism, unlike the rejection of marriage and motherhood, the separatism and economic independence, that Katherine Frank claims is intrinsic to an emerging African feminism.[32]

The women's movement has provided one of the spaces where many different drums can be beaten to many different tunes at the same time. Consequently, women in Africa and the diaspora can use this space as a place where they can beat their own drums as well, where they can send out and receive their own messages.[33] Owing to the diverse nature of these voices, it becomes problematic for African women to adopt the word "feminist" that does not adequately speak their experiences but those of a particular Western/privileged group of women, a word that, when used in their African socio-cultural contexts, is often loaded with pejorative connotations. Often, when an African woman is associated with feminism or directly labeled as a "feminist," such labeling incongruously defines her as Western, meaning that she is either condemned or not credited for what she is or does because she is said to be deviant or simply imitating Western women (a negative statement). Carole Boyce Davies has maintained that

> [T]he obvious connection between African and Western feminism is that both identify gender-specific issues and recognize women's position internationally as one of second class status and "otherness" and seek to correct that. An International Feminism to which various regional perspectives are contributed seems acceptable to African women while the European/American model is not. The failure of Western feminists to deal with issues that directly affect Black women and their tendencies to sensationalize others creates antagonisms as does the fact that white women are often partners in the oppression of both African women and men (South Africa as the most overt example). The term "feminism" often has to be qualified when used by most African or other Third World women.[34]

The insufficiency of the word "feminism" (and the controversy surrounding its appropriation) has been asserted by many critics.[35] Some African and

"Third World" women have proposed other terms in lieu of "feminist" and/or "feminism." Alice Walker is known to have proposed the word "womanism," an all-inclusive term that should speak to all women and especially to black women.[36] But Chikwenye Ogunyemi contends that she also "arrived at the term 'womanism' independently and was pleasantly surprised to discover that [her] notion of its meaning overlaps with Alice Walker's."[37] Werewere Liking coined the word "misovire,"[38] and Molara Ogundipe-Leslie, who calls herself a Stiwanist, has advocated the term "Stiwanism" instead of feminism.[39] When these women refuse the label of feminist, it is not because they do not want to side with other feminists; as Trinh Minh-ha points out in an interview with Pratibha Parmar, "Third World" women sometimes have to refuse labels "because it is crucial to keep open the space of naming in feminism" (66). African women therefore have to modify this term to better describe their experiences and the nature of their oppressions.

One can judge from these assessments that Buchi Emecheta and Mariama Bâ combine their struggle for women with the struggles of men. For them, women's subject-hood and sexuality is intrinsically linked with that of men. Experience of this subjectivity, of agency, is an ongoing process wherein women should make choices for themselves. Ama Ata Aidoo is convinced of the importance of the "development of women"—not only African, but all women—and this development (in whatever form) becomes an issue to reckon with in her writing. Miriam Tlali identifies herself as a black woman who wants to speak specifically to the black South African woman and the multi-faceted nature of her struggles against the political, social, historical, and cultural oppression that plunges black women into a struggle not only with their men, but with white wo/men, and the racial, political power structures that erase the black South African woman's voice. As a writer addressing specifically "women's issues," she distinguishes and distances herself from the powerful political figure that Winnie Mandela was. In an interview with Schipper, Tlali laments the fact that she is still the only black South African woman who has ventured to write about feminism. "There is no equality," she says. "If you do something out of the ordinary men are more inclined to see you as a 'fellow man' than to acknowledge that you have accomplished something important as a woman. That would present too much of a threat" (66). This "threat" that men see in (the act of) women's writing is not specific to the South African context. Mariama Bâ sounds the same alarm:

> Dans toutes les cultures, la femme qui revendique ou proteste est déval-orisée. Si la parole qui s'envole marginalise la femme, *comment jugera-t-on celle qui ose fixer pour l'éternité sa pensée?*

C'est dire la réticence des femmes à devenir écrivain. Leur répresentation dans la littérature Africaine est presque nulle. Et pourtant, comme elles ont à dire et à écrire!

Plus qu'ailleurs, le contexte social africain étant caractérisé par l'inégalité criante entre l'homme et la femme, par l'exploitation et l'oppression séculaires et barbares du sexe dit faible, la femme-écrivain a une mission particulière. *Elle doit, plus que ses pairs masculins, dresser un tableau de la condition de la femme africaine.*[40]

[In all cultures, the woman who makes demands or protests is devalued. If the fleeting word marginalizes the woman, how will she who dares to set her thoughts down for eternity be judged?

That explains women's reluctance to become writers. Their representation in African literature is almost nonexistent. And yet, how much they have to say and write!

More than anywhere else, the African social context being characterized by the glaring inequality between man and woman, by the exploitation and the centuries-old, savage oppression of the so-called weaker sex, the woman writer has a special task. She must, more than her male counterparts, paint a picture of the African woman's condition].[41]

No wonder, in the interview with Harrell-Bond, Bâ maintained that "Books are a weapon, a peaceful weapon perhaps, but they *are a weapon*" (214)—one that women must seize and use for themselves. Tlali subverts and uses what others perceive as a threat by addressing in her writing those thorny issues that South African women persistently have to deal with. By emphasizing this multifaceted plight of the South African, she gives voice and a platform where there was voicelessness. That is why Bâ insists that African women owe it to themselves, they have a specific mandate to write, to draw up and review the African woman question.

One can therefore infer that African women writers do not categorize their problems in linear/hierarchical, either/or dichotomies, as would some Western feminists who would privilege a specific agenda: sexism over racism, or sexuality/the erotic over material experiences and the sexual division of labor. These women do not separate one form of oppression from another; neither do they advocate such a separation as might only sensationalize certain issues and sweep equally important issues under the carpet, reinforcing the general ignorance and neglect of the problems of African women. The experience of identity, be it constituted or constituting; and the experience of difference, be it racial or sexual; and the process of reconstructing subjectivity—these are all experienced and lived out simultaneously in the realm of specific sexual politics.

I will take a critical feminist look at the ways in which the women writers whose works are the object of this study subvert (gender) and redefine the contradictions inherent in gender relations by appropriating feminist theories of gender in the African literary context. But I will also examine these post-colonial women's texts through a complementary interrogation of (Western) feminist theories of gender and African (feminist) literary criticism. My intention is to discuss women's subjectivity through the critical use of gender as a category of analysis in feminist research grounded in African women's writing, bringing my lived experiences as African woman/subject to bear on my discussion.

Teresa de Lauretis has stated that gender, both as representation and as self-representation, is constructed through multiple techniques and discursive practices that she has described as "technologies of gender."[42] It is this multiplicity inherent in the use of gender, the complexity of gender relations, and the ways in which they are subverted by sub-Saharan women writers that will foreground my discussions on identity, sexuality, and difference. This study will demonstrate that the subversion of difference and the simultaneous construction of identity, subjectivity, and sexuality are all interlocking issues. In their portrayals of women, these writers actively seek to (re)construct the subject/object dichotomy that has often been used to define the female subject. For millennia, African women have learned to juggle many things at once, and these multiple ways of simultaneously experiencing identity, sexuality, and difference in the construction of subjectivity have come to ground their strengths, not weaknesses.

Chapter 1 will take a critical look at the use of gender by feminist theorists and advance ways in which their theories, as well as those of post-colonial theorists, can be modified and/or appropriated by an African/feminist literary critic for the purposes of feminist research, thereby setting the theoretical parameters that will govern my literary analysis. Chapter 2 will explore the construction of identity in Buchi Emecheta's *The Joys of Motherhood*, Ama Ata Aidoo's recent novel *Changes—A Love Story*, and Tsitsi Dangarembga's first and only novel to date, *Nervous Conditions*. Chapter 3 will examine sexuality in Delphine Zanga Tsogo's *Vies de femmes*, Calixthe Beyala's *C'est le soleil qui m'a brûlée* and *Tu t'appelleras Tanga* (two novels that explore very similar themes and are almost an extension of one another), and Werewere Liking's *Elle sera de jaspe et de corail [journal d'une misovire . . .]*. Chapter 4 will deal with difference in Mariama Bâ's *Un chant écarlate* (translated as *Scarlet Song*), Miriam Tlali's *Muriel at Metropolitan*, and Bessie Head's *Maru*.

After reading these texts, both as "fictionalized theory" and as "theorized fiction," finding and naming African indigenous theory that is autonomous and self-determining, I will conclude that these women writers have used their writing as a weapon to delve into the African woman question, concurrently offering reconstructive insights into feminist and post-colonial theories and the reading of non-Western literatures.

1   Gender, Feminist Theory, and Post-Colonial (Women's) Writing

The concept of gender has influenced, defined, and oriented much of feminist discourse in the past three decades. Donna Haraway has stated that all the modern feminist meanings of gender have roots in Simone de Beauvoir's insight that one is not born a woman. Gender, explains Haraway, is a concept that developed to "contest the naturalization of sexual difference in multiple arenas of struggle. Feminist theory and practice around gender seek to explain and change historical systems of sexual difference, whereby 'men' and 'women' are socially constituted and positioned in relations of hierarchy and antagonism."[1] According to Elaine Showalter, gender has been used within Anglo-Saxon discourse to stand for the social, cultural, and psychological meaning imposed upon biological sexual identity. She further states that while earlier feminist literary criticism was interested primarily in women and women's writing, "[t]he introduction of gender into the field of literary studies marks a new phase in feminist criticism, an investigation of the ways that all reading and writing, by men as well as women, is marked by gender."[2] Feminist scholars were now able to theorize gender beyond the limits of sexual difference. This shift was necessary and significant because sexual difference had been central to the critique of representation in feminist writings and cultural practices of the 1960s and 1970s. Indeed, Sandra Harding has referred to feminist inquiries into the sex/gender system as "a revolution in epistemology."[3] Feminist theorists in recent decades have thus generally drawn from the diversity inherent in feminism(s).

Gender and Feminist Theory

Most feminists differentiate sex from gender.[4] Sex is understood as a person's biological maleness or femaleness, while gender refers to the nonphysiological aspects of sex, a group of attributes and/or behaviours, shaped by society and culture, that are defined as appropriate for the male sex or the female sex.[5] Gender is not a given at birth; only the actual biological sex is. Gender identity then begins to intervene through the individual's developing self-conception and experience of whether he or she is male or female.

Feminist theory has introduced gender as an important category of analysis—one with sociological, cultural, political, anthropological, historical, and other implications, depending on what aspects of gender the theorist is most interested in elucidating.[6] For some feminists, gender is a system of meanings within cultures used to categorize male and female sexuality in hierarchical terms. They argue that men and patriarchal ideologies control women's reproductive and sexual capacities, and that as a result, women are trapped by their reproductive anatomy and by a dogma of compulsory heterosexuality.[7] Other feminists have rewritten the woman's body and reconceptualized the feminine,[8] while others bring to the forefront the importance of mothering and early identification to gender relations, with the assumption that the family is the primary site of gender struggle.[9] Gender has also been seen as a play of power relations that offers men's and women's activities as public and domestic respectively. This opposition rigidly controls the organization of production and manipulates the division of labor into "male" and "female" categories.[10] Some feminists have argued that gender is a social and/or cultural process involving a complex set of relations that inevitably interlock with other relations of age, race, class, ethnicity, ideology, et cetera.[11] Still others stress the importance of the politics of spaces, locations, margins, and identities as they interlock with and alter gender relations.[12] The concept of gender therefore comes to feminist theory and criticism from many different areas.

Feminist literary criticism has for some time sought to apply some of the insights provided by gender theory. But within African literary circles, feminist literary criticism began to gain some ground only as of the late 1980s. As Jean O'Barr rightly points out, the concept of gender is still "rarely a theme for analysis" among African critics.[13] Consequently, the theories on gender that will ground my arguments will more often than not be Western theories. For this reason, I have chosen to include this theoretical chapter, which I deem necessary and important because of my primary sources; and also because, although I am writing this book in North America for a predominantly North American audience, I am also strongly aware of the African audience that must not, cannot, be excluded from its readership.

As an African literary critic working with Western feminist theories, I am confronted with the issue of what I can appropriate for the purposes of my feminist analysis of an African, postcolonial literature. I have therefore opted to take a critical look at some of the different approaches to gender that have been formulated within various areas of feminist theory and criticism, which relate specifically to issues centered on women's bodies; and also to look at how issues of identity and difference directly influence the construction of subjectivity in women's bid for agency and self-determination. I would posit that gender and feminist theory, especially vis-à-vis identity, sexuality, and difference, has not been formulated in ways that are wholly adequate and appropriate for African, "Third World" women's lives and literature. This does not in any way suggest that existing "Third World" or post-colonial theory is not without its own pitfalls.

Post-Colonial Literary Theory

Some critics of "Third World" or post-colonial literature have suggested methods for the reading of these texts that I believe are more often than not grounded in Eurocentric thinking and biases. If Frederic Jameson, for one, views "all third-world texts" as "necessarily" national allegories, Homi Bhabha speaks of an ambivalence in colonial discourse that is captured within post-colonial texts in the form of "mimicry."[14] I contend that it is limiting to treat these texts simply as national allegories or reflections of colonial experience. Although I agree with Bhabha that there is, often, an "ambivalent" element of mimicry embedded in colonial discourse and reflected/transgressed in/by post-colonial texts, I will argue that some of these texts—including the ones I will be analyzing—decisively move beyond "camouflage" and beyond being "almost the same, but not quite." These texts present the cohabitation of a multiplicity of contradictions that cannot be contained only in an "ambivalent," mimetic economy. Such texts can be read as representation that is much more than just "mimetic" and/or oppositional, or continually producing a slippage. My interest lies not with the constant fracturing and undermining of colonialist discourse but, rather, with how these texts offer alternative scripts that subvert internal systems of power, texts whose gaze is not necessarily directed toward the colonialist text.

Ashcroft, Griffiths, and Tiffin take this discussion one step further when they write in their 1989 book, *The Empire Writes Back: Theory and Practice in Post-Colonial Literatures*, that

> The idea of 'post-colonial literary theory' emerges from the inability of
> European theory to deal adequately with the complexities and varied
> cultural provenance of post-colonial writing. . . . Post-colonial theory
> has proceeded from the need to address this different practice. Indige-
> nous theories have developed to accommodate the differences within
> the various cultural traditions as well as the desire to describe in a com-
> parative way the features shared across those traditions. (11)

Although the need for a post-colonial literary theory is undoubted, the difficult issue becomes one of "developing" theo[ries] that in themselves do not simply reflect Eurocentric tendencies. Such theories should neither position these literatures only in opposition to the center (for example, Salman Rushdie's statement on the back cover of the book that "the Empire writes back to the centre") nor posit false notions of the universal. Arun Mukherjee has questioned "the totalizations of both the post-colonialists and the postmodernists that end up assimilating and homogenizing non-Western texts within a Eurocentric cultural economy."[15] The problem with such totalizations, as some critics have argued, is that the term "post-colonial" ends up being a monolithic term that ignores historical specificity and the vital differences between the experiences of colonization, past and present, among both white settlers and non-white (post)colonials.[16] Mishra and Hodge have argued that such homogenization "is clearly aimed at making the diverse forms of the post-colonial available as a single object on the curriculum of the centre,"[17] while Stephen Slemon maintains that center/periphery dichotomies end up "privileging the kind of post-colonial writing which takes resistance to colonialism as its primary objective."[18] As Mukherjee has rightly stated:

> When post-colonial theory constructs its centre-periphery discourse, it
> also obliterates the fact that the post-colonial societies also have their
> own internal centres and peripheries, their own dominants and margi-
> nals. . . . When it focuses only on those texts that "subvert" and "resist"
> the colonizer, it overlooks a large number of texts that speak about
> these other matters [of race, class, gender, language, religion, ethnic-
> ity].[19] (6)

An undifferentiated concept of postcolonialism and postcolonial theory therefore not only robs the so-called postcolonials of their differences but also ignores the power relations inherent in such totalizing categorizations. For, within the broad "post-colonial" category, and further, within those internal centers and peripheries of post-colonial societies, post-colonial women and post-colonial women's writing would "require a different order of theorising, since postcolonial women are like a fragment, an oppositional system, within an overall colonised framework. Women therefore function here as burdened by a twice disabling discourse."[20] I will add that women are not just "a" fragment, but multiple fragments burdened by a discourse that is disabling in multiple ways. As we will see in later chapters, this heterogeneity is captured and contested in post-colonial women's writing using a variety of methods. What is therefore important here for me is the fact that there can be no one, "unified" post-colonial literature or theory, just as there is no one, "unified" feminist theory, but rather feminist theories that offer diverse and differing voices within feminism(s).

When one speaks of the development of indigenous theories as mentioned by Ashcroft, Griffiths, and Tiffin, much therefore depends on one's point of view. I do agree that some indigenous theories have been developed to accommodate the West as well as the differences within various indigenous cultural traditions, but I will add that these theories also question the predominance of the West. It is my contention that indigenous theories have always been there, in the languages and cultures of Africa, in orally transmitted texts, and later on in published fiction. They were not looked into or read as such, however. This point already forecasts the most important theoretical argument that I will make in this chapter, which is that the novels I am analyzing are theoretical texts. The theory is embedded in the polysemous and polymorphous nature of the narratives themselves. These texts reinscribe and foreground teleological, ontological, and epistemological insights and praxes relevant to the specific histories and politics that preceded the fictional texts. I contend that "indigenous" theory is autonomous, self-determining, and exists in unconventional places like fictional texts; such theory can qualify as a kind of performance in print. Werewere Liking's writing offers a good example of what I am talking about. Her writing is heavily grounded in Bassa rituals. Bassa oral tradition therefore provides the theoretical foundation and framework on which her fictional texts are built. In order to fully understand her work, one must have some understanding of the theoretical fabric embedded in her writing and into which the writing is woven. When a *mvet* (instrument) player or griot narrates a *mvet* (epic poem) late into the night, continuing for hours on end, there is a theoretical framework that governs and directs his or her oral performance. In *African Oral Literature: Backgrounds, Character, and Continuity*, Isidore Okpewho maintains that:

> African oral literature is studied side by side with modern African literature because many modern African writers consciously borrow techniques and ideas from their oral traditions in constructing works dealing essentially with modern life. These writers would like to feel that even though their societies have changed drastically from what they were several generations ago and even though they communicate with the world in a language that is not their own, there must be certain fundamental elements in their oral traditions that they can bring into their portraits of contemporary life.[21]

That is why, when I read the texts in this book as fictionalized theory or as theorized fiction, feminist gender theory will find itself both alongside and embedded in the texts.

I will also use personal insights and speak in the first person so as to distance myself from subject/object dichotomies. Feminist theory has reclaimed personal experience and, by so doing, has opened up a space within academe that has hitherto been deemed non-academic, non-abstract. But, although feminist theory has lifted the ban on the first person, it has not necessarily included my personal voice. I am even more comfortable with including my personal insights because African women as scholars and critics have not often had the chance to bring their own voices and experiences to bear on most scholarly research available in print (in articles or especially in book-length analyses). My critical analysis, sometimes grounded in my everyday experience as African woman, can only enrich the arguments that will be made, given that I will be "finding and naming critical theory which is African, melding it with western feminist theory and coming out with an overarching theory that enriches both western and African critical perspectives: [breaking] the cycle of dependency on western critical theory."[22] I also come from an oral traditional background that encourages and demands communal participation in day-to-day creative activities. The personal voice, especially during sessions of oral literature and performance, is encouraged and valued. That is why Achebe once described African art and literature as a "restoration of celebration."[23] The individual voice and participation, therefore, are part and parcel of the theoretical and (communal) critical process. I agree with Barbara Christian who, while condemning what she regards as "the race for theory" driving Western literary criticism, also urges minority and Third World critics to develop ways of reading their own literatures that do not necessarily reflect the often prescriptive ideas of the Western literary theoretical establishment.[24] I also value Henry Louis Gates' suggestion that the challenge of the critic of Afro-American literature is "not to shy away from literary theory, but rather to translate it into the black idiom, *renaming* principles of criticism where appropriate, but especially *naming* indigenous black principles of criticism and applying these to explicate [their] own texts."[25] That is why Anthonia Kalu has argued that it "has become necessary and, in fact imperative, that new approaches to the problem incorporate African ways of knowing. However, that avenue requires the development of strategies that enable the African scholar/researcher to address the African problem from an authentic viewpoint."[26] Or, as aptly put by Kenneth Harrow: "Change and a literary tradition are inextricably linked. To deny African literature the emergence of its own tradition [and critical theories, I might add] is to deny it the power to differ from 'world' literature, or European literature. And to accept that difference without accepting the process of emergence is to impute a stagnation to one corner of literature while generally accepting the power of writers [and critics] to create traditions elsewhere."[27]

My aim in this chapter is therefore twofold: one, to provide a critical discussion on aspects of gender that are relevant to my analysis of gender relations in the novels I am examining, given that gender theory is only beginning to make its way into African literary criticism. Two, to modify (where necessary) or express some of my arguments in ways that can be valuable to a feminist critique of gender in the context of African literature, given that most of the feminists who were writing the theories under consideration did not have African women or their literatures, cultures, or societies in mind. Frankly, Western feminists and critics are notorious for neither reading nor citing Third World critics nor giving them the place within theoretical discussions that they deserve (except for the few that have been "recognized", integrated, and named, and therefore fall within their parameters of thinking). We are often referred to as scholars who cannot and do not "theorize." Such statements are meant to keep us ("Third World" scholars) perpetually at the consumption end of Western theory, as opposed to the production end. They reinforce what Ketu Katrak has described as a "new hegemony being established in contemporary theory that can with impunity ignore postcolonial writers' essays, interviews, and other cultural productions while endlessly discussing concepts of the 'Other,' of 'difference,' and so on."[28]

I contend that African writers and critics are not merely receivers but are makers of theory as well. The nature of their theories and the "rules" (for lack of a better word) that govern their theoretical production and practice is that which needs to be outlined, given that Western readers often have a narrow or limited perspective. I agree with Adrienne Rich's suggestion that theory is nothing else but "the seeing of patterns, showing the forest as well as the trees—theory can be a dew that rises from the earth and collects in the rain cloud and returns to the earth over and over. But if it doesn't smell of the earth, it isn't good for the earth."[29]

Rethinking Feminist Theory and Post-Colonial Women's Writing

The institutions of motherhood and heterosexuality have become central to feminist analysis of gender and sexuality.[30] Although Catherine MacKinnon has stated that sexuality is *the* locus of male power,[31] radical feminists have championed the notion that women's oppression and the disparity in gender relations is to be found in sexual asymmetry (the division of society into two distinct biological sexes) and the sexual division of labor—in the patriarchal, universal male control of women's sexual and procreative capacities. They have challenged the patriarchy's control of women's bodies, especially the constitution of sexual difference through the phallic symbolization described by Freud and Lacan, and have reclaimed the irreducible reality of women's concrete experiences.[32] Sexual asymmetry and women's lack of control over their bodies as it relates to their procreative capabilities and sexual pleasure have thus received much attention within feminist criticism.

I find these contributions valuable, but I will also argue that sexual asymmetry is not as clearly distinct nor as universal as some theorists present it to be. The Nigerian feminist and sociologist, Ifi Amadiume, has shown in *Male Daughters, Female Husbands: Gender and Sex in an African Society* how Igbo women of Nnobi in Eastern Nigeria once drew power from the fact that male-female relationships were mediated by flexible gender ideologies. Obioma Nnaemeka has noted that this flexible gender system permitted women "to assume positions of wealth, power, and authority which, under strict gender definition, would have been the preserve of men."[33] Though not a common phenomenon throughout Africa, and though sometimes class-related, such flexible gender ideologies are important to the discussion of texts by African women writers, given that issues of sexuality and male domination will be grounded in specific cultural tenets associated with male-female social and sexual relationships. For example, Buchi Emecheta shows in her writing how when women are displaced out of the rural areas where the sexual division of labor grants women certain roles and autonomy, and move to urban areas where flexible gender systems are almost non-existent, women often find themselves in a disadvantaged position compared with their men.

What Amadiume describes accounts for a different and new argument within feminist theorizing on sexual asymmetry, male domination, and women's sexuality. Without necessarily glorifying pre-colonial gender relations in these societies, it must be noted that most of the flexible gender relations she describes were rigidified during colonial rule and have become part of the post-colonial heritage in African urban communities. These more rigid, masculinist gender roles failed to assimilate the earlier gender-integrated power structures in which women played major roles. Certain gender roles became fixed in that they had to be performed by either men or women. Among the Ibgo, for instance, indigenous spiritual practices empowered women in the person of the powerful goddess Idemili. Women assumed the roles of goddesses and their high priests could be men. There were also male deities with female high priestesses. When women became Christians, the powerful goddesses were dethroned. Women could no longer assume the roles of deities that had the right to stand in judgement over men or humankind. Of special relevance is the fact that men were generally powerful, but so too were/could be women.

Amadiume has been criticized by Elleke Boehmer for "not always deal[ing] satisfactorily with the continuing predominance of *de facto* patriarchal authority in the community, and the status commanded by the roles of son and husband." I would insist, though, that the separation of gender from sex roles not only creates a clearly defined women's sphere but also accounts for what Boehmer describes as "the independence and self-coherence of women's lives within that 'sphere.' "[34] A good example of the effects of this separation is seen in our (West African) local market economies, where women have long established their own places in the public sphere and are a powerful force to reckon with. In Beba, where I come from, women have spaces/rituals that are exclusive to women that men cannot invade, though they can share in, and vice versa. An example would be our *ndzang* (women's) and *ndoto'* (men's) dances. Either gender can partake in the celebration, on the sidelines, but cannot take control of the space/ritual. The separation of gender from sex roles provides unique spheres, spaces, and locations from which women can constitute and construct identities.

The feminists discussed earlier have limited their analyses of gender inequality to woman's biology and/or her sexuality and how it has been sanctioned either by patriarchy or by the Phallus. Women's sexuality is, on the one hand, controlled by an unbalanced sexual division of labor that manipulates women's procreative activities; on the other hand, woman's body is presented as a pleasure-based entity whose drives have either been sanctioned or repressed. Adrienne Rich's and Monique Wittig's condemnation of compulsory heterosexuality and the marginalization of lesbian women is crucial to delineating the ways in which these practices affect gender relations. But, the critique of motherhood (that views women as forced mothers) and heterosexuality (that views women as sexual slaves), despite its emphasis on women and their rights over their bodies, can be problematical to most African women simply because motherhood and family have historically represented different experiences and social practices to Western and African women. Motherhood is a theme that runs through the writings of many African women writers, and they question whether women are merely forced mothers and/or sexual objects. Emecheta and Bâ show how the presence or absence of children can have devastating and/or empowering impacts on women's lives.

Whereas many Western women may view multiple childbirth as both oppressive and restrictive (to their work, careers, economic well-being, et cetera), most African women find empowerment in their children and families. They use their status as mothers to challenge some of the demands their cultures place on them. They even use this status to make demands and obtain tangible concessions for themselves. Emecheta and Bâ, for example, illustrate how a woman who is a senior wife has at least three things that stand in her favor. These she can use with impunity: one, her position of senior wife; two, her status as a mother; and three, her status as the mother of sons, since her sons are the direct heirs to the family's property. The major problem for African women will not necessarily reside in control over their bodies or motherhood as such, but with a combination of other interrelated issues, such as discriminatory cultural and patriarchal practices that give better socio-economic and/ or political status to mothers, especially mothers of sons as opposed to mothers of daughters (Adaku, one of Buchi Emecheta's characters, suffers discrimination on the basis of the gender of her children, who are all girls); the lack of sex education for young teenage girls; birth control that is nonexistent or subject to restrictive policies; infant mortality and insufficient health care facilities that force some women to lose children and bear more to make up for the numbers that they really desire, or have more children in their search for the sons that they might not have. We will see in the following chapters that the women writers do not separate these issues either. They are all problematized as different facets of women's struggle against patriarchal oppression in their societies.

Women's pleasure and the denial of pleasure for women has also been one of the thorny issues addressed by feminists. In an African context, the exclusive theorization of the erotic is not without its pitfalls, as that conception of the woman's body as openly pleasurable to the *woman* is not often openly debated by either men or women. For some men, woman's pleasure is not spoken of or meant to be spoken about. In some cases, it can be spoken about so long as it gives credit to their virility—in other words, so long as the Phallus both as sexual organ of pleasure and as transcendental signifier is affirmed. For others, women can affirm their pleasure so long as it is done in private with other women-friends; otherwise, she is seen as a slut! The expression of sexual pleasure becomes an even thornier issue in instances of polygamy. As we will see in the next chapter, the protagonist of *The Joys of Motherhood*, Nnu Ego, resents her co-wife, Adaku for her open display of pleasure. The senior wife of a male character in the same novel dies the night that her husband openly gives pleasure to his mistress in their courtyard.

For women, the picture is slightly different. Women do talk among themselves about their bodies. Women teach one another secrets and practice rituals concerning sexuality that they hand down from generation to generation. They sometimes talk about their sexual pleasure, but it is more often than not in relation to that of men. In most African societies where women's pleasure is most often inferred from what they say or do, from how they say or do it, in their day-to-day interactions with men, the theorization of their pleasure as exclusive to women would drive an intolerable wedge between men and women. Moreover, a theory of sexuality that limits itself to the presence, lack of, or denial of sexual pleasure is not only problematical but also negative to those women in Africa who have had to undergo the cruel practices of "female circumcision." I am aware of the fact that some critics might find the expression "female circumcision" to be inappropriate because of the obvious connotation of maleness/manhood in the term "circumcision"; and also because the pain and trauma, as well as the infection, hemorrhaging, sickness, and death that sometimes ensue from excision and infibulation, is not comparable to that experienced with male circumcision. I am using this expression for two reasons: one, because most Africans use it; and secondly, as an all-encompassing term, given that some women writers have used the "egg ritual" in their writing, which does not have a specific term like, say, clitoridectomy, and cannot be subsumed under female genital surgeries, either.

Western feminists tend to zero in on specific issues concerning women in the "Third World," and then sensationalize those hand-picked issues for Western consumption. Many other equally important (contextual) problems that plague the lives of these women are ignored. It is not uncommon to hear some Western feminist scholars at conferences who, when they include a few sentences or paragraph(s) on "Third World" women in their paper, immediately narrow their focus to clitoridectomies/infibulation in Africa. What happens more often than not (and this is from personal experiences as well) is that African women's sexuality seems to end up being synonymous with "clitoridectomy" in Western feminist circles.[35] The fact that this practice is limited to certain areas in Africa, and that the vast majority of African women have not been victims of this awful ritual, does not seem to matter, and neither do the various and multiple contexts of their oppression(s). The fact that these women seem to be condemned and left by the wayside by feminist discourses is more disconcerting given that feminist intellectual exercises tend to stress one thing only, the inability of these victims to experience sexual pleasure.[36]

What I find negative is the fact that a good majority of the feminists who address this issue often *do not* delve into the reasons why it happens, nor do they propose any solutions that can be helpful in the lives of these women. We are told that circumcision takes away their pleasure for life. This is sometimes followed by a plethora of examples that depict African men as inherently savage and violent. What ends up happening is unfortunate, given that in the bid to match African women's (sexual) victimization with African men's brutal nature/patriarchy, the women seem forgotten or remain in the shadow of the discussion that is (supposedly) about them and their sexuality. This issue is particularly problematical to me because my awareness of female circumcision was sparked and has been sustained only since my arrival in North America (Canada and the United States).

I have often wondered why concerned Western feminists do not crusade, for instance, for funding to set up psychotherapeutic clinics (something Western, of which they have a better understanding, although these might not necessarily work) in the countries involved, or more practically, to crusade for funding to be made available to local women's networks in the countries involved, so that these African women, who have proven time and time again that they are masters at networking, can afford to travel (given the economic status of most women) around their communities/countries, come together, talk to one another and seek solutions as individuals within groups, to solving the problems that touch their lives in so many important ways. Local women can therefore obtain valuable counseling and support from each other that can empower them either to collectively or individually protest against this practice (something that is happening already) and/or enable them to deal with their loss, heal, and live fulfilling sexual lives.

The Malian feminist, Awa Thiam, interviewed many African women who spoke and offered viewpoints about their experiences of excision and/or infibulation. Thiam assesses some reasons that are mythical, cultural, and historical associated with these practices. She concludes that the struggle against these practices can work only if the current social structures are challenged within the countries involved. Men and women need to be informed and educated, "so that everyone may take a stand against them."[37] The Egyptian physician, feminist, and activist Nawal el Saadawi has demonstrated in her book *The Hidden Face of Eve*[38] that the circumcision of girls exists in and is re-enforced by a plethora of conditions within patriarchy that range from socioeconomic, to cultural, to political reasons. For example, those who perform these acts find them economically profitable and resist change because they will lose one or their only means of making a living. Under-development and poverty are therefore closely linked with the practice. Men use this practice as a cultural and political weapon to keep women in a position of subjugation in a society where the hierarchization of sexes is important to men, so that they can always define the female sex as inferior to the male sex, thereby legitimizing the prevalent male control over the female sex and especially over her sexuality. Saadawi also describes the devastating psychological traumas that circumcised women suffer, and are, therefore, in dire need of clinics or spaces within which a healing process can begin and thrive. She is convinced that the practice of clitoridectomies, excision, and/or infibulation on women cannot be separated from all the other economic, cultural and political conventions that have fostered, influenced and still advocate its existence. She insists on "recognizing linkages between the individual, community, society, and state" (xv). To dissociate these phenomena would be dangerously limiting and would lead to obvious stereotypical assumptions and definitions, especially of the women who are scarred for life by these practices. Getting men and women, and especially women, to stand together and challenge these social structures is of the utmost importance. I contend therefore that, when (all) African women's sexuality is restricted to an issue of sexual pleasure, reductive and negative feminist politics are the result. In her insightful essay, "Arrogant Perception, World Travelling and Multicultural Feminism: The Case of Female Genital Surgeries," Isabelle Gunning cautions us that "as feminists, we must develop a method of understanding culturally challenging practices, like female genital surgeries, that preserves the sense of respect and equality of various cultures. The focus needs to be on multicultural dialogue and a shared search for areas of overlap, shared concerns and values."[39] It is our inability to develop complex methods of understanding and describing "culturally challenging practices" that I find wanting in feminist discussions on this subject.

Let me use an example from my specific cultural experience to illustrate this point. Violence against women among the Beba is considered a taboo; indeed beating one's wife is as serious a crime as committing suicide through hanging. Both acts are punishable by Beba custom. The perpetrators of battery are made to pay heavy fines. In the case of hanging, libations have to be carried out to cleanse what is considered an abomination, the stigma from which on the one hand weighs down a family for generations, but on the other hand acts as a potent sanction and deterrent of suicide within the larger Beba community. Individuals are thus encouraged to seek other avenues within their families/society in solving their problems instead of resorting to suicide. Similarly, two things are said among the Beba: a man has no right to lift his hand to a woman; only women "physically" fight other women. A man who beats his wife is, by the same token, feminized. Although this feminization of physically abusive men can be interpreted by feminists as insulting to women, as "typical macho" behavior or as an oppressive patriarchal way of thinking, the fact remains that, within Beba culture, women are protected from male violence by the same patriarchal reasoning and punishment. Language and culture thus function in complex, challenging ways and, in this instance, offer an "ambiguous" choice. As a Beba woman I might question this option theoretically, but in practical terms, I am prepared to accept and even embrace it—the deterrence of male violence against women, against me. We need to develop a more complex outlook toward these issues. The problems that define and construct African women's sexuality, therefore, need to be explored beyond the denial or lack of sexual pleasure.

As was mentioned earlier, African women do talk among themselves about their bodies and their sexuality. They have been able to create strong woman-to-woman bonds that empower them with a valuable network of practices from which men are excluded. But the vast majority of these African women have not pushed or are not able to push these bonds to the limits of celebrating lesbian sexual pleasure. They seem to be hemmed in by repressive cultures or what Rich considers to be institutionalized heterosexuality. It is my conjecture that some homoerotic feelings could and do possibly develop between some women in Africa, but they are maintained at a primal level and do not necessarily become sexual. Homosexuality in this case becomes taboo, something whose existence is sometimes "known" but heavily repressed and rarely spoken or spoken about. We will see how Beyala uses the character Ateba to question the silences (specifically women's silences) and prohibitions that for millennia have repressed and suppressed homosexuality in the language, beliefs, customs and culture of her people.

I attended the 17th Annual African Literature Association Conference in 1991, which was exclusively on the African woman (writer). When the issue of lesbianism in the work of Beyala was raised, the reaction of most of the African women in the audience fluctuated between indifference, anger, aggressivity, and even outright contempt. One woman said that lesbianism was not a "problem" in Africa, it simply was not "our problem." The chair of the panel, who evidently agreed, took the floor and angrily said that "we" have other pressing and more important "problems" to worry about. In not so many words, they dismissed the matter except for a vicious undercurrent of presuppositions and insinuations that permeated the room until the end of the discussion. Most African women sometimes have a presumptuous way of talking about lesbians, especially their diaspora lesbian "sisters," either as women who do not know how to handle their men, or as women who have the luxury of "buying into" a culture alien to theirs.

In other words, those women vehemently affirmed their heterosexuality. Reflecting back on this, I can conjecture that affirming their heterosexuality might appear to have been the right thing to do, strategically. Such affirmation gives us better chances of fighting gender oppression than endorsing a poorly understood and universally stereotyped lesbianism, whose chances of "public" acceptance will almost be nil in our African societies. Although, strategically, one might choose to risk this stance, I will maintain as well that this choice continues to stigmatize and perpetuate prejudice against what one can conjecture to be a "silenced" number of lesbian African women, who cannot speak openly about their sexuality and therefore cannot publicly and politically fight for their rights. Heterosexual women find themselves in an "enviable" bargaining position, but it is won at the expense of these silenced others.

I learned at the ALA conference that most African literary critics are not concerned with lesbian or gay issues because this topic is very sensitive and often controversial, or because they view other issues as more pressing. Or, they fall back on the excuse that homosexuality is shunned or repressed by their culture and thought by many not to exist. Furthermore, not many African writers address the issue of homosexuality in their writing, and even when they do, as Chris Dunton has shown in his essay, " 'Wheyting Be Dat?' The Treatment of Homosexuality in African Literature," its use is often either "crudely stereotypical" or "monothematic", one that sees homosexuality as directly linked to and grounded in the African's encounter/experience with the exploitative and alienating Other, in this instance, the West.[40] Dunton also notes that for the few writers who do "exhibit a much deeper imaginative engagement in the condition of homosexuality and in its social psychology . . . the presentation of homosexual relationships remains schematic, intentional" (444–45). I contend that the texts that will be analyzed in chapter 3 are accomplishing the opposite of what some critics are not ready to do, or are reluctant to do. Some critics, for instance, have condemned a writer like Beyala for creating a character with "homosexual tendencies," while others claim that what she writes about is not really homosexuality but strong friendships between women. These texts will thus be inscribing themselves beyond radical feminist protest and at the crossroads of African (literary) critical reticence and resistance.

Most African women would also judge a feminist rejection of heterosexuality as separatist. They would prefer to view sexuality as a contested terrain, one that, as Foucault points out, deals with "a multiplicity of discourses produced by a whole series of mechanisms operating in different institutions" and historical periods.[41] The socio-economic and political implications of male power embedded in the sexual division of labor must be combined with the multiple and varying meanings of women's bodies and sexualities inscribed in the novels that will be under discussion. There can be no clear-cut separation between sexuality, history, economics, and politics in texts that are written about women's lives in a post-colonial context, where some flexible gender ideologies have been replaced by less flexible ones, and where power relations have shifted drastically and have put women in more disadvantaged conditions. An important point that I will make is that these texts are not "duplicating," "reflecting," or "writing back" to radical feminist critiques on sexuality. They are creating a space for themselves by questioning a combination of oppressive conditions that are both traditional and specific to their colonial heritage and post-colonial context, a context that positions their protest beyond the limits of radical feminism.

Women-to-women bonding and networking has been specific to African women's existence and agency for millennia; so too, has been the complementarity of gender roles between African men and women. When a woman writer questions the repression of homoerotic bonding among women, when these writers critique marriage, motherhood, the male use of economic and political power to control women's sexuality and lived experiences, I contend that their texts are, within the context of African and postcolonial literature, doing within the canon something comparable to what radical feminist writings did for the feminist movement starting in the 1960s. The similarity lies not in content, but in the way both reinscribe identity. These texts are not just giving voice, nor are they just reinscribing the question of African women's identity; they are begging and forcing readers, critics (the majority of whom are men), to reflect on the issues that they have hitherto forgotten, neglected or simply brushed aside.

Susan Hekman has written that "[t]he subject/object dichotomy that excludes women from the realm of the subject has had a profound effect on the status of women in the modern era" (94). Hekman is here referring to the universal, unified subject, "Woman." If women have been excluded from the realm of "the subject" in Eurocentric discourses, then Third World women have been "objects" of discourses (Eurocentric, colonial and post-colonial) even more so than Western women. Being the Other of man, the Other of the West, the Other of other (Western/non-Western) women has been as problematical as the place(s) of post-colonial women "as writing and written subject."[42] African and "Third World" women seem to find themselves in an indescribable position within this metonymic chain of otherness, one that I will describe, to borrow Spivak's words, as that of "the historically muted subject of the subaltern woman,"[43] with a difference. If Spivak's subaltern woman is historically muted, I contend the reverse, which is that she has always spoken, she has spoken in alternative ways that have challenged and continue to challenge not only imperialism and colonial discourse but us, the critics as well, who have been slow to or have refused to hear and acknowledge when and how these voices have spoken.[44]

If African and "Third World" women are often left in the shadows, this brings problems of identity and difference to the forefront in post-colonial women's writing. Post-colonial women need to claim a specific identity, one that is crucial to what Patricia Collins has described as that of the "outsider within," because claiming an identity gives to all marginalized groups of women not only the chance to critique gender hierarchies within their own communities from the margins but also the dominant power structures.[45] They can fluctuate between what bell hooks has termed "the margin and the center," they can draw on what Chela Sandoval has described as "oppositional consciousness"[46] while simultaneously using what Linda Alcoff has called "positional perspectives" to construct meaning, subjectivity, and agency.[47] I will contend that African women need to claim an "identity politics" that foregrounds their ability to fluctuate between the margin and the center, wherever these margins and centers might be, but will also enable them to move beyond constructed and constituting margins and centers, creating their own margins and centers along the way.[48] As we shall see later, in Buchi Emecheta's *The Joys of Motherhood*, Nnu Ego's co-wife, Adaku, is a woman who quickly pinpoints the roots of discrimination against her and looks for methods to combat it: she sends her daughters to school instead of marrying them off; she sets up a trade, et cetera. Most of the texts that I will discuss demonstrate a conscious and constant weaving of personal identity politics and positionality.

Since different groups of marginalized women can create new spaces and social locations for themselves within the dominant culture, marginality (be it represented as racial, sexual, historical, or cultural difference) will therefore be the point of intersection for identity politics, the location where identity politics finds full expression. By creating these new spaces and locations, women take the margins to the center and vice versa. This constant shifting subsequently subverts dominant political, economic, cultural conceptions of gender, both at the center and at the margins. What this means for post-colonial women is that they can and need to problematize "their own internal centres and peripheries, their own dominants and marginals" (Muhkerjee 6). If I were to go back to Cameroon today, I would be confronted with different kinds of struggles at different levels and contexts. For example, on the one hand, I will have to explain to other scholars why I call myself a feminist, what I mean when I call myself a feminist, how I practice my feminism; and on the other hand, I will have to explain to many people why I do not want to have any more children when most of them believe that three is not enough, given my social and financial status. These are two very different battles but are very much related.

Post-colonial women therefore have to make use of multiple identity, of the "I" that Minh-ha maintains has "*infinite layers*" (*WNO* 94).[49] They bring to the politics of identity and gender-as-difference, as otherness, a struggle that must actively involve the dominant and dominated, the colonizer and colonized, the First and Third Worlds. That is why, Minh-ha contends, the story of gender-as-difference is a story that places both insiders and outsiders in an arena of contestation and negotiation, because:

> The moment the insider steps from the inside she's no longer a mere insider. She necessarily looks in from the outside while also looking out

from the inside. Not quite the same, not quite the other, she stands in that undetermined threshold place where she constantly drifts in and out. Undercutting the inside/outside opposition, her intervention is necessarily that of both not-quite an insider and not-quite an outsider ("Not You" 76).[50]

What this means is that identity must be constantly constructed in the context of other identities, always shifting depending on whom one encounters. We will see in the next chapter how, in Dangarembga's *Nervous Conditions*, the protagonist's cousin Nyasha's identity constantly shifts depending on her (re)actions towards her father, her mother, or her cousin, Tambudzai. Fixed identity must therefore be de-stabilized and by so doing, fixed relations of gender and power hierarchies can also be dis-organized. This disruption creates simultaneous margins where sexual difference or gender inequalities will find themselves in potentially fluid, though still problematized, shifting locations. African women can, therefore, not only fluctuate between and within identities and subject positions, they can redefine their racial, cultural, historical difference(s).

My arguments can be summarized as follows: my treatment of identity here synthesizes post-colonial and gender theory and moves beyond the strictly "academic" parameters that are assigned to critical theory and practice. This book not only confronts the lack of and neglect of women's fiction writing but, in the same vein, is reclaiming and recovering this fiction and a practice of theory not common to feminist politics and praxis. Recovering women's fiction, therefore, also belongs in the realm of indigenous theory. I emphasise the point that these texts move beyond conventional academic definitions of theory. For instance, after she bears a (male) child, Nnu Ego is told, "You are now a woman," or "You have become a woman." These statements are loaded with a number of gender-related definitions: It is as if gender were discontinuous (as if she is not a woman until the birth of a child then confers womanhood and femininity); is sometimes biologically achieved or lost; and in her cultural context ushers in a status that can either be rejected or assumed and manipulated.

The theoretical framework that I have delineated will show how the writings of African/post-colonial women writers create and redefine the new spaces in the margins of feminist and hegemonic discourses. When Spivak asks, "Can the subaltern speak?" she is also questioning the "desire to conserve the subject of the West, or the West as Subject" (271). My analysis begins in the next chapter with three writers: Buchi Emecheta, Ama Ata Aidoo, and Tsitsi Dangarembga. This chapter will demonstrate how they have reconstituted and reconstructed the multiple, shifting, and sometimes contradictory identities and subjectivities of African women in their writing. They show how these same contradictions are valuable and empowering tools necessary to subverting gender(ed) dichotomies and exigencies, contradictions that are paramount to describing African women's identity, subjectivity, and agency.

2 (Re)Constructing Identity and Subjectivity: Buchi Emecheta, Ama Ata Aidoo, Tsitsi Dangarembga

> Efuru slept soundly that night. She dreamt of the woman of the lake, her beauty, her long hair and her riches. She had lived for ages at the bottom of the lake itself. She was happy, she was wealthy. She was beautiful. She gave women beauty and wealth but she had no child. She had never experienced the joy of motherhood. Why then did the women worship her?

This epigraph is the last paragraph of Flora Nwapa's novel *Efuru* and is the fulcrum from which Buchi Emecheta spins off the story of Nnu Ego in *The Joys of Motherhood*. If Efuru's story is that of one woman's struggles for self-definition despite her barrenness, Nnu Ego's story is that of one woman's attempt toward self-actualization through her ability to bear and raise children. I begin this discussion on the construction of identity by women writers with motherhood not only because these writers "are preoccupied with sexual roles and identity" (Brown 13), but also because motherhood has been the predominant framework of identity for women in African literature, be it from the perspective of male writers or from that of female writers. This is probably because motherhood is so closely linked to understanding African women's lives and identities within their sociocultural contexts.

Male and female writers approach this topic differently. Men have been criticized for their equation of mother with Earth, with Africa, with eternal Beauty; as eternal nurturer, and as metaphor for the creative and/or (nationalistic) revolutionary process. In short, the majority of these men have been accused of idealizing and romanticizing African women by positing an essentialist, beautiful, nurturing, marginal, and often submissive African woman (for example: Chinua Achebe's *Things Fall Apart*, Okot p'Bitek's *Song of Lawino*, Cyprian Ekwensi's *Jagua Nana*, Elechi Amadi's *The Concubine*). What one notices in the writings of most male writers is the fact that they treat "woman as peripheral to the larger exploration of man's experience."[1] A reading of women writers, by contrast, shows how they seek to break away from the dominant male stance, by depicting *women and women's experiences*, women's ways of knowing in women's spaces and locations. *Efuru* and *Idu* are titled after the women whose stories are told by Flora Nwapa, in the same way that *The Joys of Motherhood* is Nnu Ego's story and her struggle with African institutions of motherhood and the awful ironies of "success" as a mother. Similarly, women seem to challenge in their writings that which Davies has described as the "fairytale ending of children, success and happiness" prevalent in the writings of men (249). Molara Ogundipe-Leslie has shrewdly, though sarcastically, noted that "the way African writers enthuse about motherhood, one wonders if there are no women who hate childbirth or have undeveloped maternal instincts."[2] And Mariama Bâ aptly stated that

> As women, we must work for our own future, we must overthrow the
> status quo which harms us and we must no longer submit to it. Like
> men, we must use literature as a non-violent but effective weapon. We
> no longer accept the nostalgic praise to the African Mother who, in his
> anxiety, man confuses with Mother Africa. Women have a place within
> African literature, the place due to them on the basis of their participa-
> tion—side by side with men—in all phases of the liberation struggle,
> and their contribution to economic development. But women will have
> to fight for that place with all their might. (int. qtd in Schipper 50)

For the women who write, identity and "motherhood [become a] site of struggle," with motherhood often interwoven with or presented as an intrinsic or shifting component of women's identity.[3] One would understand Ogundipe-Leslie's exasperation over the fact that "the theme of childlessness has been explored by African female writers so much so that one would wish they would seek other themes" (9) and we will see how the opposite stance is addressed by Emecheta.

In this chapter, I am going to look at the lives of three generations of fictional women. These characters will include Nnu Ego in Buchi Emecheta's *The Joys of Motherhood*, Esi Sekyi in Ama Ata Aidoo's *Changes—A Love Story*, and the cousins Tambudzai and Nyasha in Tsitsi Dangarembga's *Nervous Conditions*.[4] The first group or generation of women are those whose lives extend from the pre-colonial period to the end of colonialism. They are illiterate women, like Ma'Shingayi, Tambudzai's mother, whose lives have been shaped solely by their traditions and cultures, or women, like Nnu Ego, who are trying to make the transition from traditional, rural life to modern, post-colonial life in the cities. The second group of women are children of illiterate women who, in the post-colonial era, get the Western education that their mothers never had. These are women like Esi and like Maiguru, Nyasha's mother. The third group of women are young girls growing up in families and homes in which either the parents or other family members are all very educated people. These are women like Nyasha and Tambudzai. I will discuss the different ways in which their creators (re)construct their identities and subjectivities in a changing African sociopolitical and literary scene, with the intention of bringing out what can be learned from this portraiture of characters by women writers.

Nnu Ego:
Beyond the Problematic of Biological Determinism

Nnu Ego's story in *The Joys of Motherhood* is about childlessness but even more about "child-ness" and Nnu Ego's need for the many children she finally bears, as well as how childbearing shapes her identity. Emecheta uses this theme of motherhood not only to construct Nnu Ego's subjectivity but also to reconstruct women's sexual identity, to move beyond gender as sexual difference. Gender identity is portrayed as biologically achieved through birth and nurturing (especially, of sons). Nnu Ego's experience is no idealized or romanticized picture of motherhood. Her identity, though biologically achieved through childbirth, can only be understood within the context of sexual politics around which having children is inscribed and valued in Ibuza society.

The story begins with Nnu Ego about to commit suicide because of the death of her four-month-old son. The representation of woman's "madness" and mother's milk and breasts are those that capture one's attention from the onset. One begins to wonder why a woman would want to kill herself just because of the loss of a child. One is thus confronted with the centrality of wifehood and motherhood to Nnu Ego's identity, and it is only by understanding and piecing both together that one gets the picture of how the physical and the psychical are intrinsic to one another.

The exchange of women, marriage, child-bearing, and child-rearing are the components around which male-female relationships are grounded in Nnu Ego's society. It is this exchange of women and the right to patrilineality that Nnu Ego grows up to accept as the standard, and which directly shapes her expectations to bear and raise children. Men exchange and inherit daughters and wives (Agbadi inherits daughters and wives through war victories, Nnaife inherits his elder brother's wives when the latter dies). By so doing, they maintain and promote a sex/gender system that "transforms biological sexuality into products of human activity" (Rubin 159). The purpose of these wives is to bear children and to maintain continuity in the family without which they have no place in society. They are nothing.

Nnu Ego is thrown out of her first marriage because she is said to be barren and, to crown it all, she so desperately wants to have a baby that she engages in breastfeeding her co-wife's son. Inducing physical motherhood via breast-feeding becomes the sine qua non of her psychic balance. The flow of milk from her breasts confirms to Nnu Ego that she can bear children. She does not choose the second husband she is married to. This husband is chosen by her father, and even though she does not love Nnaife nor his job as a "laundry man" for a white woman, a job that in her eyes feminizes him, Nnu Ego does not and cannot leave the marriage because of her profound need for children. Nnu Ego is the type of woman who can only validate herself or prove her womanhood by bearing a child. In answer to her threat to leave him because he is, in her words, a "woman-made man," Nnaife retorts:

> "I wonder what good father would take his pregnant daughter back into his home, just because his son-in-law's job doesn't suit her? Your father is well known for his traditional principles. I'd like to see his face when you tell him you don't like the second husband he has chosen for you, es-pecially since your *chi* has consented to the marriage by making you pregnant. If you were not pregnant, it might be more understandable. But not now that the gods have legalised our marriage, Nnu Ego the daughter of Agbadi. As I said earlier, you have to do what I say. Your father cannot help you now."
> "You are not even happy to see me pregnant—the greatest joy of my life!"
> "Of course I am happy to know that I am a man, yes, that I can make a woman pregnant." (*JOM* 50–51)

This verbal exchange delineates a number of points concerning gender rela-tions: (a) Marriage is an institution. The institution of marriage does not change its traditional principles, even if the woman is distinguished by her class (Nnu Ego is the daughter of the powerful and wealthy chief of Ogboli, Nwokocha Agbadi). Marriage and fertility thus define gender. Gender identity is achieved in adult reproduction and procreative capacities, and not in the resolution of the Oedipus complex. (b) Pregnancy legitimizes marriage, be it in the traditional or cultural sense, in the eyes of humans as well as in the eyes of the divine, the gods or the *chi*. (c) Marriage and motherhood domesticate women (Emecheta describes Agbadi's wives as originally arrogant and saucy women who "sink into domesticity and motherhood" after marriage [*JOM* 10]). (d) Pregnancy and reproduction make a woman, a *woman* and a man, a *man*. Pregnancy becomes Nnu Ego's proof of womanhood and Nnaife's proof of manhood, defining their "femininity" and "masculinity," a femininity and a masculinity that is first of all affirmed in strictly sexual terms, and further complicated by the cultural trappings that this affirmation can be brought to bear on men and women.

Nnu Ego's desire to commit suicide is at first incomprehensible to the onlookers who stop her at the bridge. The breasts dripping with milk, milk that signifies that she has borne a child, is adequate proof to the onlookers that she is deviant or even mad, since no woman in her right senses who has borne a child would run away from her mothering responsibilities and her biologically achieved gender. That is why Nwakusor, one of the onlookers, rebukes her, "What are you trying to do to your husband, your father, your people and your son who is only a few weeks old? You want to kill yourself, eh? Who is going to look after your son for you? You are shaming your womanhood, shaming your motherhood" (*JOM* 61). Nnu Ego is even physically assaulted by a woman bystander who accuses Nnu Ego of "disgracing the man who paid for [her]," for forgetting "the tradition of our fathers" (*JOM* 62) and for thinking only of herself. It is interesting to note what little consideration is accorded Nnu Ego, i.e., the woman, the subject who is about to die, and her predicament. All concerns are geared toward the child, the son, her husband, and fathers—the tradition. Only after learning about the death of Nnu Ego's infant son can they rationally reconcile her suicide attempt with the wet breasts. Her predicament is reaffirmed and reinscribed within the Law of the Father. We are told that everyone is relieved that "she is not mad after all," since "they all agreed that a woman without a child for her husband was a failed woman" (*JOM* 62).

Failure to bear children "for one's husband" can therefore be seen as an adequate and acceptable reason for women's madness and death. Foucault has described this type of "madness" as one that guarantees "the solidarity of the family institution, and the safeguarding of society" through the hysterization of women's bodies (*HS* 147). Motherhood is so ingrained in women's psyche that the alternative to the loss of a child is the loss of self, of gender and of identity. The woman's body has no raison d'être when it cannot fulfill its procreative function. Adrienne Rich has aptly criticized the devastating consequences that institutionalized motherhood and the practice of patriarchy has had on women over the centuries. According to Rich, "[t]he woman's body is the terrain on which patriarchy is erected" (*OWB* 55). That is why she has argued for motherhood to be an experience of choice for women, not an institution. Were the practice of motherhood left as a choice, Nnu Ego would not necessarily have yearned for so many children. Nnu Ego is one of those women who would fit the cultural script described by Rich. But, even more so, Nnu

Ego's story brings a new element to Rich's standpoint by clearly demonstrating how gender can be biologically achieved through the experience of motherhood.

Nnu Ego is a woman only by being a mother. Sexuality is fertility and child-rearing. As she proclaims in her own words, "I don't know how to be anything else but a mother" (*JOM* 222). Motherhood is that which gives meaning and agency to her life, without which she vacillates into madness. When she gets married to her first husband, she cannot "give" him any children. When she gets married the second time, she is continuously haunted by dreams of babies, babies being given or taken away from her by her *chi*. These dreams push Nnu Ego into worrying about her own sanity. Her brother-in-law consoles her with these words:

> "I shall come and visit you again when you are really 'mad.'"
> "Mad? Brother-in-law, did you say mad? . . . If you think I shall go mad, brother-in-law, I'd like to go back with you." . . .
> "New wife, I don't mean that kind of madness. I mean the kind that goes like this—" he crossed his arms, couched his shoulders as one would when holding a small baby and rocked his arms —"cootu, cootu! Ha, ha, ha! Cootu, cootu, cootu!"
> Then Nnu Ego laughed too. She returned to the raffia mat bed and did not dream anymore, understanding what he was saying: that women talk and behave like mad people with their infants who are too young to make sense of any such noises. (*JOM* 45–46)

Here again is the implicit, intrinsic link between bearing children, motherhood, happiness, and madness. Women are "mad"—i.e., happy—when they have children, just as women are "mad"—i.e., physically and mentally disturbed—when they cannot have children or when they lose children. In other words, maternal validation is necessary for women's physical and psychical well-being. Nnu Ego only sleeps comfortably without those horrible nightmares because of the consolation that she can and will have children. She learns to tolerate Nnaife as a husband only because he has made her pregnant, "has made [her] into a real woman—all [she wants] to be, a woman and a mother" (*JOM* 53). She finally accepts this man as her husband, and "father of her child, and the fact that this child was a son gave her a sense of fulfillment for the first time in her life" (*JOM* 54). One therefore understands her suicidal enterprise when her first child dies, because losing that child means losing that fulfillment, it means (un)becoming a woman, the only other recourse being madness or death.

Buchi Emecheta has been criticized for presenting "stereotypic portraits of

Africans,"[5] for placing emphasis on sexual roles in the portrayal of her charac-ters, often creating heroines who are confined to their sexual identity.[6] Or, her main concerns are described as evolving around the "biological and marital aspects of women's lives" central to which are "motherhood, bridewealth and polygamy."[7] *Joys* is a case in point, given the centrality of motherhood to Nnu Ego's identity and subjectivity. Some critics, among them Bryce-Okunlola, ar-gue that "the longing for a child on the part of fictional women . . . is a para-digm for feminine desire itself, the longing for what is *absent* from their lives" (201). But others maintain, more convincingly, that Emecheta's purpose "is clearly to show the tragedy of woman's existence when it remains circum-scribed by motherhood alone" because women accept that which in turn en-slaves them for the rest of their lives (Davies 253). I will go a step further by claiming that womanhood is equal to motherhood and Nnu Ego's suicide at-tempt is a response to her loss of gender.

Filomina Steady has stated that the most important and vital role that women play in African traditional society is that of mother, because mother-hood is central to all other roles. She observes that, "[e]ven in strictly patri-lineal societies, women are important as wives and mothers since their repro-ductive capacity is crucial to the maintenance of the husband's lineage and it is because of women that men can have a patrilineage *at all*."[8] Although Steady's comment on reproduction and the "maintenance" of patrilineality carries much truth, it also seems to say that the struggle for control over women's reproductive and childbearing capacities is *the* site of struggle for Af-rican women. One therefore wonders why Nnu Ego, after giving proof of her womanhood, keeps on having more and more children.

I will argue that Nnu Ego's tragedy lies not only in the restrictions of sexual identity conferred on her by Emecheta, or in the fact that her existence remains circumscribed by motherhood. A plethora of contradictory issues accumulate and compound her very existence as a woman in both Ibuza and Lagos. There is no doubt that she has bought into the patriarchal and patrilineal laws that govern her society at Ibuza, but because of the allowance made there for the separation between sex and gender roles, these laws are not all-oppressive. This separation allows women to be autonomous from their husbands even though motherhood still strongly binds them to a male lineage. But Nnu Ego's inability to separate sex from gender, and her stubbornness and resistance to change, compound her situation, diminish her faith in her own identity, and stifle her agency when she moves to Lagos and starts having children.

She suddenly finds herself in a situation where she has to depend on her husband for everything, especially money for food. All that she is left with is a now isolated and ever-growing family, and therein lies the dilemma:

> In Ibuza, women made a contribution, but in urban Lagos, men had to
> be the sole providers; this new setting robbed the woman of her useful
> role. Nnu Ego told herself that the life she had indulged in with the
> baby Ngozi had been very risky: she had been trying to be traditional in
> a modern urban setting. It was because she wanted to be a woman of
> Ibuza in a town like Lagos that she lost her child. (*JOM* 81)

This shift in location and the sexual division of labor has devastating consequences for a "traditional" woman like Nnu Ego, whose quandary lies in her
desire to maintain the Ibuza way of life in Lagos. Where Ibuza men do respect-
able jobs like farming and hunting (according to Nnu Ego), the men in Lagos
have menial jobs such as being cooks, domestics, "washermen," laborers for the
white colonial master. Nnu Ego's friend and neighbor, Cordelia, even claims
that all their men have lost their manhood in Lagos:

> "You want a husband who has time to ask you if you wish to eat rice, or
> drink corn pap with honey? Forget it. Men here are too busy being
> white men's servants to be men. We women mind the home. Not our
> husbands. Their manhood has been taken away from them. The shame
> of it is that they don't know it. All they see is the money, shining white
> man's money. . . . They are all slaves, including us. If their masters treat
> them badly, they take it out on us. The only difference is that they are
> given some pay for their work, instead of having been bought. But the
> pay is just enough for us to rent an old room like this." (*JOM* 51)

Whereas men in Ibuza are masters of themselves and their household, men in
Lagos are "mastered." The constant juxtaposition of manhood in Ibuza versus
manhood in Lagos pushes the wives of Lagos men to feminize them, to treat
them as "women." One can infer that women are those who are normally "mastered," not men. Established hierarchies and gender/power relations therefore
find themselves inverted in Lagos. Nnu Ego's first impression of her husband
is that of "a man with a belly like a pregnant cow" (*JOM* 42). Without knowing
that this man who has just wobbled into the house is her new husband, she
remarks to herself that "marrying such a jelly of a man would be like living
with a middle-aged woman!" (*JOM* 42). She finds herself comparing Nnaife to
Amatokwu, the very man who repudiated her for her barrenness. She describes
Amatokwu as "that native Ibuza man. That African" (*JOM* 72). An African
who would refuse "to wash for a woman, a skinny shrivelled-up one with un-
healthy skin. . . . That was the sort of man to respect" (*JOM* 72). Nnu Ego's
reaction is laced with sexism, classism, racism, and ageism. In Nnu Ego's eyes,
the perfect figure of a man therefore "was not a washerman, washing women's

clothes. And he was not a ship-worker, neither was he a labourer cutting grass somewhere" (*JOM* 78). It was that of a man who was not part of the economy of colonialism.

The oppression of women like Nnu Ego in urban post-colonial cities becomes a form of protest against colonialism and contemporary "colonial" relations (most, if not all, "Third World" countries are still treated as colonial property on whose terrain "First World" politics are experimented with and played out). Nnaife has become part of what has been described as the capitalist sexual division of labor in which men's work is remunerated and valued, as opposed to women's daily experiences and work in the home that are neither remunerated nor valued. But these colonial work and class relations "feminize" men in Nnu Ego's eyes. Her reaction can therefore be seen as a protest against a system that does not give her "work" the value that it deserves. That is why she regresses into comparisons between Ibuza and Lagos. I will also add that Emecheta is not only "writing back" in protest "to the center." She is also protesting against that which, within our own traditional spaces, oppress women like Nnu Ego, forcing them to resign themselves to circumstances that they normally would not. If Nnu Ego had not been repudiated by a husband who wanted to increase his lineage, she would have preferred spending her life with a man like Amatokwu instead of with Nnaife.

By romanticizing manhood as defined by Ibuza culture, by feminizing her husband, by failing to understand the difference between living and working in Lagos as opposed to Ibuza, and by not bridging the gap created by the different realities that govern gender relations in these two locations, Nnu Ego fails to make the transition from village life to urban life. She instead blames herself for the death of her son and gives up her petty trading to care for the second child (a mistake, given that she would have combined childcare and petty trading were she at Ibuza), until her husband loses his job and the little money he used to make. He then has to leave his family, first for Fernando Po to work on a ship, and secondly for Burma to fight on the British side during World War II. Not only does she bear more children throughout these deteriorating circumstances, but her economic situation crumbles as the years go by. She has to fend for her children solely on her own, without a subsistence community. But despite such poverty and economic degradation, she continually finds it difficult to reconcile traditional Ibuza life with her life as wife, senior wife, and mother in Lagos.

Nnu Ego also fails in her responsibilities towards Adaku, Nnaife's second wife. She is discourteous towards Adaku and very jealous of her. Adaku does not become the co-wife, companion, friend, and confidante with whom she should share secrets about her husband, house chores, and child-rearing duties, as would be the case at Ibuza. Instead Nnu Ego treats Adaku as a rival, envies Adaku her independent spirit, sexual pleasure, and well-fed daughters, and proceeds to confront and alienate herself and her children from Adaku. Adaku's ability to combine traditional and urban values are no match for Nnu Ego. For example, when Adaku astutely convinces Nnu Ego, the senior wife, that they boycott serving their husband food as a measure to force him to increase their food allowance, Nnu Ego agrees, but defeat is snatched from the jaws of victory when Nnu Ego gives in at the last minute, under the pretext that unlike her co-wife, she has children to feed. This battle for more rights for themselves as women, wives, and mothers is used by Nnu Ego as a weapon against Adaku. Her "crime," in Nnu Ego's eyes, is her personal ambition and her independence, a free spirit that Nnu Ego both dreads and secretly covets.

Instead of ridding herself of some of the shackles that tradition holds over her head as Adaku does, Nnu Ego invests her energy in mistreating and hurting Adaku by flaunting both her position as senior wife and her claim to hierarchy, property, and power in the persons of her sons. As she feminizes her husband, Nnu Ego consciously and laboriously places a barrier of class, power, and hierarchy between herself and Adaku. Even though she does not love Nnaife, she clings to her sons to assert her anger and frustrations. These emotions are aimed not only at Nnaife but at Adaku as well, in a society where boys are the "valuable" offspring who ensure men's immortality; a society in which daughters are mere helpers, appendages to men to be disposed of, transferable chattel whose purpose is to look after sons (*JOM* 127, 204, 207). Sons are those who harvest yams, who go to school, those who carry the "precious seed," values that Nnu Ego has accepted (unlike Adaku). Nnu Ego can be said to invert Audre Lorde's statement that "the Master's tools will never dismantle the Master's house," given that she can be accused of using the Master's tools instead, for she employs these very chauvinistic ideals as the basis for her attacks on her co-wife, reminding Adaku relentlessly that she has only daughters and by definition, no rights. Their kinsman Nwakusor likewise invokes the ideals in siding with Nnu Ego:

> "Don't you know that according to the custom of our people you,
> Adaku, *the daughter of whoever you are*, are committing an unforgivable
> sin?" Nwakusor reminded her. "Our life starts from immortality and
> ends in immortality. If Nnaife had been married only to you, you would
> have ended his life on this round of his visiting earth. I know you have
> children, but they are girls, who in a few years' time will go and help
> build another man's immortality. The only woman who is immortalis-

ing your husband you make unhappy with your fine clothes and lucrative business." (*JOM* 166, my emphasis)

This rebuke is meted out to Adaku even though she is within her rights to complain about the senior wife's disrespect towards a member of her own family who comes to visit, a family that is not recognized since Adaku herself has no sons. Adaku is referred to as "the daughter of whoever you are," a reference that confirms her status as a nonentity, in spite of the fact that she has worked very hard on her own to build the lucrative business that becomes a threat not only to the men, but to Nnu Ego as well. This rebuke is the last straw that gives Adaku the adequate reason to give new direction and meaning to her own life. She decides to break the cycle of poverty and non-personhood that buries her in Nnaife's house.[9] Adaku sees no reason to be living in a stuffy room with her children when she can work hard on her own and make her life comfortable. Economically, therefore, she seeks her independence. Unlike Nnu Ego, she puts more value on her daughters: she decides to stop taking them to the market with her and sends them to school instead, an intelligent move that she believes will "benefit them in the future" (*JOM* 168). It is a shrewd move that proves how resourceful Adaku is in a fast-changing world where the Ibuza way of life is fading into a thing of the past. Adaku thinks in revolutionary and positive terms about herself as a woman; about herself as a wife; and about herself as a mother of daughters whose future she is determined to change, instead of letting that future be mapped out and controlled by a blatantly discriminating cultural script. In an illuminating statement, she remarks:

> "*I am not prepared to stay here and be turned into a mad woman, just because I have no sons.* . . . I'm going to be thrown away when I'm dead . . . whereas people like you, senior wife, have formed roots . . . the more I think about it the more I realise we women set impossible standards for ourselves. That we make life intolerable for one another. I cannot live up to your standards, senior wife. *So I have to set my own.*" (*JOM* 169, my emphasis)

By refusing to "kill" herself physically, psychologically, and economically, Adaku rejects the equation of childlessness or having female children with madness for women. Most of all, she rejects the lack of sons that only perpetuates the Phallus and the Law of the Father. She is also rejecting the radical feminist stance that might posit women's oppression and women's powerlessness as resulting from (absolute) male power. She sets her own standards because she has realized that women like Nnu Ego set impossible standards for themselves.

If patriarchy is to blame for women's oppression, then patriarchal women should carry some of the blame.

Emecheta has said that the main themes of her novels are "African society and family: the historical, social, and political life in Africa as seen by a woman through events. I always try to show that the African male is oppressed and he too oppresses the African woman."[10] When asked by Adeola James what the questions at the center of her creative works were, Emecheta replied, "First of all, I try to ask: why are women as they are? Why are they so pathetic? When you hear about traditional women who were very strong, you wonder, why are we today so pathetic, so hypocritical?"[11] She has repeated in interviews that her "main criticism is of women enslaving themselves."[12] She claims to sympathize with and "forgives" uneducated women, but has no patience for educated women who "still submerge themselves into this type of system which they know is wrong" (Granqvist and Stotesbury 17). She has criticized writers like Chinua Achebe and Cyprian Ekwensi for the distorted image of women that they present. She has argued that in the eyes of these men, "the only good woman is the woman who slaves for her children, no matter what the cost. She must ask nothing for herself" (Schipper 45). She goes on to tell Schipper that she thinks "there is a tendency to consider a woman who works outside the home, and is thus not a mother in the traditional sense, as a threat to her husband" (45–46). Her answer to such tendencies is seen in the portraits of Nnu Ego and Adaku.

Nnu Ego therefore epitomizes that woman who enslaves and lets herself be enslaved not only by her gender but by her tradition as well. One therefore wonders, how different is Nnu Ego from all the subordinate women portrayed by male authors that Emecheta criticizes? The main difference lies not only in the fact that this woman is the center of her story, but also that we are led into her thought processes as she battles with the contradictions inherent in her life and the multiple demands that these same contradictions make of her as a wife, as a senior wife, as a mother, and most of all, as a mother of sons.

The reader is led through a journey into the intricate ways in which patriarchal discursive practices are inscribed in women's minds and bodies, right from the beginning through the end of the novel. Nnu Ego is born of a woman, Ona, whose hand the father refuses to give in marriage. He has no sons and wants his daughter to bear sons that he could claim as his own. Ona in turn respects her father's wish, refuses to marry her lover, Agbadi, but strikes a bargain with him when she is pregnant to give her child to her lover if it is a daughter or give the child to her father if it is a son. This constant shifting between two powerful men and the politics that they represent (that of using her as a bargaining chip in their separate struggles to uphold and assert their masculinity) makes her feel suffocated and caught in between, so much so that she cries out for help when she pleads with her lover with her last breath, "see that however you love our daughter Nnu Ego you allow her to have a life of her own, a husband if she wants one. Allow her to be a woman" (*JOM* 28).

Unfortunately, Nnu Ego is socialized in accordance with the same contradictions that plagued her mother's life, with the difference that Nnu Ego has neither the will, the strength, nor the determination to make the kinds of independent decisions that her mother made (despite the fact that Ona also lived in the shadow of two men). The eloquent (feminist) statement that brings out the most significant shift in Nnu Ego's identity is expressed in her own voice when she bears her second pair of twin daughters. This shift in her subjectivity and awareness to different subject positions is the potent moment of self-realization:

> The arrival of the new twin daughters had a subduing effect upon Nnu Ego. She felt more inadequate than ever. Men—all they were interested in were male babies to keep their names going. But did not a woman have to bear the woman-child who would later bear the sons? "God, *when will you create a woman who will be fulfilled in herself, a full human being, not anybody's appendage?*" she prayed desperately. "After all, I was born alone, and I shall die alone. What have I gained from all this? Yes, I have many children, but what do I have to feed them on? On my life. I have to work myself to the bone to look after them, I have to give them my all. And if I am lucky enough to die in peace, I even have to give them my soul. They will worship my dead spirit to provide for them: it will be hailed as a good spirit so long as there are plenty of yams and children in the family, but if anything should go wrong, if a young wife does not conceive or there is a famine, my dead spirit will be blamed. *When will I be free?*"
> But even in her confusion she knew the answer: "*Never, not even in death. I am a prisoner of my own flesh and blood.* Is it such an enviable position?" (*JOM* 186–87, my emphasis)

This is the truly potent feminist statement made in this story about the plight of Nnu Ego and all women who must reject being defined solely by their gender in relation to men. Nnu Ego strives not only to come to grips with her condition, but also to give voice to the multiple and varying contradictions and yearnings that have gradually shaped her sense of self. She questions the father's Law that posits sons/male supremacy over women/daughters without whom patriarchy can neither be perpetuated nor reinforced. Her plea to God (and not Man) for a "woman who will be fulfilled in herself" desperately brings out Nnu Ego's belief that only a supernatural force (not herself) can change what she has subjected herself to and this is confirmed by the tragic lack of freedom that she feels both in life and in death.

Nnu Ego finally realizes that even though patriarchy is to blame for the tragedy in her life, she has herself in many ways been the active agent of that tragedy. She aptly describes herself as a prisoner of her own flesh and blood. This feeling, which Florence Stratton describes as one of "enclosure and entrapment," [13] permeates the whole novel. Nnu Ego is said to be the reincarnation of the slave girl that was killed and buried with her father's first wife. This allusion and indirect link to slavery automatically spells out that lack of freedom. Just as the slave girl struggled unsuccessfully to beg for and earn her freedom, so are Nnu Ego's futile attempts to free herself from the bonds of her husband and children. Another example of closure is seen in the living quarters that are shared by the Owulum family. Such closure is another significant legacy of colonial administration whereby the white masters lived in huge houses while their "boys" were forced to live with their families like sardines, in very restricted quarters (often one-bedroom houses), with no consideration for the African extended family system. We see so many adults and children cramped to the point of suffocation in a one-bedroom house, aptly described by Nnu Ego as a "choked room." Adaku makes the smart choice by escaping this claustrophobic atmosphere before it asphyxiates her and her children, but Nnu Ego prefers to tough it out.

Nnu Ego is offered valuable assistance in Lagos through a reliable network of women around her. This network, if exploited to the fullest, would have opened up many doors that could have helped her out of her "prison" or at least opened up new windows to let in breaths of fresh air. But Nnu Ego embraces this network hesitantly or hardly at all, and consequently cannot learn from her own mistakes by listening to or emulating other women. Cordelia warns her very early in the story, "We are like sisters on a pilgrimage. Why should we not help one another?" (*JOM* 53). True to Cordelia's words, many women do help Nnu Ego as a fellow "pilgrim" in an alienating, modern location like Lagos. When Nnu Ego's son dies, Ato makes "Nnu Ego understand that the dividing line between sanity and madness was a very thin one" (*JOM* 74). Mamy Abby puts her education and experience in Lagos at Nnu Ego's disposal. Iyawo discreetly brings food to Nnu Ego and her son (without hurting Nnu's feelings and dignity) when she diagnoses Oshia's illness as hunger and malnutrition. Her co-wife at Ibuza, Adankwo, gives her advice to go back to her husband's home in Lagos (after Nnu Ego spends seven months at Ibuza to mourn her father). In other words, she is advising Nnu Ego not to relinquish her rights as Nnaife's senior wife.

When Nnu Ego does not get the help that she had cultivated, nourished, and anticipated all her life from the sons who abandon her to her misery (by leaving for the United States and Canada), Nnu Ego realizes the grievous mistake she made in giving up the friendship that had been offered her by other women:

> Nnu Ego told herself that she would have been better off had she had time to cultivate those women who had offered her hands of friendship; but she had never had the time. . . . [S]he had shied away from friendship, telling herself she did not need any friends, she had enough in her family. But had she been right? (*JOM* 219)

Obviously not. The biggest mistake she makes in her life is that of shutting out the women's network and relying on her children, especially her sons, as an insurance policy for her old age. She needs to unlearn such patriarchal rules of happiness by learning instead, as Nancy Bazin has suggested, that freedom "must begin with rejecting the patriarchal glorification of motherhood."[14] One understands her bitterness when she questions herself about who made the law that women not have hope in their daughters. By finally questioning these "laws," Nnu Ego is advocating a "rewriting" of these laws, a rewriting that is not unilateral, one that must accommodate her as "woman" and speak for and about her experiences. When she cannot find an adequate answer to her question she concludes: "We women subscribe to that law more than anyone. *Until we change all this*, it is still a man's world, which women will always help to build" (*JOM* 187, my emphasis).

Statements like this one have drawn disparaging remarks from critics (such as Palmer and Ogunyemi) who state that this is feminist propaganda on the part of Emecheta.[15] Although I agree with Palmer that the male characters in this novel are not fully developed or given as much attention as they should have (though Emecheta consistently shows how, when the men are oppressed, they in turn oppress the women), it is my view that Nnu Ego's story can be read as a rebuttal to the so-called "joys" of motherhood, since her life does not end in happier circumstances than that of a childless woman. Emecheta can therefore permit herself the luxury of such direct statements that can be read by some as an indictment of all men and patriarchy without necessarily being accused of "propagandist attitudes." Indeed, Rolf Solberg has quoted Emecheta in a 1980 interview as refusing to be called a feminist because she "think[s] our men have an excuse to oppress us, because they are not free themselves, even in the so-called independent states. They cannot see that they are being used. So until they are free you can't really . . . claim to be a feminist."[16]

Only by means of direct critique of the negative dimension that motherhood brings in the lives of some women is Nnu Ego's story transformed from tragedy to hope for women. Cynthia Ward has observed that

> While it is possible to "read" in [Emecheta's] texts a narrative of African woman's oppression, it is equally possible to "hear" in her texts a multiplicity of often contradictory stories, perspectives (and meanings) that may tell us our own significance. Thus, we can "hear" that in Igbo, the term *mother*, while extremely significant, does not circumscribe one's possibilities for self-identity; it encompasses many simultaneous possibilities within the matrix of one's—and others'—subjectivity."[17]

Nnu Ego, who has admitted that "the trouble with me is that I find it difficult to change" (*JOM* 127), realizes too late that women must not necessarily subscribe to the Law but must themselves be active agents in the process of change. They will succeed, not only by putting the blame on "the cultural practice of polygamy that creates most of the knotty problems in this particular novel," as Elinor Flewellen claims,[18] or by establishing "a countercommunity—a matriarchal family," as Stratton suggests,[19] but also by subverting, when necessary, those very laws that entrap and enslave them. They need to develop other, counterdiscursive strategies for themselves. The statements made by Nnu Ego are proof of her awareness of the part she ought to play in her own life, foregrounding a process through which she "names/re-names" herself. Being named by men, with "their" words, exposes the intrinsic, powerful connotations of sexual inequality and power relations that women's lives are subsequently infused with: *ona*, meaning an ornament, "a priceless jewel" (*JOM* 11); or names like *nnu ego*, "twenty bags of cowries," meaning priceless as well (*JOM* 26).

This endeavour to rename herself, to question the father's Law, becomes the subversive moment of redefining her marginal position as an Other. Nancy Hartsock has stated that when marginalized Others "begin to demand the right to name [themselves], [they are demanding the right] to act as subjects rather than objects of history."[20] A reading of Nnu Ego's identity would, as Haraway has suggested, cherish "ambiguities, multiplicities, and affinities without freezing identities" ("Reading Buchi" 121). It is therefore no irony that in death, Nnu Ego, who dies quietly by the roadside "with no child to hold her hand and no friend to talk to her" (*JOM* 224), like Flora Nwapa's "woman of the lake" in

Efuru, does not "answer prayers for children" (*JOM* 224). Women therefore must cease to be necessarily defined by their sexual identities. Motherhood can be rewarding, but most of all it can also be enslaving.

If Buchi Emecheta's Nnu Ego is an illiterate woman who let herself be enslaved by her traditions and culture, who learns to affirm agency too late in her own life, Ama Ata Aidoo's Esi in *Changes—A Love Story* is a literate woman who, by comparison with Nnu Ego, appears to have made the decision to become the agent for change in her life. On closer examination, though, she proves to be beset with the same kinds of multiple and varying contradictions that plagued Nnu Ego's own life. It is in the light of these multiple contradictions that Esi's character will be read in this section. For the purposes of this study I will situate Esi as the representative of the next generation of women after the Nnu Egos, that is, those children born of women like Nnu Ego who then obtain an orthodox Western education, one that their mothers never had a chance at. The question is, how do issues of identity differ for these two generations? How is the self-understanding of the second generation different from that of the generation that bore them, raised them, and saw to it that they got a decent education from "the Whiteman"?

Ama Ata Aidoo is one African woman writer who has not only encouraged women to get an education, but has also questioned its advantages and disadvantages—the doors that education opens up for women and the obstacles it poses for them in African societies. In her essay, "Ghana: To Be a Woman," she speaks in favor of (Western) education, recognized in her own family as that which offers "alternative lives for children." Her father had come to consider education as "the answer to the limitations of the untrained mind, and to the definite waste that was the sum of female lives." She recollects one of her aunts telling her, " 'My child, get as far as you can in this education. Go until you yourself know you are tired. As for marriage, it is something a woman picks up along the way.' " Marriage is here posited as incidental in a(n) (educated) woman's life. Aidoo therefore questions why people (men especially), "believe that marriage is what a woman was created for? And that higher education for a woman is an unfortunate postponement of her self-fulfillment? That any successful career outside the home is naturally for men—and a few 'ugly' women?"[21] Throughout the essay, she discusses what being African, educated, career-oriented, and unmarried means to being a woman. She examines the frustrations, the stigma of "doing anything 'like a man' " (261), and the "freeze" that is put on one's work just because of one's gender. Aidoo's own constant struggles against such stigmatization and discrimination nourish her insights. It is therefore no wonder that educated women like Esi, the protagonist in

Changes, have a prominent place in Aidoo's work as a writer. She begins the novel with a disclaimer:

> To the reader, a confession, and the critic, an apology
>
> Several years ago when I was a little older than I am now, I said in a
> published interview that I could never write about lovers in Accra.
> Because surely in our environment there are more important things
> to write about? Working on this story then was an exercise in words-
> eating! Because it is a slice from the life and loves of a somewhat privi-
> leged young woman and other fictional characters—in Accra.

By writing this disclaimer at the beginning of the novel, Aidoo is saying that *Changes* is not just *a love story,* a Harlequin novel to be read for escape or a fulfillment of fantasies.[22] *Changes* presents a complexity of issues with love as one component of the myriad problems a woman like Esi has to face. In an interview with Adeola James, Aidoo had this to say:

> I am beginning to say that love or the workings of love is also politi-
> cal. Even when it is a so-called a-political treatment of love, if there is a-
> political of anything, it is very important that one explores the nature
> of human relationships, including sexual relationships. So in a way,
> maybe, I am not really eating all of those words. I have just written a
> play which explores polygamy and people in love. (14)

Aidoo is addressing the same theme in this statement and in the disclaimer at the beginning of *Changes.* Both the play and the novel seem to grow out of Aidoo's reevaluation of love. It is noteworthy that for Aidoo love is political. Thus I will read this story not just as a love story for the purposes of relaxation, but rather with emphasis on the complex and political nature in which the edu-cated, "privileged young woman," Esi, deals with her career and love interests in the process of constructing both identity and subjectivity.

Esi: The Context of an Alternative Lifestyle

Esi, a data analyst with the urban bureau of the Department of Statis-tics, holds a master's degree, loves her job and career, is married (with one child, a daughter) to Oko, himself a teacher and soon-to-be principal of a sec-ondary school. Esi and Oko are unhappy with their marriage. Esi believes that Oko demands too much of her body and her time. Oko wants not only to have at least one more child, preferably a boy, but firmly believes that his wife "definitely put[s] her career well above any duties she owed as a wife. She was a great cook, who complained endlessly anytime she had to enter the kitchen" (*CLS* 8). Oko resents her professionalism. She would leave her home at dawn and return at dusk, sometimes bringing some work home with her, has an elderly woman as her house help, and attends numerous conferences all over the globe. Oko is completely frustrated with this new breed of African woman of whom "there are plenty around these days . . . these days . . . these days" (*CLS* 8, Aidoo's ellipses). In order to assert his manhood, he takes out his anger on his wife by assaulting her sexually:

> 'My friends are laughing at me,' he said.
> Silence.
> 'They think I'm not behaving like a man.'
> Esi was trying to pretend she had not heard the declaration. . . .
> Oko flung the bedcloth from him, sat up, pulled her down, and moved on her. Esi started to protest. But he went on doing what he had determined to do all morning. He squeezed her breast repeatedly, thrust his tongue into her mouth, forced her unwilling legs apart, entered her, plunging in and out of her, thrashing to the left, to the right, pounding and just pounding away. Then it was all over. . . .
> For some time, neither of them spoke. There was nothing else he wanted to say, and there was nothing she could say, at least, not for a while.
> What does one do with this much rage? This much frustration? This much deliberate provocation so early in the morning, and early in the week? (*CLS* 8–9)

Marital rape is the final straw that helps Esi make up her mind about this shaky marriage. The assault on her body forces her to take things into her own hands by divorcing her husband. This is a big step for Esi because within her cultural context, what happened between her and her husband is not considered rape. The sexual division of labor assigns her body, all of it, to her husband as a right:

> But marital rape? No. The society could not possible [sic] have an indigenous word or phrase for it. Sex is something a husband claims from his wife as his right. Any time. And at his convenience. Besides, any 'sane' person, especially sane women, would consider any other woman lucky or talented or both, who can make her husband lose his head like that. (*CLS* 12)

What does this mean and represent for women like Esi, like myself, other African women? By refusing to comply with her husband's demands, Esi subverts an age-old tradition that silences women's feelings about their own bodies. She seeks to create a space within which African women can protest the subjugation of their bodies by those African men who see this as a right. One would ask, couldn't she have worked this out with her husband and made him understand that sexually assaulting her is rape? The answer in this case is no, because, as the text makes clear, Oko knows it is rape but does not think that he needs to apologize for his act:

> [Oko] was already feeling like telling Esi that he was sorry. But he was also convinced that he mustn't. He got out of bed, taking the entire sleeping cloth with him. Esi's anger rose to an exploding pitch. Not just because Oko taking the cloth left her completely naked, or because she was feeling uncomfortably wet between her thighs. What really finished her was her eyes catching sight of the cloth trailing behind Oko who looked like some arrogant king, as he opened the door to get into the bathroom before her. (*CLS* 10)

Oko triumphs in his abuse and further humiliates her by arrogantly displaying his pleasure and affirmation of his "manhood."

Esi is a woman who enjoys moving around her house naked. She loves exposing and enjoying the comfort of her naked body. Oko's taking of the cloth would therefore normally not have infuriated her. But the fact that she feels this rage at her nakedness in front of her own husband, and especially "dirty" from the wetness between her thighs, proof of his physical triumph over her body, is indicative of how deeply hurt she is, how much such a violation has cost her. She realizes two things. First, that it is wrong for women to internalize (and see themselves as "lucky or talented or both") the fact that a husband lusts after their bodies, even if it is clearly for his own gratification. Should women let their husbands get away with marital rape just because they want to keep the men, and by so doing subscribe to their sexual roles as wives? And second, if women do not take a stand against the subjugation of their bodies, neither will the men. There must be a point at which a woman comes to consciousness about what *she* wants.

Her choice of bearing *one* child, and in a society just like Nnu Ego's where boys are preferred and valued over girls, is already problematic. Esi consciously takes that bold step of controlling her procreative capabilities, a choice that is not accepted by her family and least of all by her husband's family. She finds herself attacked and verbally abused by Oko's "mothers" and sisters who call her a "semi-barren witch" (*CLS* 70). It is ironical to see how two women, Nnu Ego and Esi, are oppressed either by their inability or ability to make choices about issues of childbearing. Nnu Ego, who almost goes mad to the point of killing herself, dies an embittered mother of eight children. By naming Esi a witch, her own mothers and sisters-in-law metaphorically place her in that group of women whose actions are characterized by their madness. In their eyes, she joins that group in reality when she decides to divorce her husband.

It is interesting to note how in Nnu Ego's case, non-motherhood and madness are interrelated as motherhood and divorce are in Esi's case. By divorcing Oko, she positions herself within that group of single women for whom her society has no respect or pity. Esi is aware of the confusion and contradictions this will pose in her life and discusses them with her friend, Opokuya:

> 'It is even more frightening to think that our societies do not admit that single women exist. Yet . . . '
> 'Yet what?'
> 'Single women have always existed here too,' she said with some wonder.
> 'Oh yes. And all over the continent . . . '
> 'Women who never managed to marry early enough.'
> 'Or at all. Widows, divorcees.'
> 'I wonder what happened to such women.'
> 'Like what?'
> 'Think about it carefully.'
> 'I am sure that as usual they were branded witches.' Esi said, laughing.
> 'Don't laugh Esi, it's serious. You may be right. Because it is easy to see that our societies have had no patience with the unmarried woman. People thought her single status was an insult to the glorious manhood of our men. So they put as much pressure as possible on her—'
> '—until she gave in and married or remarried, or went back to her former husband.'
> 'And of course if nothing cured her they ostracised her and drove her crazy.'
> 'And then soon enough, she died of shame, loneliness and heartbreak'
> (*CLS* 47–48, Aidoo's ellipses).[23]

Being single is as much a problem for Esi as being married to Oko was. In her marriage, she did not have as much free time for herself as she wanted. As a single woman she has the free time but runs the risk of "shame, loneliness and heartbreak." She chooses not to be single by opting to marry Ali, a married man with whom she has fallen in love. But the problem for Esi does not lie with the second marriage itself, but with the fact that she radically ignores all the traditions that go with polygamy. Unlike Nnu Ego, who exploits her position of senior wife and mother of sons, Esi chooses not to adhere to the laws that govern the position of second wife.

She does not know Ali's first wife, neither does she seek to meet her co-wife-to-be. Opokuya is alarmed by this first and major mistake because Esi could possibly form a strong aversion for the first wife and avoid a polygamous marriage in which there would be no entente but obvious chaos; or, the two women could become friends, in which case both would exchange views "about Ali's strengths and occasionally trading gossip about his weaknesses" (*CLS* 97). In the latter case, the wives would not become rivals competing for his favors and attention, reinforcing his dominant position, and giving him personal gratification. On the contrary, a close bond between the two would serve as a checking-point for the husband who would then be conscious of the friendship, collaboration, and complicity between his wives. This friendship could either work positively for him and the family, or it could be catastrophic to his own needs and familial power position.

We saw earlier how Adaku wanted to use such co-wife collaboration but failed because Nnu Ego gave up the hold that they had on their husband, by breaking the strike on food preparation. When one has made the decision to marry into a polygamous home (as Esi has), then as co-wives, women have the chance to make things work for themselves through close bonding and collaboration, a point that Opokuya makes abundantly clear to her friend who does not even know what the first wife of her husband-to-be looks like.

Esi therefore usurps the traditional rights of the first wife to give her consent. Although the need for the first wife's "stamp of approval" (*CLS* 97) smacks of authority, hierarchization and more power to the first wife, this period of meeting and of familiarizing oneself is paradoxically invaluable in that it gives both women the chance to begin identifying their mutual interests. The cooperation that later has to develop between these women begins with this early alliance. Because she will live in her own house alone and manage her work according to her tastes and desires, Esi decides to walk like a blind person into a marriage, as if she were living in a vacuum. This so-called "alternative lifestyle" frightens Opokuya, who finds it unrealistic:

> 'My dear, don't look so sad. You'll be alright.' What she wanted to add
> but which she didn't, was that it was meaningless for Esi to say that she
> and Ali were going to be happy. In a polygamous situation, or rather in
> the traditional environment in which polygamous marriages flourished,
> happiness, like most of the good things in this life, was not a two-person enterprise. It was the business of all the parties concerned. And in
> this case it would have included the first wife of Ali whom Esi had not
> even met! (*CLS* 98)

Home and the Politics of Location

Esi's "modern" marriage to Ali Kondey depersonalizes the subject and woman Esi, and redefines the traditional concept of "home." Traditionally, families share the same compound. If a man has more than one wife, the man has his house and each of his wives has her own house that she shares with her children. But all these houses must be situated in one compound. In the middle of the compound is a big yard (in Beba we call it *nsaa*) where the children meet and play together. The situation has changed significantly in urban areas. Because most men cannot financially afford many houses in one compound, they usually rent houses with many rooms. The husband and the wives each have their respective rooms (or in lower-income homes, the husband has no room of his own but shares those of his wives), while the children share the rest of the rooms. The point of the matter is that the whole family has to live together, in spite of economic restraints. We saw earlier in this chapter how Nnaife had to live with his two wives and children in a one-bedroom house. Increasingly, there are polygamists who are using the Esi-Ali model.

Esi alienates herself not only from her only child and her mothers, but also from her society as a whole. She becomes an Other within the context of an ever-changing post-colonial world in which she struggles to lay down her own rules. How would Esi get married to a man without even knowing what his first wife looks like, that she has three children, and is called Fusena? I would say that she makes an individualistic choice in a context where individuality is thought of strictly in relation to the collective. By creating a void between herself and Ali's wife (as Fusena is often referred to) she discursively constructs Fusena as Other, as nonexistent, as an absence, as if Fusena were dead, buried and forgotten. Unlike her friend, Mrs. Opokuya Dakwa, midwife and mother of four, who successfully juggles hospital rounds, a husband, his/her family, and work in the home, Esi retreats from the collective responsibilities that she is expected to combine with her career; being married to a husband "and his family." Opokuya's advice is meant to help her friend see that she needs to treat Fusena as a presence, if she wants her marriage to work.

Her marriage to Ali fails because she ends up finding herself alone and lonely in the vacuum that she helped create and perpetuate. Love and economic independence alone do not suffice. That is probably why Aidoo portrays love as not only personal, sensual, and sexual, but also as something that is political, that moves beyond personal, individualistic experience. Love is shown to depend on a more familial, collective, cultural context, governed by customs and traditions that are therefore beyond any individual's control. Despite Aidoo's vehement condemnation of the marriage practices that have enslaved and exploited women "through out history and among all peoples," she nevertheless warns women that

> [T]he solution does not lie with you, the individual woman, married or unmarried, no matter how keenly aware you are of the problems in your environment. Naturally, to keep up some kind of sanity through the working day, you may have to adopt a position of combative protest of your own against the continuous and veiled insults. On the other hand, over-personalising the issue exposes you to the growth of some rather dangerous convictions. ("To Be a Woman" 263–64)

Aidoo is making a specific point about women working together and putting collective action to their benefit against oppression, yet her statement could also be used as a comment on the plight of the fictional character, Esi. By over-personalizing her relationship with Ali, she leaves by the wayside many people whose input, no matter how little, is necessary to constructing a more acceptable or convenient relationship in Accra.

The distance that Esi creates between Fusena and herself finally envelops her own relationship with Ali like a shroud. Ali's visits to her home dwindle as the months and years go by. His marital duties are transformed from sexual fulfillment to material compensation. Ali showers her with gifts from all around the world to compensate for his absence, although she prefers his physical presence. She even finds herself asking Ali a question about her new car: " 'but what would your wife say?' " (*CLS* 147). She finds herself in the position described by Collins as that of the "outsider within," because she has been unable to assume the position of what Minh-ha has described as that of the insider who "looks in from the outside while also looking out from the inside" ("Not You" 76). Although married to Ali, nothing, except the presents she receives, are proof a marriage exists. Not even her home is *home* to Ali who always finds himself rushing off to what he considers *home*, as he does on New Year's Day after giving her the new car:

> [L]ike a spirit newly released from the body, Esi sat and remembered all the other times in the past that Ali had announced he had to leave her— after a short or a long stay—and how intensely she had hurt each time then.
> 'I must be running home . . . '
> 'I have to go home . . . '
> 'I'll phone from the office before I go home . . . '

'I'll pass by on my way home . . . '
And they had both known that he had always meant where he and his
wife, Fusena, and children lived. (*CLS* 150)

Inclusion and exclusion, openness and closure, plague Esi's life as her mother
had feared and warned. She had hoped that her educated daughter "should
have everything better than she has had" (*CLS* 95). She was not against polygamy as such. She had simply wanted her daughter to have "her own" husband
or at least be a senior wife. Things had not turned out that way and the older
women from both sides (Esi's and Fusena's) were shocked at "how little had
changed for their daughters—school and all!" (*CLS* 107).

One therefore wonders whether education, as depicted by this novel, makes
any difference at all for women. One might say with respect to Esi that education can be both a handicap and a strength. As a handicap, formal schooling
tailored on Western models can substantially undermine the traditional values
of the self, one that is viewed as an intrinsic component of the community
(Africans often talk of every soul as belonging to the community). Undermining these values is detrimental to compromises in gender relations between
husband and wife and most of all between husband, wife, and their respective
family members. As an educated, economically independent woman, Esi erro-
neously or naively believes she can live a life of "isolated" love with Ali in Accra
as if she were in London, Montreal, or New York, i.e., adopting "First World"
attitudes where family ties are not as important or as demanding as they are in
Ghana. The impact of her education, in this instance, becomes an alienating
factor instead of a strength. Esi's Western education lays the ground for this
kind of problematic experimentation in the context of Accra. The many questions that she asks about the uses and influences of her own education, when
she eavesdrops on her mothers, are proof of this dilemma:

Why had they sent her to school?
What had they hoped to gain from it?
What had they hoped she would gain from it?
Who had designed the educational system that had produced her sort?
What had the person or those persons hoped to gain from it?
For surely, taking a ten-year-old child away from her mother, and away
from her first language—which is surely one of life's most powerful
working tools—for what would turn out to be forever, then transferring
her into a boarding school for two years, to a higher boarding school
for seven years, then to an even higher boarding school for three or four
years, *from where she was only equipped to go and roam in strange and
foreign lands with no hope of ever meaningfully re-entering her mother's*

> *world* . . . all this was too high a price to pay to achieve the dangerous
> confusion she was now in. (*CLS* 114, Aidoo's ellipsis, my emphasis)

Having lived most of her life in another culture and in strange lands, Esi loses
contact with her own roots, and with her mother's world. She loses contact
with other philosophies that give different kinds of meanings to her life and
experiences. She has to unlearn some of the practices that Western education
has inscribed in her thinking by taking steps towards "re-entering her mother's
world," first by realizing that her attitude towards marriage in Accra is more
alienating than fulfilling. Going to see Ali's family (which she does basically as
a necessary stepping-stone towards getting married) and receiving them in her
home is not enough. As I noted earlier, Esi not only treats Ali as an isolated
individual but his first wife, Fusena, as an absence, as an Other. This process
of othering grounds and perpetuates the contradictions in her identity that are
part of the construction of subjectivity.

Only she can save herself from the hasty way in which she galloped into the
second marriage. Her education then becomes a strength. Because she is economically independent, she can do without Ali's financial support, given that
husbands' economic support is often held as a guillotine over the heads of poor,
dependent women. Without the financial constraints that otherwise could have
left her perpetually indebted to Ali, Esi has to make a decision that is primarily
emotional. She comes to the realization that even though Ali loved her, "his
fashion of loving had proved quite inadequate for her" and breaks off the relationship (*CLS* 165). They do not annul the marriage but agree to live separate
lives, neither accountable to the other.

In both instances, Esi has been the agent of her own self-destruction, self-
reconstruction, and self-determination. She makes many mistakes, but eventually, she redefines herself in the context of her society's relations of gender. Her
friend Opokuya is proof that educated, career-oriented, married women can
juggle the contradictions that they encounter in their daily lives with their husbands, children, and families, and still be able to live fulfilling family and love
lives. Herein lies what most critics have applauded as Aidoo's strength, her social criticism and literary realism.[24] Rooney notes that Aidoo records "the social
and cultural upheavals as well as the continuities, the aspirations as well as the
traditions, and in doing so, [she informs] the present and future with the past"
(243). Wilentz suggests that Aidoo's vision and writings aim toward "the bet-
terment of women's position as well as a global concern for the liberation of
Black peoples everywhere (39), while Brown points out that Aidoo's "insistence
on portraying the woman's experience without transcendental resolutions remains a consistent strength of Aidoo's short fiction" (120) and of her novels, I

might add. Although Esi and Ali's type of free-floating relationship may not be the ideal for women (Opokuya represents an invaluable alternative), Esi's capacity to think and re-think issues concerning her body, her career, her marriage, and her ability to make choices for herself (though not always the right ones) becomes her strength.

Esi has the ability as well as the means to enable her to assess the damage and move on in new and different directions. She realizes that she is not a very maternal woman and limits childbirth; in the same way, she realizes that her marriage cannot work on her terms and calls it off. Such an outlook is also important to a character like Nyasha in Tsitsi Dangarembga's *Nervous Conditions*. She, too, has to deal with alienation and contradictions in her young life, and she struggles to be rational about these contradictions. Children of Nyasha's generation are located in this study as the children of educated parents like Esi, that is, the third generation of women.

Women as Victims of Their Femaleness: Entrapment and Escape

The story of *Nervous Conditions* evolves principally around two first cousins, Tambudzai (Tambu) and Nyasha. Tambudzai's narration at the beginning sets the tone of the novel and highlights the issues that will be discussed.

> I was not sorry when my brother died. . . . I shall not apologise but begin by recalling the facts as I remember them that led up to my brother's death, the events that put me in a position to write this account. For though the event of my brother's passing and the events of my story cannot be separated, my story is not after all about death but about my escape and Lucia's; about my mother's and Maiguru's entrapment; and about Nyasha's rebellion—Nyasha, far-minded and isolated, my uncle's daughter, whose rebellion may not in the end have been successful. (*NC* 1)

"I was not sorry when my brother died," is the first sentence and opening statement of *Nervous Conditions*. The speaker is a young *woman*, Tambudzai, and this simple statement about a young *man*, her brother, is loaded with the gender-related hierarchies and dualisms that prescribe and ground women's entrapment as told in the novel.

"I was not sorry when my brother died." This is an unbelievable statement proffered by an African woman. The first shock one has to get over is, how could she not be? How could she say such a thing? First of all, given our African extended family system that demands close family ties, no one in their right mind would say such a profane thing. Secondly, this is an African woman talking about the death of her own brother, Nhamo, her only brother, and an only son and heir, essential to the continuity of the patrilineage. Yet Tambudzai is not being callous. Her statement is a blanket truth about what it means to grow up as a woman in her society. She recounts that "the needs and sensibilities of women in my family were not considered a priority, or even legitimate. That was why I was in Standard Three in the year that Nhamo died, instead of in Standard Five, as I should have been by that age" (NC 12).

The fact that she is gendered female excludes her from education, to the boy's comparative advantage. Tambudzai's education can be suspended or terminated just because she is a woman, since women's education is thought to be purposeless. Women stay at home and men go to school. The essentializing linkage between men/education and women/home is foregrounded in both Emecheta and Dangarembga, who critically show how their societies link intellectual advancement to men's biology and needs, while finding the same unnecessary for women. Feminine living depends on "natural" (unschooled) inclinations. These authors depict and criticize such either/or, mind/body dichotomies that have plagued women by repressing their strengths. Tambudzai's father, Jeremiah, rebukes his daughter's yearning for education:

> [M]y father called me aside to implore me to curb my unnatural inclinations: it was natural for me to stay at home and prepare for the homecoming [her uncle's]. . . . He did not like to see me over-absorbed in intellectual pursuits. He became very agitated after he found me several times reading the sheet of newspaper in which the bread from *magrosa* had been wrapped as I waited for the *sadza* to thicken. He thought I was emulating my brother, that the things I read would fill my mind with impractical ideas, making me quite useless for the tasks of feminine living. (NC 33–34)

For Jeremiah, cooking, not intellectual pursuits, defines womanhood and feminine living. He views education as that which ruins women, distracting them from their gendered role. Contrary to what Jeremiah thinks and believes, Tambudzai tries to subvert this ideology by combining intellectual pursuits with cooking. She refuses an either/or split by refusing to confine and define herself only in terms of the domestic sphere (like her mother who asks her to "learn to carry [her] burdens with strength" [NC 16]), but to make both the spheres of home and school work for her. Combining cooking and reading is only one of several examples. When she is pulled out of school she asks for and obtains land from her grandmother (farming is women's work) on which she grows "mealies" that she sells to pay for her education. As a woman, she strives to work with the tools that are hers, and by so doing she redefines what is seen (especially through male eyes) in her society as a naturalized woman's place. In this social context, male/female conflicts are grounded in what Tambudzai states is the "question of femaleness. Femaleness as opposed and inferior to maleness" (*NC* 116).

Nyasha rebels against this binary opposition, one that is often played out in her relationship with her father, Mukoma, the quintessential patriarch. Tambudzai describes her cousin Nyasha as a very intelligent young woman, with very vigilant eyes, always observing people, with a capacity of "switching" herself on and off, and most of all, a very independent spirit. She has an incessant thirst for knowledge; she has read more books than all the girls of her age. But Nyasha's greatest foe lies in the hybridization that takes place when she goes to England.

Nnu Ego is illiterate, married, mother of many children; Esi is literate, married, and mother of one child; Nyasha, the third-generation woman, is a teenager, unmarried, literate, with an insatiable thirst for knowledge and personal well-being. Her inability to speak her native *Shona*, and the alienating effects of her stay in England, create a void in her while simultaneously shaping her identity and subjectivity. After living the first five years of her life in Zimbabwe, the next three in England, and then returning to live her early teenage years back at home, Nyasha is deeply troubled. She is keenly aware of something lost and is not happy at what she seems to have become, the post-colonial female subject caught in a negative process that she needs to affirm, transgress, and displace:

> 'We shouldn't have gone,' Nyasha was saying, looking disheartened. 'The parents ought to have packed us off home. They should have, you know. Lots of people did that. Maybe that would have been best. For them at least, because now they are stuck with hybrids for children. And they don't like it. They don't like it at all. It offends them. They think we do it on purpose, so it offends them. And I don't know what to do about it, Tambu, really I don't. I can't help having been there and grown into the me that really has been there. But it offends them—I offend them. Really, it's very difficult.' (*NC* 78)

This hybridization has affected Nyasha in multiple ways: going to England was frightening and confusing because it has made her forget "what home was like . . . what it looked like, what it smelt like" (*NC* 78). As a result, it made her forget how to speak Shona. That is why she gets really alarmed when her cousin and only true friend, Tambudzai, is offered a place in an all-girl secondary boarding school run by Roman Catholic nuns. Because of her experience in

England, Nyasha is afraid that growing up in such a space colonizes the self through the process of assimilation that encourages one "to forget who you were, what you were and why you were there" (*NC* 178–79). Tambudzai understands her cousin's fears. Tambudzai was herself alarmed to find that Nyasha's loss of Shona seemed to affect every facet of her life. Tambu realized that "[their] conversation was laboured and clumsy and because *when Nyasha spoke seriously her thoughts came in English*, whereas with me [Tambu], the little English I had disappeared when I dropped my vigilance to speak of things that matter" (*NC* 77, my emphasis).

What can be more assimilating and colonizing to Nyasha than the fact that her most serious thoughts came to her in English and not in Shona? I would like to take us back to Esi's predicament as narrated by the critical authorial voice, which connects part of Esi's confusion to her being torn away at age ten from her first language, that "which is one of life's *most powerful working tools*," that which grounds subjects ontologically and epistemologically. Thinking in English demonstrates how disruptive this process of assimilation can be to her selfhood.[25] Nyasha presents a devastating crossing of political colonization and the construction of subjectivity in the post-colonial woman and subject. Assimilation alienates and negates Nyasha's Shona-self, positioning it as Other, while affirming and reinforcing her English-self, one she is not comfortable with. The story shows how, for Nyasha, forgetting to speak Shona is the worst thing that could have happened to her because it made her forget who she was and where she came from: her roots and her history. Nyasha, who finds herself shifting from one identity to an-other, who, as Tambu tells us, can "switch" herself on and off, decides to fight the paradox of forgetting by "learning" through the difficult process of listening (especially to Tambu), reading, and remembering. Nyasha happens to come from a society in which women are not only storytellers but also custodians of history; this custodial role opposes the patriarchal rationing of other kinds of education for women. Her grandmother is said to give Tambudzai history lessons, "history that could not be found in textbooks; a stint in the field and a rest, the beginning of the story, a pause. 'What happened after, Mbuya, what happened?' 'More work, my child, before you hear more story' " (*NC* 17).

It is important to observe how and why Shona/African women are the storytellers and the custodians of history. First, they hand down what they know to their children, especially their daughters, who will then continue the process of remembering and transmission. This seems to work constructively and positively for women in a society where sex roles are tailored along the lines of a specific sexual division of labor that predetermines and defines what men and women should do. Tambudzai, for instance, has no right to go to school because of assumptions about gender. The little money that her mother can scrape together is reserved for her brother. As her father is quick to say, "Can you cook books and feed them to your husband? Stay at home with your mother. Learn to cook and clean. Grow vegetables" (*NC* 15). It is an injustice in patriarchal society that Tambudzai cannot at this point go to school, but this same injustice puts her in an advantageous position where her brother can never be, *at the source of history.*

The knowledge of her roots, history, and culture turn out to be the most important and the most rewarding thing in Tambudzai's life. They create a balance for her when she goes to the "whiteman's" school that, as Nyasha has pointed out, assimilates and erases one's history, making one forget who one is. Tambudzai therefore does not have the same kind of struggle Nyasha faces to relearn the forgotten. She is better equipped to resist assimilation than either Nyasha or her brother, Nhamo, whose situation is worse than Nyasha's. Nyasha has the excuse of having been whisked out of her cultural background to England and is determined to fight the forces that further her alienation.

Nhamo, "educated" in the colonizer's knowledge, has never left his motherland. He becomes a budding arrogant elitist (with the help of his overbearing "been-to" uncle) whose open bigotry towards women is questioned by his sister, Tambu. He not only looks down on his illiterate and lazy father—indeed, he proclaims that by going to live and study at a better school run by his uncle he no longer is Jeremiah's son—but he also decides to forget his Shona. He prides himself with his command of the English language, using his Shona strictly on occasions "when a significant matter did arise so that it was necessary to discuss matters in depth, Nhamo's Shona—grammar, vocabulary, accent and all—would miraculously return for the duration of the discussion, only to disappear again mysteriously once the issue was settled" (*NC* 53). Nhamo's mother is extremely unhappy about her son's attitudes because although she wanted her son to be educated, even more "she wanted to talk to him" (*NC* 53). His mother's deep hurt and frustration towards a son with whom she cannot communicate show how being alienated from his family because of his education is bad enough, but forgetting his Shona is unforgivable. It means forgetting his people, his mother, and most of all, his history. Sue Thomas has rightly observed that "Englishness alienates the Shona of the black colonial elite from their ancestors . . . it kills psychically and spiritually, if not physically." [26]

By learning, questioning, and nurturing the history handed down from her grandmother, mother, aunts, and later from Nyasha, Tambudzai strikes a balance in her life. She thus becomes an acceptably *whole* person, of a sort that anyone confronted with a clash of two cultures, one colonizing the other, might strive to be. She is not necessarily inside or outside of these cultures, but simultaneously not quite an insider and not quite an outsider. Tambudzai's ability to nurture and carry on her tradition can be interpreted in the larger context of collective recollection and consciousness. For someone like Tambudzai, who is well versed in her own history and prepared, though awkwardly, to confront another colonizing history, the task is made easier by her knowledge of her own history. Only she can piece together the different stories, his-stories and her-stories, that redefine the larger context of women's lives, de-naturalize women's gendered oppression within a patriarchal culture, and explain her own inability to be remorseful at her brother's death.

Another reason why Shona/African women are important as storytellers and custodians of history is written into the cultural text that defines sex roles for men and women. Women subvert this cultural text to their own physical, historical, and spiritual advantage. Tambudzai's grandmother, Mbuya, weaves storytelling into the work-text, and by so doing achieves two inseparable goals: both women get to share stories, stories that also serve as a medium that makes work less burdensome. I grew up listening to stories told by my mother. In the evenings, after a hard day's work on the farms, we always did some kind of work while waiting for the evening meal to cook. During this period, we engaged in telling riddles, jokes, and especially folktales. When I think back on those moments of collective communion, what I remember is that by telling or listening to stories as we worked, shelling groundnuts (peanuts) or pumpkin seeds, the work went faster, we even enjoyed doing it, and it also helped us forget how tired and hungry we were after a hard day's labor on the farms. None of us ever worked as hard as my mother on the farms, yet she was there telling those stories, kindling that same flame in us because she, more than anyone else, understood the historical, cultural, and most of all individual implications that storytelling should have in/on our lives. Yes, one had to work, but work was not necessarily seen as a foe, work could also serve as a driving force, as a space within which other valuable experiences and roles can infuse themselves and interact. It is this type of interaction that Mbuya constructs and reconstructs with her inquisitive granddaughter, Tambudzai. Nyasha cannot share this interaction with her own mother, but she seeks it within herself and with the collaboration of her kindred spirit, cousin and friend, Tambudzai. This explains why African women writers, like those studied in this chapter, infuse their written works with *oraliterature*.[27] Orality permits the writer and her fictional characters to reenter the mother's world, and negotiates the constant shift between the mother's world and the larger context of the world of patriarchy.

Contradictory, Multiple and Shifting
Perspectives of Subjectivity

Nyasha has lost part of her history, and she struggles to fill in the blanks that two different types of histories (a fragmented one and an alternative alien one) have created in her life: one history that is patriarchal, that views female-ness as opposed to and inferior to maleness; the other that is racist, that views and uses colonization and assimilation as a potent weapon of power and control. These different histories, though, cannot be read totally in negative terms. The perpetual struggle to redefine herself, endlessly shifting from her privileged background and all that goes with it, to Tambudzai, her invaluable friendship, love, and the stories that they share is an important step, not only to consciousness, but to the construction of subjectivity and agency. Without them, Nyasha would have been a tragic character. Teresa de Lauretis has stressed that subjectivity is a continuous process, a constant renewal based on interaction between shifting though still problematized subject positions, and determined by experience. She notes that "what is emerging in feminist writing is ... the concept of a multiple, shifting, and often self-contradictory identity, a subject that is not divided in, but rather at odds with, language, an identity made up of heterogeneous and heteronomous representations of gender, race, and class" ("Feminist Studies" 9). Subjectivity, in Nyasha's case, becomes en-gendered through personal experiences and interactions with other subjects that are open (like herself) to self-analyzing practice.

This unique position offers Nyasha the possibility of defining an identity politics and a positionality that offers her an almost integrated though still problematized understanding of both histories. I would agree with Brenda Bosman, who suggests that "Tambu's story is equally inseparable from identity politics and positionality, and ... it presents most forcefully a feminist argument for the usefulness of the problematic of identity and difference in the context of a history that is always in motion—and thus in contradiction."[28] Nyasha has the luxury and capacity to mock Tambu's enthusiasm for going to the Catholic, all-girl, "multiracial convent. A prestigious private school that manufactured guaranteed young ladies," one in which "you wore pleated terylene skirts to school every day and on Sundays a tailor-made two-piece linen suit with gloves, yes, even with gloves!" A multiracial convent that offered "two places for all African Grade Seven girls in the country," a place where all the black heads that could be seen belonged to porters carrying all the trunks in sight, except those trunks that belonged to the Tambudzais (NC 178). Tambudzai rightly celebrates her access to further education, especially that in light of the qualifying examination, she is one of the two most intelligent girls in the country. She is therefore as intelligent as her own brother, whose education was given priority over her own, if not more intelligent. But only Nyasha can evaluate and understand the extent of racism, discrimination, and contempt exuded by these missionaries. This she can do because of her dual knowledge. Tambudzai recognizes Nyasha's ability to constantly look for "alternatives and possibilities" very early on, when Nyasha returns from England (*NC* 76). Tambu learns to take her problems to Nyasha because Tambu comes to identify "her multi-dimensional mind" as a strength (*NC* 151).

Nyasha's multidimensionality places her in a position to confront women's oppression head-on, without much tact. Nyasha's combined knowledge of her Englishness and lack of or rejection of certain traditional Shona values force her to be tactless when she confronts the problems that attend her ways of thinking and seeing things. She imagines that every question must have clear-cut answers. She openly confronts her domineering father, who dismisses his daughter's confrontations by likening her to a prostitute. He equates her rebellion to that of a "free-woman," for only such women can dare to confront him, the ultimate patriarch. Tambu rightly resents "Babamukuru condemning Nyasha to whoredom, making her a victim of her femaleness, just as [Tambu] felt victimised at home when Nhamo went to school and [she] grew [her] maize" (*NC* 115).

Nyasha resents her mother (university-educated, holder of a master's degree like her husband) for not standing up to her husband, for letting him feed off her emotions and sympathies, becoming the Woolfian looking-glass that reflects him at twice his size; for letting him control her income, for settling into her role as wife and mother without thinking of herself, for becoming a Woolfian angel in the house.[29] Although Nyasha rightly confronts women's oppression in her society, the main hurdle lies within herself, in the intransigent and almost chaotic streak embedded in her rebellion. She leaves no room for dialogue and gradual reconciliation with her parents and especially with her father. She expects radical changes and when they do not happen, she seems to fault herself. Her self-censorship is expressed by her many attempts to starve herself that result in anorexia. She becomes seriously ill. Her body becomes the battleground on which she fights traditional notions of femininity and the displacing effects of colonialism. As Susan Bordo observes, in anorexia

> the woman's body may . . . be viewed as a surface on which conven-
> tional constructions of femininity are exposed starkly to view, through

their inscription in extreme or hyperliteral form. They are also written, of course, in languages of horrible suffering. It is as though these bodies are speaking to us of the pathology and violence that lurks just around the edge, waiting at the horizon of "normal" femininity. It is no wonder, then, that a steady motif in the feminist literature on female disorder is that of pathology as embodied *protest*—unconscious, inchoate, and counterproductive protest without an effective language, voice, or politics—but protest nonetheless. ("The Body" 20)

I agree with Marina Percy's assessment that "[d]espite her bodily deterioration, which conveys that she can no longer consume or be consumed by the history of colonization—a history that endorses the silencing and subjugation of her race and sex—Nyasha refuses to relinquish her subjectivity."[30] Nyasha rebels against the one-sided history she has been taught and in a murderous, self-emancipatory rage, she tears up her history book with her teeth, the book that has taught her "lies" and given her her Englishness.

These are only part of the ongoing contradictions that are embedded in her sense of self. Her own mother describes her head as "full of loose connections that are always sparking" (*NC* 74). One cannot help but visualize with horror the day when these sparks might ignite in a short circuit that will kill her. As Nyasha herself puts it, "I'm not one of them but I'm not one of you" (*NC* 201). Only after her near-death experience through self-starvation does she realize that change cannot be radical, and that she needs to diversify and redistribute her energies.

> But Nyasha's energy, at times stormy and turbulent, at times confidently serene, but always reaching, reaching a little further than I had even thought of reaching, was beginning to indicate that there were other directions to be taken, other struggles to engage in besides the consuming desire to emancipate myself and my family. Nyasha gave me the impression of moving, always moving and striving towards some state that she had seen and accepted long ago. (*NC* 152)

Unfortunately for Nyasha, her thirst for knowledge, her struggle to oppose oppressive institutions, and her drive towards excellence isolate her from her family, schoolmates, and age-mates. In her struggles to fill in the historical and cultural gaps in her life, Nyasha looses sight of living, of being a child, of being a teenager. As Sally McWilliams observes, Nyasha "realizes that she can't continue to absorb and be absorbed by the histories of colonialism."[31] Tambudzai's departure serves as an impetus for the sixteen-year-old Nyasha to rethink the contrary instincts that almost drive her to madness. I see this reassessment as a positive step toward a subjectivity that would evidently continue to be in contradiction and in flux.

Nyasha cannot fully resolve these contradictions, not when her own mother and her patriarchal father (who also epitomizes the colonizer) do not change their own oppressive attitudes towards their daughter. They do not fully grasp the extent of their daughter's despair that is expressed through her self-starvation. Bhabha has stated that "[c]olonial power produces the colonized as a fixed reality which is at once an 'other' and yet entirely knowable and visible" ("The Other Question" 76). Mukoma remains a "fixed reality," with the stereotypical and pejorative trappings of the colonized within colonial discourse, because he does not strike a balance between his Western education and his traditional, patriarchal power struggles with other members of his family, and especially with his daughter. Nyasha is, paradoxically, the one who understands not only her father's intransigence, but also how, in his bid to play the revered (educated) patriarch, he becomes a tragic representative of the post-colonial subject that she resents and can never become, nor emulate. The content of one of her letters to Tambu is quite revealing of the gradual change that ushers in the need to (un)learn past/colonizing histories:

> I am missing you and missing you badly. In many ways you are very essential to me in bridging some of the gaps in my life, and now that you are away I feel them again. I find it more and more difficult to speak with the girls at school. I try, Tambu, but there is not much to speak of between us. They resent the fact that I do not read their romance stories and if I do not read them, then of course I cannot talk about them. If only they knew that when I was ten my mother used to scold me very severely indeed for sneaking them down from the bookshelf: . . They do not like my language, my English, because it is authentic and my Shona, because it is not! They think I am a snob, that I think I am superior to men (if you can call the boys in my class men). And all because I beat the boys at maths! I know that I should not complain, but *I very much would like to belong, Tambu, but I find I do not.* I spend a lot of time reading and studying now that you are not here for us to distract each other, but I must admit I long for those distractions—it's not virtue that keeps me so busy! . . . . I cannot help thinking that what antagonises is the fact that *I am me*—hardly, I admit, the ideal daughter of a hallowed headmaster, a revered patriarch. (*NC* 196–97, my emphasis)

Tambudzai does not find the time to reply to Nyasha's letters but the fact that Nyasha keeps on writing reinforces the need to recollect and retell, and the healing that it engenders. What finally happens to Nyasha is analogous to Tambudzai's reference to her own long and painful "process of expansion," one that taught her to begin "to assert herself, to question things and refuse to be brainwashed" (*NC* 204). It gave her the strength to retell the story of her life, of Nyasha's, and of all the other women whose lives intertwined with and shaped her subjectivity. Tambudzai's "process of expansion," equivalent to an effort of self-definition, illuminates the questions she keeps asking herself upon leaving for boarding school. Those close to her insisted she "not forget," to which she wonders:

> Don't forget, don't forget, don't forget. Nyasha, my mother, my friends.
> Always the same message. But why? If I forgot them, my cousin, my
> mother, my friends, I might as well forget myself. And that of course,
> could not happen. So why was everybody so particular to urge me to re-
> member? (*NC* 188)

For Tambudzai, remembering is a given; but Nyasha, who had once been made to forget her African history, as well as her own self, best understands why remembering is important. Finding that self then becomes an obsession that she has to struggle with throughout her youthful life. Remembering and retelling, which is women's work, becomes empowering and subversive. In an interview, Dangarembga has said that Tambudzai has one advantage that enables her to appreciate some of the chaotic aspects of Nyasha without being drawn into them or becoming chaotic herself. It consists in the fact that "she has this very solid background. She knows exactly where she's come from. She may be leaving it, but it's there for her" whenever and wherever.[32] Nyasha, by contrast, has to redefine her struggles, extend her interests beyond the boundaries she has traced around books and her friend, Tambudzai.

In her learning process, Nyasha will have to emulate women like her aunt Lucia and reject the obvious naturalization of gendered roles, sexuality, and women's oppression epitomized by another aunt, Mainini Ma'Shingayi, Tambu's mother. When we last see Nyasha, she is beginning to heal (physically) from her anorexia, coming to terms with her body as a site of power contestation and control. This physical and mental healing is a gradual process that could restore faith in her mental capabilities and enable her to see power, to use Willis' words, not as "a monolithic system [represented by Mukoma] but as a system of overlapping contradictions."[33] It will also restore her own faith in her ability to control her body in ways that are not destructive to selfhood. She will see her body and "sexuality as a more complicated set of dynamics, as a contested terrain, not a static area of oppression" (Willis 119). Such an understanding ushers in new dimensions to her subjectivity and agency at the end of *Nervous Conditions,* a story that is left open-ended as if a new and different Nyasha and Tambudzai would be the object of another story. In the next chapter, I will proceed from where I leave off with Nyasha, to discuss women's bodies and sexualities as contested terrains where power struggles and control are played out within preestablished hierarchies and gender relations.

3 Sexuality in Cameroonian Women Writers: Delphine Zanga Tsogo, Calixthe Beyala, Werewere Liking

This chapter has been dedicated to Cameroonian women writers for a number of reasons. First, their male counterparts from Cameroon (Ferdinand Oyono, Alexandre Biyidi alias Mongo Beti alias Eza Boto, Guillaume Oyono Mbia, Mbella Sonne Dipoko, Francis Bebey, to name a few) have received most of the attention from critics. These male authors have been (re)read in the context of Négritude, post-Négritude, and post-colonial writing. In any available critical anthology on West African literature in French, one is certain to find, at the least, something on Ferdinand Oyono or Mongo Beti. Cameroonian women writers have been virtually ignored in favor of their Francophone women colleagues from West Africa. Mariama Bâ and Aminata Sow Fall, for instance, have been given far more critical attention than their Cameroonian counterparts. True enough, Calixthe Beyala published her first novel only in 1987, but Werewere Liking's works were in print as early as 1977. Liking is widely known for her work as a playwright, and her *théâtre rituel* has been given considerable critical attention (although more still needs to be done). Her novels, though, have been neglected. Fortunately, there seems to be some growing interest in the novels of both authors. I therefore devote an entire chapter to these Cameroonian women writers.[1]

Some critical works have dealt specifically with Cameroonian writers. These include Josette Ackad's *Le roman camerounais et la critique*; David Ndachi Tagne's *Roman et réalités camerounaises*; *Le roman camerounais d'expression française* by Claire Dehon; Richard Bjornson's *The African Quest for Freedom and Identity: Cameroonian Writing and the National Experience*, and Eloïse Brière's *Le roman camerounais et ses discours*. Apart from Brière's work, which devotes one chapter—her final chapter, titled "Retour de la voie féminine"— specifically to women's writing, these books mention the women writers only in passing or simply gloss over their work in a few paragraphs. Bjornson's impressive work on Cameroon literature pays attention to texts by women writers, but the author does not allocate a chapter or an in-depth study to any woman writer as he does with some male authors.[2] I will address this omission by discussing Delphine Zanga Tsogo's *Vies de femmes*, Calixthe Beyala's *Tu t'appelleras Tanga* and *C'est le soleil qui m'a brûlée*, and Werewere Liking's *Elle sera de jaspe et de corail (journal d'une misovire . . .)*.[3]

Buchi Emecheta dedicated *The Joys of Motherhood* to all mothers. Delphine Zanga Tsogo dedicated *Vies de femmes* to her three daughters, her sisters, to all her friends who encouraged and helped her, and, last of all, to all those women whose experiences brought into being and molded the story. No wonder she simply titles the story "vies de femmes," literally "lives of women." Women's lives are seen through the eyes of Dang, who tells the first part of the story, comprising two thirds of the text, and then disappears in the last part, which is told by the omniscient narrator.

Zanga Tsogo legitimates her title by stating that she decided to give her voice to all the women who have confided in her and never have a chance to speak openly:

> Toute jeune, j'aimais beaucoup lire. J'aime la lecture. Petit à petit, je me suis dit que je pouvais peut-être exprimer et livrer certaines de mes réflexions, d'autant plus que je reçois beaucoup de confidences tant à mon bureau qu'à la maison. Je voudrais partager certaines situations vécues avec un plus grand nombre afin de fixer par quelques récits la vie actuelle de notre société, les mutations que nous vivons et en faire prendre conscience. C'est pour cela que j'ai accepté de prêter ma voix aux femmes qui se confient à moi et qui n'ont pas le courage de s'exprimer directement.[4]
>
> [When I was young, I loved reading a lot. I love to read. Bit by bit, I told myself that I could perhaps express and convey some of my thoughts, especially because many confide in me, at my office as well as at home. I would like to share some lived experiences with more people so as to set down through some accounts the present state of our society, the changes that we are living through, and awaken people's consciousness. That is why I have agreed to lend my voice to the women who confide in me and who do not have the courage to express themselves openly].

When Delphine Zanga Tsogo wrote this novel, she was one of the few women at the head of a government Ministry. She was the Minister of Social Affairs, a ministry that had women, and gender issues, on the forefront of its agendas. Politically, besides her ministerial post, she was also the president of "l'Organisation des femmes de l'UNC, l'Union nationale camerounaise," the women's wing of the CNU, the Cameroon National Union, the only/ruling party in Cameroon at the time. As a woman, a writer, and a powerful political figure, Zanga Tsogo had to lend her ears to "women's affairs," to stories of women's lives told by women and about women. As the Minister of Social Affairs, she was in a unique position to learn more about polygamy, prostitution, conjugal violence, infidelity, rural exodus, and illiteracy, to name a few, and how these issues directly affected the lives of women. Her position also gave her relatively easy access to publication in Yaounde, unlike most other Cameroonian women. Zanga Tsogo could therefore integrate the lives and experiences of other women into her own and rewrite these stories in fictional ways, thus unburying buried lives.

One of the main issues that I see in this novel concerns women's bodies, women's sexuality, and the way sexuality is related to polygamy and exploited by economically well-off men. Most of the women in this story are in polygamous marriages. They are not white-collar workers like their husbands. Nor do they have jobs with the civil service. Although many of the stories about the lives of these women sound familiar, each woman seems to live out her sexuality on her own terms. Zanga Tsogo's fictional analyses of sex, marriage, and patriarchy will be read as an open protest against discriminatory practices towards women and their sexuality.

Dang and Sexual Politics

Dang interweaves her own story with those of two categories of women: prostitutes and married women. Women's lives and bodies seem to depend on and be controlled by men, mainly for economic reasons. Dang sets out to establish a different pattern of life for herself, but a lack of sex education and financial independence and stability stand in the way of realizing such dreams. She goes through a succession of lovers, experiencing one disappointing affair after another. Each man seems to lust only after her body, and once she gets pregnant or has the baby, they vanish into thin air. She bears four daughters with four men. She is sexually abused as well by a Roman Catholic priest who takes advantage of her after offering her a job in his house. The priest also demands and gets sexual services from two other girls who live and work in his house. Dang escapes this one "unholy" relationship without getting pregnant.

What happens to Dang is representative of two phenomena: the displacement of women, and the disruption in the sexual division of labor and gender relations that adversely affected women's lives at the end of the colonial era. This displacement and disruption had many facets. Women lacked the necessary education to find work, in a post-colonial context of white-collar jobs that automatically absorbed men (who had had access to education under colonialism). Some women became economically dependent on men, especially in urban centers. Jeanne Henn has noted with reference to southern Cameroon (the geographical setting of *Vies de femmes*) that, in the years following independence in 1960,

> [t]he limitation of wage labor positions to women [in urban and semi-urban areas] reflects the impact of the traditions and contemporary functioning of the social relations of patriarchy on the development of the capitalist mode of production in Cameroon. Men oppose making labor opportunities available to women because this would allow women to fulfill her traditional obligations to her husband (subsistence food production, domestic services, etc.) by means of which the husband appropriates a good deal of his wife's surplus labor. With wage labor opportunities, a woman could more easily join the rural exodus without the eventual need to marry and become a subsistence farmer on her husband's land.[5]

But these wage labor opportunities for women were few and far between. We see how women's sexuality in the novel is intricately linked with procreation and poverty. Women had little access to wage labor in urban and semiurban areas, and because of that, unfortunately they, mostly found themselves dependent on men, and vulnerable to other forms of exploitation. Men's opposition to making labor opportunities available to women was clearly advantageous to the men. Therefore, if men (as owners of the land) exploited women's labor in the rural areas, men (as power brokers, civil servants, white-collar workers, etc.) exploited women in the urban areas, first by denying them "wage labor opportunities" and second by taking advantage of their predicament as jobless women who needed to survive. The lack of sex education as a social program for young teenage girls had devastating consequences. Those who got pregnant had to submit to older, working, powerful privileged men for subsistence. Dang's narration brings out how most men use their powerful positions to exact sexual favors in return for job (promises) that do not materialize. Women therefore have to put their bodies in a position of exchange, at the mercy of men, in order to survive. This is exactly what happens to Dang when she moves to the town of Ongola, where she becomes Evoundi's lover. A young man claiming to be the nephew of a Minister, Evoundi "offers" her a job. Dang's attitude towards Evoundi appropriately describes women's predicament:

> Le chômage me pesait terriblement. Je ne l'aimais pas. Mais devenir son amie afin de travailler, ne constituait pas une épreuve au-dessus de mes forces. Nombreuses sont mes camarades qui étaient passées par cette voie, mais je ne voulais pas d'enfant. Cependant je ne savais comment

faire pour les éviter. Je n'en avais que quelques idées vagues glanées dans des journaux. . . .

Puis je me retrouvai enceinte. J'en informai Evoundi qui changea aussitôt d'attitude. (*VF* 20)

[Unemployment weighed heavily on me. I did not love him. But becoming his girlfriend so as to get work did not constitute an insurmountable task. Many are my friends who took the same path, but I did not want to get pregnant. However, I did not know what to do to avoid it. I only had a few vague ideas gleaned from newspapers. . . .

Then I got pregnant. I informed Evoundi, whose attitude changed immediately].

Dang has seen many young girls choose suicide over carrying a pregnancy to term, and her anger forces her to contemplate suicide or murder many times during her numerous pregnancies. However, she can never bring herself to implement her plans. Although she does not desire to have the babies, feeding and taking care of them becomes a priority once they are born.

What revolts Dang the most in what she sees as sexual exploitation and women's inability to control such oppression is the fact that men blame women for what happens to their bodies, taking little or no responsibility for the physical and emotional degradation that women experience. Her first lover, Kazo, who abandoned her with their baby, reappears in her life nine years later, with no excuses but only blame:

[T]u me reproche d'avoir gâché tes études. Toi aussi, tu as gâché les miennes, car lorsque tu m'annonças ta grossesse, j'avais dû sécher les cours pendant une semaine, cherchant le moyen de m'en sortir. N'est pas assez? L'avais-je fait exprès, puisque vous accusez les hommes de ne pas prendre des précautions. Lorsque j'allais avec toi, je n'avais aucune intention délibérée de te mettre enceinte. La grossesse a été une surprise pour nous tous. . . . Vous les femmes, vous voulez toujours nous faire endosser vos responsabilités. Tu n'avais qu'à ne pas concevoir après tout ! . . . Comment l'homme peut-il, à ce point, feindre d'ignorer les conséquences des rapports sexuels ? Il faut donc toujours que ce soit la femme seule qui en porte la responsabilité ? (*VF* 32–33).

["You blame me for ruining your studies. You also ruined mine, when you broke the news about your pregnancy, I had to skip classes for a week, looking for a way out of it. Isn't that enough? Did I do it on purpose? since you accuse men of not taking precautions. When I was going out with you I had no deliberate intention of getting you pregnant.

The pregnancy was a surprise to us all. . . . You women, you always want
to make us bear your responsibilities. All you had to do was not get preg-
ant, after all! . . . "
How can a man feign such ignorance of the consequences of sexual relations? So the woman alone always has to bear the responsibility?].

There are two issues at play here. Kazo rightly points out his ignorance about
the consequences of teenage pregnancy. Most young men view sex with a girl
as play, without any conscious awareness of the potential tragedy that lies
ahead for the young woman. More importantly, they view it as a stepping-stone
to the discovery and affirmation of their manhood. Consequently, just as
young women need to be educated, so too do young men like Kazo. Some
of them can be as confused as the young women they make pregnant. Kazo is
therefore right when he claims that neither of them were expecting Dang to get
pregnant. But the other side to this argument lies with the fact that although
men, at certain points in their lives, can claim not to be aware of the consequences of their sexual acts, there comes a time when they need and have to
be accountable. But because men like Kazo are rarely held accountable, they
can easily brush aside responsibility and put the blame squarely on the woman
without any qualms.

When the men who have children with single women like Dang disappear from their lives, these men are not apprehended and taken to court, be it
a traditional court or otherwise. We are presented instead with a network of
women, mothers, aunts, cousins, sisters, that helps raise the abandoned children. The community of women becomes a resource for most women in such
circumstances. Procreation ends up a women's issue and women's responsibility. Furthermore, Kazo has seen neither Dang nor his daughter in nine years,
during which time one would expect him to have "matured," to have at least
acquired a better understanding of women and their bodies. But his retort to
Dang about his having missed one week of school, and his resentment at
women always blaming men instead of preventing themselves from getting
pregnant, reinforces her conviction that men do not care and cannot be trusted.
It does not bother Kazo that Dang had to quit school for good (he does not
even inquire about that); all he wants is to have sex once again. But this time
Dang gets rid of him. I infer from the story the strong point that women are
those who are damaged by such experiences and have to protect themselves,
themselves. Such women refuse to see sexuality as "a static area of oppression"
(Willis 119). I see in women's networking a refutation of what MacKinnon has
described as absolute male power and female powerlessness; of women's sexuality converted to male domination.[6] Dang and the women's community make

some choices that demonstrate how "sexuality, gender, and reproduction need not be fused; on the contrary, they can be separated into distinct systems of power."[7]

Experiences similar to the one with Kazo force Dang to use her own body both as a defense mechanism and as an escape from male sexual advances. Dang tells her friends, Hadja and Tobbo, that she has decided to stay away from men in order to defend herself against them, but also against those women who may see her as a rival competing for men's financial favors:

> Et c'est une autre femme qui s'en prend à moi! Si elle aime son travail d'objet sexuel, c'est son affaire. Moi, j'ai été bafouée, humilée. Aussi, je tiens à vivre par mes propres moyens (*VF* 35–36).
> [And it is a woman who attacks me! If she likes her job as a sex object, that's her business. I, I have been ridiculed, humiliated. So, I intend to live by my own means].

The woman Dang is referring to here is a neighbor. She has become a prostitute rather than work at menial service jobs such as being a housemaid, hospital ward servant, or laundry woman. These are precisely the job positions that Dang had occupied before she got a better position with the civil service as a social worker.

The choice that Dang's neighbor makes directly reflects the political context within which this story is written. The story takes place against a social upheaval as Cameroon emerges from colonialism. Paulette Songue has suggested in *Prostitution en Afrique: L'exemple de Yaounde* that the face of prostitution among women took a new and different turn during the colonial era in Cameroon, and continued to flourish in the post-colonial period. Rural exodus and the lack of adequate jobs for women were the main reasons for this rise in prostitution. Women who had been subsistence farmers were mainly housemaids in the city to white colonials or wealthy Cameroonians. Their incomes and those of their husbands, who were mostly blue-collar workers, could not suffice for their family needs. Some women turned to petty trading and some resorted to prostitution.[8]

Like the prostitutes, the married women in this story seem condemned to wait on the men in their lives for all their financial support. Marriage is not necessarily pictured as "legalized" prostitution, but some women do choose marriage simply for survival. As Henn points out, "[t]o state that women were economic dependents is not to say that they were incapable of supporting themselves and their children. On the contrary, nearly every investigation of African women's farming and craft activities shows that they were always physically and intellectually capable of economic independence. But this evident capacity was repressed by traditional and colonial practices of land and crop control, ideological restrictions on rights to mobilize 'family labor,' which gave such powers primarily to patriarchs, and customs defining women as dependents."[9]

Most of the married women in this story regret having given up their education in order to get married, either because they wanted a position in society through their husband's status, or because their own families forced them into marriage so that the husband could then take care of their siblings and parents. It is this exchange that puts women's bodies at the mercy of men. Edanga, the District Administrative Officer, uses his position and power to sexually harass women who work in his office, or he marries them. For instance, Dang's co-worker Nnomo, who is also Edanga's secretary, must choose between marriage or loss of her job. Edanga, the prospective husband, showers Nnomo's family with food and gifts, taking care of her mother and siblings, so all she can say is yes to the marriage. Women in *Vies de femmes* seem to internalize this type of oppression that leaves them open to exploitation by men. Edanga, for one, ends up marrying seven wives, each of them a prize from his tours within his administrative district, with whom he bears over forty children. Even Catholic priests use their positions within the church to take part in this subjugation of disadvantaged women who, as domestics, can no longer compete economically on the same terms as their men. Dang has to run away from her job in the priest's house, not only because she is sexually abused, but also because of the rivalry that ensues. The other two girls resent the fact that Dang might become "the favourite."

In *Vies de femmes*, Zanga Tsogo seeks to dispel certain myths about women's ability to live together in harmony and sharing. Because of the nature of women's economic dependence on men, women tend to hurt other women by flaunting either their sexual strengths (good looks, their ability to satisfy a man's desires) or the little education that they might have. The expectation that women will be faithful to one man, or, in the case of polygamy, that the wives will harmoniously share their husband raises problems, given that they do not have the same rights to pick and choose other men in their lives as their husbands or lovers do. Sharing one man or having one's sexual needs and rights not fulfilled by the husband becomes an issue to reckon with.

Abomo, Edanga's first love, his childhood sweetheart and senior wife, laments the fact that when a woman gets married and starts having children, she needs "help"—and this help comes in the person of another woman who also has "the right to a place in the husband's heart" (*VF* 95). Abomo best explains this dilemma and the contradictions women face in polygamous relationships.

C'était très dur à supporter que de voir son mari entrer chez d'autres; deviner ses gestes, ses mots. Tout ce qui avait fait partie de sa joie d'épouse. Comment allait-elle partager son mari avec une autre ? Chaque mot pour l'autre était un coup de poignard qu'elle recevait en plein coeur. Souvent, leurs murmures, leurs éclats de rire la faisaient pleurer. Son coeur, petit à petit, se vidait de tout l'amour qu'elle avait pour son mari, et Abomo n'était plus que l'ombre d'elle-même (*VF* 95–96).

[It was very difficult to endure seeing her husband enter other [women's] houses, to guess his gestures, his words. All that had made up part of her happiness as wife. How was she going to share her husband with someone else? His every word to the other was a stab that went straight to her heart. Often, their murmurs, their outbursts of laughter made her cry. Her heart, bit by bit, emptied itself of all the love she had for her husband, and Abomo was no more than the shadow of herself].

As in *Joys*, women are the most united and divided by issues centered around the body (childbearing, childrearing, sexual fulfillment). We saw in chapter 2 how Nnu Ego paradoxically resented Adaku's open display of sexual pleasure with a man (Nnaife) that Nnu Ego tolerated simply as a legal husband and father of her children. She never treated him as a friend or lover. Her reaction, in some ways, displayed her own lack of sexual fulfillment with Nnaife, while highlighting the deeper feelings and joyful (sexual) experiences she had had with Amatokwu, who had repudiated her as a wife. We noted how Agbadi's senior wife, Agunwa, fell ill and died the same night that her husband had openly made love to his mistress in his courtyard. People said "she had sacrificed herself for her husband" while a few observed that "it was bad for her [Agunwa's] morale to hear her husband giving pleasure to another woman in the same courtyard" (*JOM* 21). The intimate and personal nature of lovemaking had been put on public display by a husband who had used his and Ona's "privacy" to violate that of the other women who also legitimately shared private spaces in the same courtyard. It is Agbadi's duty to conform to, cultivate, and maintain those personal private spheres that belonged to his wives but that, as the story revealed, he transgressed with impunity.

We see Abomo here expressing the same anger, the same hurt. It is not just her husband having sex with another woman but the pleasure that goes with it: the touching, the whispering, the giggles or outbursts of laughter that also are no longer confined within a private space. The public display of that which

Nnu Ego or Abomo think ought to be expressed privately seems to turn a knife in the wound of sharing. For women like Abomo, reproduction gradually takes precedence over sexual pleasure, procreation gradually defining their sexuality. Bearing children becomes detrimental to sexual pleasure because reproduction might become the only end of intercourse. As their husbands marry more and younger women, women like Abomo are neglected by these husbands. Abomo's co-wife, Yondo, openly cheats on her husband, and her cheating is tolerated. It does not become a reason for divorce, especially since Edanga believes himself "superior" to all the men with whom she cheats on him.

In *Vies de Femmes*, I see in Zanga Tsogo's fictional analyses of sex, marriage, and patriarchy an open protest against those practices that are discriminatory toward women and their sexuality. I read in her protest an equivalent to the consciousness-raising of radical feminist discourses on the subjugation and appropriation of women's bodies by men and patriarchal ideologies. What is more, Zanga Tsogo is (re)inscribing other women's protest through the medium of fiction. I noted at the beginning of the discussion of *Vies de femmes* how Zanga Tsogo made it clear, in the interview, that she was telling her story and the stories of many women who shared their experiences with her. Fiction then becomes what Bâ has maintained, "a weapon" that women writers can use, one revolutionary device that can serve this purpose for women who have no other avenue. While radical feminists had to begin with consciousness-raising, Zanga Tsogo realizes that most of these women's stories show they are already beyond that point. They are fully aware of their predicament. They want solutions and social change, especially of the men who benefit from these practices that oppress women. Fictional storytelling becomes one agent of change, just as storytelling or folktale narration has been predominantly used for didactic purposes in traditional societies. Cameroonian folklore repertoires abound in etiological tales, which explain the courses or origins of various phenomena (e.g., why there are diseases in the world, why the leopard has its spots, why mosquitos buzz around people's ears), and women are often the primary narrators of folktales. I see a correlation between fictional writing by women, who tell not only their personal stories but those of other women, and the roles that folktales play in the lives of those who share them.

Zanga Tsogo presents women's sexuality as circumscribed by economic dependence and male control. Men control not only the woman's body but her womb as well—the womb which Spivak maintains is "a workshop," a place of production that can be managed and controlled in terms of use value and surplus value (*IOW* 80). Since housework and childrearing is not seen as paid labor, it is what women as mothers "happily" do. Zanga Tsogo therefore paints a bleak picture not only of polygamy and the strained gender relations that have been erected and nurtured by an unbalanced and precarious post-colonial era, but also of women's sexuality as controlled by men. In the same vein, she is also criticizing post-colonial practices of Cameroonian men in positions of power in a system that devalued women's work that had been hitherto valued (as discussed in the previous chapter). These men did not integrate women into the system; neither did they change the system itself.[10]

The only way out of such control is to become economically independent, as does Dang, who consciously makes the decision to stop depending on men and start fending for herself. She achieves this goal, but it immerses her in bitterness towards men that she cannot seem to overcome. Her body becomes shielded in armor. She can be friends with men but cannot bring herself to share more than her friendship. She refuses to "offer" her body. Even when she truly falls in love with Essi, she is ashamed of showing him her older, "scarred body" and of loving him sexually (VF 77). She turns down his offer of marriage not only because of her fear of loving a man sexually again, but most of all because he asks her to quit her job, to become a wife and mother who stays at home, something she cannot afford to do after working so hard and getting so far. She obviously cannot see herself sitting at home doing nothing but having more babies, caring for a husband and family.

Although her rejection of Essi constitutes a negation of all those practices that determine sexuality defined through the abuse of power, one begins to wonder what then happens to women like Dang. Does the search for economic independence by these women necessarily lead to a negation of one's sexuality? One wonders why the only positive image for women, the character Dang, is not developed further in the novel, an issue for which Zanga Tsogo has been criticized. Anny-Claire Jaccard, for instance, questions why Dang's story or women's stories are abandoned and replaced by Edanga's tribulations. She wryly suggests that the last part of the story might have been the author's revenge towards irresponsible polygamous men and their treatment of women.[11] Although Zanga Tsogo defends her style as one that presents slices of many lives in different "tableaux," the fact that Dang disappears completely from the story leaves a void and perplexity in the structure of the story and the mind of the reader.

When Dang refuses to marry Essi, she leaves Abang for Ayos where a new life begins for her—and that is the last we hear of her. All we have learned of Dang is that she is a young woman who has had a number of bad experiences with men, who decides to work hard to make her life better, and who takes the pain to describe the multiple problems that many women face in her society in their relationships with other women and especially with men. Jaccard has suggested that this female view of gender relations, the act of giving voice to women's look on men's socio-familial, sexual behavior, is one of the strengths of Zanga Tsogo's text (125). Bjornson has also suggested that Zanga Tsogo's "implicit thesis is that men as well as women need to realize that dominant attitudes and prevailing social institutions must be changed," (390) and he contends that for Zanga Tsogo, "feminism implies both a more intense awareness of female individuality and a heightened solidarity among women" (389). But, unfortunately, Dang's awareness of her individuality and her construction of healthy relationships with others (especially men) is not resolved in the story. Some feminists have argued that a polarized discourse of sexuality—for example, reproduction vs. sexual pleasure, pro-pornography vs. anti-pornography, gay vs. straight, women vs. men—can only be limiting and inadequate for women, given that these splits do not actively problematize the complexities and contradictions (which should include race, class, ethnicity, etc.) that are all intricately linked with women's sexuality.[12]

Dang, the progressive heterosexual woman through whom the feminist statements are made in the novel, seems to have acquired economic freedom to the detriment of sexual plenitude. She refuses to be economically dependent on men and substantially reduces the harassment she might face from men who would use their money and position to exact sexual favors from women. What I find disturbing is her "vow" to remain celibate as a solution to the treatment she has received from men. She effectively severs all sexual relations with men. Since Zanga Tsogo does not develop her character further in the novel, we therefore do not have the chance to meet a Dang who has bridged the gap, a Dang who regains confidence in her body and finds new ways and possibilities of enjoying her own sexuality. She vanishes from the story at the point where she has severed sexual links with men, repressing all her erotic and sexual needs and simply being content with her present economic freedom. It is this dilemma of exchange and control involved in sexual relations that Dang and Zanga Tsogo do not resolve. However, it is an issue that Calixthe Beyala addresses head-on in *Tu t'appelleras Tanga*.[13]

Tanga and the Objectification of Women's Bodies

This story opens up with two women in a prison cell, a seventeen-year-old African woman, Tanga, and a French-Jewish woman, Anna-Claude. Tanga is about to die and is being cajoled by Anna-Claude into telling the story of her life. Tanga agrees to share her story on condition that her prison-mate "feel" and "become" herself. The story then becomes a journey of self-definition for both women as they seek to merge their identities and her-stories.

Unlike the women in *Vies de femmes* who are married or choose to be prostitutes, Tanga has been forced into prostitution by her own mother. Tanga's story is an indictment of human depravity in African urban slums, of a patriarchal society that condones child abuse, child slavery, and child prostitution—a society that is not only oppressive to women, but one in which women also act as oppressive agents toward other women. Through Tanga, Beyala subverts and politicizes not only "Woman" but the woman's body experiences. She achieves this by articulating a sexual politics that need not necessarily define womanhood in relation to motherhood. Identity, subjectivity, and sexuality are intricately linked in this novel. Beyala shows how women's selfhood and sexuality need not be limited to or defined by their gender and procreative capabilities.

Tanga often refers to herself in binary terms—for example, "la femme-fillette" [the woman-girlchild]—in order to describe the duality of a child forced to live as a woman, and of a woman who dreams of recapturing a lost childhood. She comes from four generations of women who are referred to in hyphenated terms: "femme-mère" [woman-mother, wife-mother], "femme-maîtresse" [woman-mistress, woman-concubine], "femme-enfant" [woman-(girl)child], "pute-enfant" [whore-(girl)child], "enfant-parent" [child-parent]. The text abounds in such hyphenated references. Naming women in binary terms is a discursive act that not only discloses their hyphenated identities as a reflection of the hierarchical society in which they live, but also exposes the problematic nature of womanhood as it relates to mothering, reproduction, and to sexual pleasure. Embedded in these dichotomous descriptions is the oppression of women and the objectification of their bodies.

Tanga's grandmother is raped many times over. She gives birth to Tanga's mother, gives the child away to her own mother, and vows against motherhood. Tanga's mother grows up a vagabond who tries to escape brutal treatment from men by forcing her virginity with palmnuts at the age of thirteen. She falls in love with Tanga's father, hoping to break the chain of misfortune encountered by her maternal forebears. But her husband turns out to be a womanizer who verbally and physically abuses her. He also rapes and impregnates his twelve-year-old daughter, Tanga. Like all the women in her family, Tanga is subjected to violent verbal and sexual abuse, and this trauma forces her to treat her own body as an absence, a not-I.

> J'amenais mon corps au carrefour des vies. Je le plaçais sous la lumière.
> Un homme m'abordait. Je souriais. Je suivais. Je défaisais mes vêtements.
> Je portais mon corps sur le lit, sous ses muscles. Il s'ébrouait. D'autres
> images m'assaillaient. . . . Je ne sentais rien, je n'éprouvais rien. Mon
> corps à mon insu s'était peu à peu transformé en chair de pierre (*TTT*
> 19–20).

[I took my body to the crossroads of lives. I placed it under the light. A
man accosted me. I smiled. I followed. I undid my clothes. I put my
body on the bed, beneath his muscles. He snorted. Other images as-
sailed me. . . . I felt nothing, I experienced nothing. My body, unknown
to me, had bit by bit transformed itself into a flesh made of stone].

Between the ages of twelve and seventeen, Tanga continuously attempts to
confront the psychological and physical pain ensuing from both the incestuous
rape and forced prostitution. Tanga's identity and sexuality are controlled and
exploited by individual men, as well as by a patriarchal society, but this control is compounded by the cooperation of her own mother. Tanga's experience
shows how women, and women's sexuality, are constructed and constituted by
a ladder of power struggles in such a way that they become accomplices in
men's domination. Women become active participants in their own objectification. Tanga's mother, for instance, subjects her daughter to a clitoridectomy.
This dismembering of body parts, which recalls the hyphenated identities in
the text, further reinforces Tanga's otherness as she who can be dominated and
manipulated. After the clitoridectomy has been carried out, Tanga's mother re-
joices while her daughter reflects on the tragic consequences of what has just
happened to her:

Je la vois encore, la vieille ma mère, éclatante dans son kaba immaculé,
un fichu noir dans les cheveux, criant à tous les dieux: «Elle est devenue
femme, elle est devenue femme. Avec ça, ajouta-t-elle en tapotant ses
fesses, elle gardera tous les hommes.» Je n'ai pas pleuré. Je n'ai rien dit.
J'héritais du sang entre mes jambes. D'un trou entre les cuisses. Seule
me restait la loi de l'oubli (*TTT* 24).
[I can still see her, my mother the old one, glowing in her immaculate
kaba, a black headscarf in her hair, calling out to all the gods: "She has
become a woman, she has become a woman! With this," she added, pat-
ting her buttocks, "she will keep all the men." I did not cry. I said nothing. I was inheriting blood between my legs. A hole between my thighs.
All that was left for me was the law of forgetting].

Tanga's mother's reaction illustrates the point that this practice of female circumcision defines her daughter as a woman. It signifies that she has crossed
over from childhood into womanhood; but simultaneously, it captures the implicit right of men to possess Tanga's body. In her own mother's words, "she
has become a woman and with this she will keep all the men," meaning that
men will always lust after her body. The more men possess her body, the more

money she makes. Tanga has no say either in the process of objectification or in the resultant alienation of her own body.

The practice of female circumcision is therefore not a simple cultural practice, but one that is as political as it is economically motivated. Tanga is ashamed of her mother. Her feeling of shame indicates she believes her mother could have protected her body from being mutilated. But just as Tanga's mother quietly looked the other way at her daughter's rape, so does she jubilate at her daughter's clitoridectomy. This ritual has economic implications for the mother for whom it is the culmination of her daughter's commercial servitude and, as she puts it, the old age insurance that she expects and demands of her daughter by forcing her into prostitution. The mother not only reinforces the ritual and cruelty to women and their bodies, but legitimizes her financial demands on her own (female) child.

In this way, the mother positions herself within that group of people whose gendered status equips them to wield power and control over others. It is important to note how, in the prison cell, one of the prison guards proposes (to the obvious amusement of his colleagues) that it might be worthwhile to "cut off" Anna-Claude's clitoris in order to silence her ("[o]n pourrait peut-être lui couper le clitoris" [*TTT* 69]). These men are fully aware of the magnitude of such action, they are conscious of the fact that amputating the clitoris is an act of abuse whose repercussion is the woman's silence. This silence is a direct consequence of the pain, trauma, and powerlessness that such practices breed in women and which they must learn to confront. The second prison guard even goes as far as saying that cutting off the clitoris would be too honorable a thing to do to this woman. The third guard opts for another method of punishment, which in his mind is "better" than sexual mutilation. He proposes to offer Anna-Claude "a cigar" (*TTT* 69) and, without hesitation, he pulls down his pants and defecates in her cell. He uses his feces as a metaphor for the penis and the Phallus via the well-known Freudian image of the cigar. What is also striking here is how the waste from his body is constructed as better punishment than removing "the waste" from Anna-Claude's own body, a body that is, in the same vein, constructed and defined as inferior—not even to his body but to the "excess" of his body.

This obvious brushing aside of the woman's body is in staggering opposition to the fanfare that surrounds the male body and circumcision. In *C'est le soleil qui m'a brûlée,*[14] Beyala skilfully crafts a parody of male circumcision as a "spectacle," a theatrical demonstration that the whole village turns out to watch. Everyone in the village partakes in this mass voyeuristic ritual where nobody listens to the cries of the boy to be circumcised, of the "real" man-to-be, who, as the story tells us, cries out to his mother for help, to stop the circumcision from happening:

> «Lâchez-moi! Lâchez-moi! Maman, aide-moi! Aide-moi, maman! Je ne
> veux pas! Je ne veux pas!» . . . Certes il crie, gesticule, mord, mais il ne
> pourra pas s'évader, il ne pourra plus s'en aller, *il fera désormais partie
> de la corporation et, comme les autres, il transmettra la souffrance.* (*CSB*
> 40, my emphasis)
>
> ["Let go of me! Let me go! Mamma, help me! Help me, Mamma! I don't
> want it! I don't want it!" . . . Certainly he cries, gesticulates, bites, but he
> will not be able to escape, he will not be able to go away, he will hence-
> forth be part of the guild and, like the others, he will hand down suffer-
> ing.]

In the boy's mind, as in Tanga's, the mother becomes the only person who can stop this display of madness, but she does not. His cries, though directed at his mother, can also be interpreted as an open plea to the community as a whole. The ceremonious attitude surrounding male circumcision puts the crowd in a trance-like state, awaiting the expert removal of the prepuce and the spurting out of blood that is greeted with ululation and applause. Male circumcision therefore has a communal dimension and cultural impact, as if the destiny and continuity of the community were embodied in that sacred moment that everyone has to watch, participate in, and remember. This underlying (re)construction and acclamation of the Phallus has to be engraved in the collective consciousness.[15] It therefore becomes the most political of statements that founds and grounds thinking and actions within the community and continually engenders that collective consciousness. The literal body then acts as "a powerful symbolic form, a surface on which the central rules, hierarchies, and even metaphysical commitments of a culture are inscribed and thus reinforced" (Bordo 13).

This dramatic element of communal participation is absent in instances of female circumcision. The collective and communal consciousness is no longer called into play. Female circumcision becomes incidental to other communal demands. Mothers or other women, on individual basis, prepare their daughters for the ritual and the duties that lie ahead. It becomes "merely" a women's issue. In *Tanga*, there are only three people present at Tanga's clitoridectomy, the "arracheuse de clitoris" (the woman responsible for "tearing out" the clitoris, "the clitoris snatcher"), Tanga herself, and her mother. In *Soleil*, when Ada takes her niece, Ateba Léocadie, to the old woman for the egg ritual, these three women are still the only ones involved. In the egg ritual, the curved head of an egg is placed on the vagina, as if in the act of penile penetration, and rotated to ascertain a young woman's virginity. The correlation between the "fictional" egg ritual employed by Beyala and female circumcision is noteworthy. Saadawi has pointed out that "circumcision of females aims primarily at ensuring virginity before marriage, and chastity throughout" (39). Even though the egg ritual in *Soleil* does not involve amputating any body parts, it is meant to serve the same purpose. Ateba feels the same loss of self, sensation, and disconnection with her body that Tanga felt at her clitoridectomy: "Travail achevé en deux minutes? En dix heures? Ateba ne sait plus. Ateba ne veut pas le savoir" (*CSB* 82) [Work done in two minutes? In ten hours? Ateba no longer knows. Ateba does not want to know].

The timeless duration is indicative of Ateba's separation of body and mind, feeling and sensation, and as with Tanga, her body does not seem to belong to her anymore. It belongs to a woman like Ada, who needs to prove that her niece is a virgin in order to restore her own honor as a "mother" and caretaker. She wants to demonstrate that she has brought up her daughter the right way, i.e., properly prepared for the marriage market. Likewise, Tanga's mother subjects Tanga to a clitoridectomy in order "to prepare" her daughter for the market of prostitution. Paradoxically, Ada has had as many lovers as she has wanted in her life. She therefore has to struggle with this image of herself as a loose woman and the need to portray herself as a good mother. She is haunted by the endless succession of "fathers," lovers, that she parades in front of Ateba and the hopelessness of her own life. She resents the fact that her sister, Betty, who had chosen prostitution as a means of making a living, has deserted her for a relationship with a man, leaving her child Ateba Léocadie in her care. She is also frightened by the prospect that history might repeat itself and her niece might follow in her sister's footsteps. Ada's deep-rooted fear and resentment push her, for both selfish and political reasons, to subject her niece to the egg ritual. In her bid to portray herself as the ideal mother, she punishes Betty by humiliating Ateba. The "purity" and good behavior that are demanded of women and embodied in their virginity are exploited and reinforced by Ada. Ateba's virginity is thus commodified, just like Tanga's. Women can, for very personal reasons, be active participants in the (dis)membering, (dis)embodying, and objectification of other women's bodies. For a true revolution to take place, women must begin from their position as women (who paradoxically seem to have the adequate powers), "to confront the mechanisms by which [they become] enmeshed, at times, into collusion with forces that sustain [their] own oppression" (Bordo 15).

Tanga, Ateba, and the boy all expect or implore their mothers to stop the circumcisions from taking place. Beyala seems to be saying that women, especially mothers, can stop this from happening to their children, if they want to or put their minds to it. In line with my discussion of Ifi Amadiume's work on flexible gender ideologies, I believe it is plausible to assume African women have some power over what happens to their children. After all, in African societies, mothers are respected for the various ways in which they shield and protect their children from illnesses and harmful experiences. In the interviews that Awa Thiam conducted with African women, an educated Malian woman, who never wanted her daughters excised and infibulated like herself, recalled coming home from work one day and finding with horror that her mother had done exactly what she did not want to happen to her children. She made this revealing statement: "I can't tell you what my feelings were at that precise moment. What could I do or say against my mother? I felt a surge of rebellion but I was powerless in the face of my mother. . . . Like many African women, my mother had just proved that she had rights not only over me, but also over my children—*her* grandchildren" (64). Saadawi holds the same conviction, but adds that educated parents increasingly are protesting and refusing the operation for their daughters, unlike uneducated parents who "still go in for female circumcision in submission to prevailing traditions" (38). What this means is that women, and especially mothers, can successfully resist these operations by refusing to submit to prevailing traditions. Rejection of the practice becomes a potent form of feminist protest.

The novel shows that men cannot always be blamed for the ways in which the woman's body is written into the cultural script. By criticizing women like Ada and Tanga's mother, the novel positions itself beyond the margins of radical protest and consciousness-raising. It is demanding that women assume their responsibilities in the (con)textual writing of this script. They must cease to be the domesticated victims that they make themselves out to be by rejecting what conditions them into subservience. True change can begin with women, one that consequently would invade and subvert the collective consciousness constructed by the Law of the Father, thus exploding the very foundations and boundaries erected by that consciousness.

Toward a Lesbian Continuum? or Reclaiming the Erotic

Calixthe Beyala illustrates this beginning in *Tanga* and *Soleil* by portraying women seeking women-centered spaces and women-grounded relationships that seem to be not as oppressive as the male-centered spaces and relationships within which their sexuality is constructed. In *Tanga*, the seventeen-year-old African woman opens up her soul to the Jewish French woman. This is the first time, during her neglected and exploited existence, that Tanga has ever spoken about herself with anyone. She tells Anna-Claude the story of her life. The story opens with the two women in a prison cell, the ultimate metaphor for the various kinds of prisons that have defined and entrapped their lives and their sexuality. Recounting her story to Anna-Claude becomes the final straw in Tanga's struggle to break her own silences, "silence as a will not to say or a will to unsay and as a language of its own" (Minh-ha 74). Storytelling in this context becomes the medium through which both women explore and subvert the very prison walls within which the experiences of their identities and sexualities have been confined for so long. It becomes the route to self-liberation and the construction of agency, one that enables them to bridge multiple differences of white/black, colonization/colonized, oppressor/oppressed.

Tanga (re)constructs the maternal link with Anna-Claude. I see this reconstruction as the continuation of what began with her adoption and breastfeeding of the little boy, Mala. Both women become what Julia Kristeva has defined as subjects-in-process, as they seek to reactivate the repressed feminine and appropriate a semiotic, maternal link[16]—one that, in the novel, facilitates the shattering of prison walls and patriarchal boundaries. As she haltingly recounts her story, Tanga insists on everything about both women touching: their stories, their minds, their bodies. Tanga begins by asking Anna-Claude to put her hand in her own: "Donne-moi la main, désormais tu seras moi" (*TTT* 18) [Give me your hand. From now on you will be me]. This act is the beginning of something psychological and physical, mental and sensual that ignites the flow of the story. Bodies, not objectified bodies, but revived bodies; bodies in the process of rejuvenation, reconstruction, and reconstitution; bodies that shatter their shields of armor through a persistent reaching out, a touching of hands, without which Tanga feels no warmth or communication. This mental and physical touching recaptures for both women what they interpret as the maternal:

> Leurs corps s'enlacent. Anna-Claude pleure. Tanga trace sur son cou et son flanc des sillons de tendresse. Elle lui dit de ne pas pleurer, qu'elles venaient de connaître le cauchemar mais que le réel était l'étreinte. Elle lui dit qu'elles frotteront leur désespoir et que d'elles jaillira le plus maternel des amours (*TTT* 72).
>
> [Their bodies embrace. Anna-Claude weeps. Tanga traces furrows of tenderness down her neck and side. She tells her not to cry, that they

had just known a nightmare but the embrace was reality. She tells her that they will rub their despair together and from them will spring the most maternal of loves].

Female bonding develops out of this sensuous, maternal love, and paves the way for both women to shift in and out of their marginality, for their silences to be broken and their stories to be told. Non-heterosexual and women-centered existence is strongly reclaimed and reaffirmed in Beyala's work. But there is a difference in reclaiming these women-centered spaces that does not exclude a male frame of reference—a difference that I see in Beyala's work as compared, for example, with Monique Wittig's *Les guérillères*. There is an active pursuit of sensuous relationships between women, but there is also a tolerance for women seeking pleasures with men, if only the women are not objectified in the process. These women-centered spaces are unlike those portrayed by the other women writers here considered. Though others do affirm women-to-women bonding, what is specific and important in Beyala's work is that it goes beyond mere "bonding" (i.e., the type of bonding within the women's network that pitches in to help other women when they are in need). Calixthe Beyala portrays a specific sensuousness and eroticization of that women-centered existence that can be likened to a modified version of what Adrienne Rich has described as a lesbian continuum. According to Rich, "*lesbian existence* suggests both the fact of the historical presence of lesbians and our continuing creation of the meaning of that existence. I mean the term *lesbian continuum* to include a range—through each woman's life and throughout history—of women-identified experience; not simply the fact that a woman has had or consciously desired genital sexual experience with another woman" (156). I will here modify Rich's definition by inserting in this continuum Alice Walker's definition of a womanist as "a woman who loves other women, sexually and/or nonsexually. . . . Sometimes loves individual men, sexually and/or nonsexually" (xi). The continuum that I see in Beyala reflects both Rich's and Walker's suggestions. The women in Beyala's work do not necessarily reject heterosexuality, nor do they necessarily turn to lesbianism. Walker would say, for example, that these women appreciate women's culture and possess a valuable emotional flexibility. Some of them (especially the main characters, Tanga and Ateba Léocadie) simply seem to find psychological, sensuous, and sometimes sexual fulfilment in other women.

The nineteen-year-old Ateba spends all her life writing letters to women, recreating a women's "world of stars," a mythological world in which women were free before men invited them and then subjugated them. Ateba's "madness" and revolt against patriarchy and the male subordination of women is mediated through this writing, in the same way that Tanga uses storytelling. Women therefore seem to be the best friends, listeners, and confidantes of other women. Women bring out the best in other women, listen to them, kindle their loves not only for living but for enjoying life. They mold each others' desires— desires that, according to Ateba, should be directed toward other women, but that in some instances could also be directed toward men. As Ateba herself puts it: "Quelquefois, je t'ai reproché ton desire de l'homme" (*CSB* 67) [Sometimes I have begrudged you your desire for men]. But then, her own pursuit of these desires and contact with men have only reinforced her closeness to women, in every sense.

The sheer cruelty of the egg ritual on Ateba's body only reinforces this belief and strengthens her friendship with Irène, the prostitute who fills a gap in Ateba's heart. Irène is like the real-life representation of her own mother, Betty, the (ideal) woman whose soul and problematic life Ateba has sought to recreate in her dreams, fantasies, and relentless quest for happiness and self-definition. Irène becomes that woman through whom Ateba's subjectivity and sexuality gain full expression. When she goes with Irène to the midwife for Irène's abortion, she tries to comfort her frightened but determined friend, telling her that woman's suffering, caused by "man", has become women's strength. As they wait in front of the midwife's office, she tries to reach out to Irène:

> Elle avance une main, elle veut la poser sur le genou d'Irène, elle tremble, son corps lui dit qu'elle pèche, tout son être lui dit qu'elle pèche. Et elle reste le corps tremblant, essayant d'écraser cette chose intérieure qui la dévore. La femme et la femme. Nul ne l'a écrit; nul ne l'a dit. Aucune prévision. Elle pèche et rien ni personne n'explique pourquoi elle pèche. Tout le monde baragouine à ce sujet (*CSB* 158).
> [She reaches out a hand, she wants to place it on Irène's knee, she trembles, her body tells her she is sinning, her entire being tells her she is sinning. And she waits, her body trembling, trying to crush this thing that is devouring her from within. A woman and a woman. It was never written of; neither was it spoken about. No preparation. She sins and nothing, no one, can explain why she sins. Everyone gabbles on this subject].

This is what I see as the erotic and (un)spoken moment of/for lesbianism in *Soleil*,[17] an issue, among others, that has been highly controversial with some readers and critics.[18] Jean-Marie Volet has rightly suggested that Beyala is "developing into one of the most provocative women writers of her generation."[19] While some reviewers of Beyala's work, like Armelle Nacef, celebrate what she refers to as a feminine way of loving,[20] Richard Bjornson maintains that "Beyala's lesbian approach to the reality of contemporary Cameroon is unusual within the context of the country's literate culture" (420). Ndache Tagne claims that "Ateba's homosexual yearnings . . . will raise an outcry from a number of African readers," and even states that readers will be scandalized by the "pornographic" content of Beyala's first novel (97). But Rangira Gallimore disagrees with critics who label Beyala's work as pornographic when they accuse her of "commercializing African eroticism."[21]

What I see in Beyala's work is an obvious eroticization of the woman's body by another woman. Audre Lorde has described the erotic as

> [A] resource within each of us that lies in a deeply female and spiritual plan, firmly rooted in the power of our unexpressed or unrecognized feeling. In order to perpetuate itself, every oppression must corrupt and distort those very sources of power within the culture of the oppressed that can provide energy for change. For women, this has meant the suppression of the erotic as a considered source of power and information within our lives. (*SO* 53)

Lorde condemns what she sees as the prevalent attempts to separate the spiritual from the political, as well as from the erotic, because she believes that "the bridge which connects them is formed by the erotic—the sensual—those physical, emotional, and psychic expressions of what is deepest and strongest and richest within each of us, being shared: the passions of love in its deepest meanings" (56). Ateba Léocadie tries to make an erotic connection with Irène, but these connections remain frustratingly muted because of their association with and definition as "sin." As Ateba muses, "She sins and nothing, no one, can explain why she sins. Everyone gabbles on this subject." Ateba questions those histories, cultures, and laws that have posited woman-woman (sensuous/sexual) pleasures as "sinning." This questioning puts into perspective Beyala's critique of institutionalized heterosexuality and patriarchal ideologies in the two texts, *Tanga* and *Soleil*. By questioning what this "sin" is, a restriction reserved for women in patriarchal culture, Ateba is, to paraphrase Lorde, making those connections between the spiritual (psychic and emotional), the political, and the erotic (physical and sensual). Women's sexuality and the repression of lesbian contacts become much more than a sensuous and sexual issue. They are a political concern to be reckoned with.

At the end of the novel, Ateba commits a murder that has personal and political ramifications. After Irène bleeds to death from the abortion, Ateba goes to the bar where Irène had always gone to pick up men, and does the same. The man takes her home, rapes her, and forces her to have oral sex on her knees because, "God sculpted woman on her knees at the feet of man" [Dieu a sculpté la femme à genoux aux pieds de l'homme] (*CSB* 173). She spits out his sperm at his feet, kills him by repeatedly hitting him on the skull with a heavy ashtray. In her mind, she destroys that which has forever subjugated her and all women and romanticized her and woman's subjugation. Then in a hallucinatory daze, she embraces, kisses, and fondles this corpse all night, calling it Irène, and professing her love to Irène.

In *Tanga*, the erotic moment of fulfilment for Tanga and Anna-Claude comes when they embrace and share physical, spiritual, and sensuous warmth as the culmination of their self-liberation of and from their her-stories. The affirmation and the use of the erotic as power can therefore be seen as an important and original weapon used by Calixthe Beyala to describe women's sexuality. This use of the erotic as a critical and powerful subverting tool is also seen in Werewere Liking's *Elle sera de jaspe et de corail*, which is interestingly, though pointedly, subtitled *journal d'une misovire* [diary of a man-hater].[22]

The use of the erotic is also deeply embedded in the style of this novel. Liking calls it a "chant roman" [chant-novel], because it is profoundly anchored in Bassa ritual. Although Liking is a novelist, poet, painter, performer, and playwright, this multitalented artist is best known for her *théâtre rituel* [ritual theatre] in which she adopts, transforms, and recreates traditional ritual content of Bassa initiation rites for performance on stage. The performances are meant to serve the same purpose that purification rituals serve in traditional Bassa society. Jeanne Dingome has noted that Liking's parents were

> "traditional musicians who introduced her to their art as well as to oral
> literature in general. But it is after her initiation into esoteric cults as a
> teenager that she developed an intimate relationship with the living cul-
> ture around her. . . . Indeed, it is her initiation at that most sensitive pe-
> riod of her life that later put her in a position to draw more readily on
> her culture's aesthetic (and essentially its theatrical) resources which are
> embedded in its myths and rituals."[23]

By combining and fusing traditional and modern elements, and by utilizing these elements to persistently question the mores of modern African society, Werewere Liking has succeeded in creating a new African literary aesthetic that clearly distinguishes itself from Western literary forms. It is within the context of this revolutionary aesthetic/ritual theatre, grounded in Bassa ritual and Liking's creative process, that the "chant roman" *Elle sera de jaspe et de corail* is written.[24] It is therefore the framework within which I read the text.

Liking incorporates many elements from different genres in this chant-novel, giving it a new form and aesthetic. In an interview with Magnier, Liking describes her chant-novel and defends her style of writing in these words:

> L'esthétique textuelle négro-africaine est d'ailleurs caractérisée, entre autres, par le mélange des genres. Et ce n'est qu'en mélangeant différents genres qu'il me semble possible d'atteindre différents niveaux de langues, différentes qualités d'émotions et d'approcher différents plans de conscience d'où l'on peut tout exprimer. . . .
> Dans mon avant-dernière publication *Elle sera de jaspe et de corail*, tous les genres se rencontrent: poésie, roman, théâtre. . . . [25]
> [Negro-African textual aesthetic is for that matter characterized, among other things, by a mixture of genres. And it is only by mixing different genres that I deem it possible to attain different levels of languages, different qualities of emotions, and to come close to different planes of consciousness from which one can express everything. . . . In my last-but-one publication, *Elle sera de jaspe et de corail*, all genres meet: poetry, novel, theatre. . . .]

It is this new and very innovative form of writing—combining genres, juggling words and phrases, defying conventional syntax, grammar, punctuation, et cetera—that has put Liking's work on a plane all its own. Critics have applauded the unique intertextuality that grounds her work and the heterogeneous voices that are woven into these complex texts.[26]

Using the Erotic as Power Or Reclaiming the Life-Force, *Um*

Not only is her style of writing innovative, Liking has also coined the word *misovire* to better capture and (fore)ground the issues she wanted debated and played out in her chant-novel, *Elle sera de jaspe et de corail*.[27] When *Elle* was published in 1983, Liking explained in an interview with Sennen Andriamirado of *Jeune Afrique* why she felt the need to create the word "misovire." I have loosely translated this as manhater (i.e., the opposite of misogynist), though, as we see from the following excerpt, misovire is a much more complex term that moves beyond the literal definition. The concept is grounded in Liking's specific understanding of what gender relations between men and women ought to be. When they fall short, that is, when men and women do not/cannot complement each other, then a woman becomes a misovire.

Jeune Afrique: Tu n'aimes pas les hommes, Were?
Werewere-Liking: Je suis une misovire.

J.A.: Je n'ai pas compris.

W.L.: C'est misogyne . . . [*le ton calin*] au féminin.

J.A.: Tu mélange le latin et le grec. Tu devrais dire misoandre!

W.L.: Tous les puristes me disent la même chose, mais je préfère dire misovire! C'est moi qui ai inventé ce mot. Pour moi, pas pour les autres!

J.A.: Que reproches-tu aux hommes?

W.L.: Disons qu'ils sont décevants. Pas convaincants! Ils ont peur, ils rampent. Ils n'ont plus accès à la beauté!

J.A.: L'homme porte tous les péchés de l'humanité! La femme n'a-t-elle aucune responsabilité?

W.L.: Bien sûr que si! Si l'homme en est là, c'est parce que la femme a accepté d'être médiocre! On a l'impression que la femme n'est plus qu'un trou et l'homme une viande! Tout se résume au sexe. . . . J'essaie de regarder l'autre face de l'être.[28]

[**J.A.:** You don't like men, Were?

W.L.: I'm a misovire.

J.A.: I don't understand.

W.L.: That's misogynist . . . (fondly) in the feminine.

J.A.: You're blending Latin and Greek. You should have said misoandre!

W.L.: All the purists tell me the same thing, but I prefer to say misovire! I'm the one who invented the word. For me, not for others!

J.A.: What do you blame men for?

W.L.: Let's say that they're disappointing. Not convincing! They are afraid, they grovel. They don't have access to beauty any more!

J.A.: Man bears all the sins of humanity! Doesn't woman have any responsibility?

W.L.: Of course she does! If man is where he is, it is because woman agreed to be mediocre. One has the impression that the woman is only a hole and the man, meat. Everything is reduced to sex. . . . I try to look at the other side of being].

Liking did not create this word because she wanted women to hate men, but out of her frustration with so many men *and* women. What she advocates through the concept of the misovire is for men and women to confront that which makes them pitiful beings and reinvent themselves. If they do so, either there will be no need for misogynists and misovires in the universe, or else when/if the two do meet, they can better understand the reasons for their hate, and they ought to be better capable of dealing with it and reconstructing themselves. The literal meaning of "manhater" must therefore be imbued with regenerative connotations to give it its full (counter)discursive feminist meaning—one that enables us, as Liking points out, to "look at the other side of being."

In *Elle*, Liking's vision and the questions that she raises about the problems that plague Africans, and humanity in general, are written into the text. Lunaï (a symbolic representation of Africa) is the place where the story takes place. The people of Lunaï have, upon colonial contact, turned their backs on traditional knowledge and wisdom and have adopted corrupt, individualistic, and materialistic attitudes that are destroying their society. They need to rethink the decadence in which they have immersed themselves, one that is disruptive to the selfhood of the community as a whole, by falling back on purification rituals, on those positive aspects of the traditions that they have "forgotten." Liking herself uses this method, incorporating the cleansing, cathartic effect of Bassa ritual into the story and structure of the chant-novel. Right from the beginning, the diarist invites everyone to think along with her, to ponder the issues at stake, and together find solutions, as they would, I might add, in any ritual performance. Bjornson has pointed out that:

> Within the contemporary African context, Hourantier and Liking be
> lieve that ritual theater offers the possibility of overcoming social and
> psychological neuroses that express themselves in the form of parasitical
> privileged classes, petty dictators, outmoded traditional hierarchies, and
> the lethargy of common people. If Africa is to recuperate its true iden
> tity, they argue, the tensions underlying these symptoms need to be
> brought to the surface and exorcised. . . . This view of the African situa
> tion has universal ramifications because, as Liking and Hourantier
> point out, a similar procedure could be applied to the neuroses that ex
> ist in other parts of the world. (449)

Women can play an especially important role in the rejuvenation process that is described in *Elle*. The readers are invited, by the diarist who acts, I would say, as an informed "*meneur de rite*" to take part in this process, along with the people of Lunaï.[29] We are guided by the critical observations, the "word-force" [mot-force] (*ESJC* 8), and constant probing of the woman, diarist, observer, author-narrator in her quest and demand for the dawn of a new race of people "of jasper and coral." She calls herself a misovire simply because she rejects the fragmentation of identities and the limited ways of thinking that the people of Lunaï have adopted. She resents the incapacity of men and women in Lunaï to look beyond their stomachs and their sexual organs, in consequence of which the people have been reduced to sex objects. She bemoans the fact that their erotic desires, thinking, and understanding of beauty, language, identity, art—their heritage, in short—are completely lost and forgotten. This loss has culminated in the degradation, desolation, and decadence that characterizes Lunaï. The diarist therefore demands that a new race be born. This new race will not come into being out of a neofascist ideology that fosters racial or ethnic cleansing. It will be made up of people who have looked into the depths of their own fractured souls and questioned what they have been doing wrong, so as to be able to strive for better self-definition and agency. As the text tells us:

> «Et l'Homme de la prochaine Race se présentera dans un corps sain plus fort et plus harmonieux avec des Emotions plus riches plus stables et plus affinées. Sa pensée sera plus rigoureuse et plus créatrice sa volonté plus ferme et mieux orientée sa conscience plus ouverte. . . . » (ESJC, 22; Liking's ellipsis)
> [And Man of the next Race will appear in a healthy body stronger and more harmonious with richer more stable and more refined Emotions. His thinking will be more rigorous and more creative his will stronger and better guided his consciousness more open-minded. . . .]

When these people redefine themselves, they will also cease to define themselves strictly in the patriarchal or binary ways of thinking that are represented in the text by the characters Grozi and Babou. The text advocates a new race of misogynists and misovires that will exist only to complement each other:

> Il naîtra une Nouvelle Race d'hommes
> De souffle humain et de feux divins
> Et la misovire que je suis rencontrera un misogyne (ESJC 9).
> [There will be born a New Race of men
> Of human breath and divine fires
> And the misovire that I am will meet a mysogynist].

The misovire's text comprises nine "pages"—that is, the diarist refers to her nine entries as pages 1 to 9, but each entry is more than a page. There is no linear continuity to these entries. The nine pages are interspersed with the conversations of other people, such as Babou and Grozi. Their reflections bring together a whole range of thought-provoking issues such as the colonial heritage and the African post-colonial predicament; the misuses of desire/pleasure; and the development of new languages or modes of expression, and their continuity. The diarist justifies this particular choice and innovative style of literary expression at the end of her entry on "page" 5. Liking has probably chosen to write nine pages because of the important symbolic function that, she contends, the figure nine has in Bassa ritual and tradition (interview with Andriamirado). She maintains that this figure represents the point from which one can begin to make any assessment, give forecasts' or draw conclusions.

In the nine "pages" of the misovire's diary, therefore, she criticizes corrupt Africans for (mis)managing their colonial heritage and for gradually losing touch with their oral traditions and identities. She contends that the people of Lunaï can regain the values embedded in these traditions and as such remold their identities and agency by learning a new language or languages—languages of art and desire; pleasure and sexuality; of fairness and selflessness, of change and continuity—as well as a politics of transcendence.

"Pages" 2 and 3 specifically describe the relationship between woman and the phallus. The phallus is condemned both as a sexual object and a way of thinking, as that which man has used for centuries to describe and reinforce relative and bifurcated notions of desire and knowledge:

> Mais Grozi me dégoûte parce qu'il y a en lui dans les gènes je le crains la pourriture de la civilisation macho qui a régné depuis tant de siècles et qui voit tout en phallus!!! (*ESJC* 66)
>
> ... [L]es hommes s'imaginent que leur seul phallus suffit à tout compenser: la pauvreté intérieure et extérieure la petitesse de vue et d'action la laideur la bassesse. . . . (*ESJC* 150, Liking's ellipsis)
>
> [But Grozi disgusts me because there is in him in the genes I am afraid the rottenness of macho civilization that has reigned for so many centuries and views everything as phallus!!!
>
> ... [M]en delude themselves that their phallus by itself is enough to compensate for everything: internal and external poverty narrow-mindedness of outlook and action ugliness vileness. . . .]

The misovire questions the sheer stupidity of using this power destructively, like a force of nature, a perennial storm or hurricane. She questions this concept of desire, sexuality, and power that can objectify and subjugate not only women but also men themselves, who have used the phallus as an instrument of power for centuries. Such power, she believes, is only ephemeral and nonfulfilling, one that persistently and mockingly hunts the subject, comparable to the drop of mucus that relentlessly hangs on to the tip of Grozi's penis after his masturbation and will not go away, will not drop off. The "unruly" drop of sperm reflects men's lascivious behavior and the degradation of morality and ethics within Lunaï. It persistently hangs on, like unfinished business, a constant reminder of lack in men, of their inability to be whole even when they try to affirm this wholeness through the use of the phallus. The phallus, therefore, is seen by the misovire as a very limiting weapon/concept. It represents and has governed a philosophy of life that is outdated, one that needs to be eradicated because, according to the misovire, desires, drives, sexuality, and power, do not have to be constructed only by defining an other, the woman as lack, as absence, or as object:

> Je parle d'un désir qui t'enrichirait sans m'appauvrir
> D'un désir qui pourrait me remplir sans te vider (*ESJC* 69)
> [I speak of a desire that will enrich you without impoverishing me
> Of a desire that could fill me up without emptying you out]

The erotic has often been confused with the pornographic, even though, as Lorde has pointed out, pornography "is a direct denial of the power of the erotic, for it represents the suppression of true feeling. Pornography emphasizes sensation without feeling" (*SO* 54). When Liking speaks of reintegrating the spirit and mind with the body, she is speaking about rejecting the pornographic need inherent in the tragic quest for the phallus, one that is a direct denial of the power of the erotic; and of recapturing the power of the erotic, one that makes possible the coming together and coexistence of sensation and true feeling. The power of the erotic becomes a fusion of a totality of desires, mind, body, creative energies, plenitude; a force that enriches without necessarily impoverishing or depersonalizing. It is a power that rids itself of the mystique surrounding the phallus. This power is not only all-inclusive but challenging as well, since it intervenes in dualistic thinking by questioning the separation of thought and body, mind and knowledge.

Women possess this power of the erotic and should use it to achieve this fusion and fulfillment. This they can do by looking deep down into their womanhood, as does the diarist, or by descending to the abyss of their own "madness" and self-imposed amnesia, for therein lies the power of *Um*, the cosmic force that redeems people from their abyss.[30] Bjornson notes that through their joint initiation and study of Bassa ritual,

> Liking and Hourantier became convinced that the cosmic force is present in every individual. However, they also observed that people in the contemporary world habitually suppress an awareness of this force as they betray each other and seek to conceal their crimes from public view. In the light of the malaise produced by these tendencies, the two of them recognized the wisdom of purification rituals that allow people to expiate their crimes and realign themselves with the force that gives order to the universe. In Bassa, this force is called Um, and when it descends upon purified individuals, they will act unselfishly, for Um is the

principle of love and community. Such individuals will also become capable of a heightened creativity because their gestures and words will be infused with the power of this force. (448–49)

According to the diarist, *Um* is the creative force that women must repossess. She claims that if Lunaï is in such bad shape, the fault goes to women: "it is because women have become real bad luck, Tsetse Flies" ([c'est parce que les femmes sont devenues de la vraie poisse, des Tsé-Tsés]) [*ESJC* 74]. These are the tropical flies that carry sleeping sickness, a disease easily curable if diagnosed but fatal when untreated.[31] The malaise of the people of Lunaï is compared to this "sleeping sickness," both as disease and as the (dis)ease inferred in their almost total amnesia—figuratively, a suicidal and/or deadly act perpetrated on valuable oral traditions. The deadliness embedded in and associated with the tsetse fly in their lives, bodies, and environment here becomes contextually revealing and poignant. Women have become bad luck because they have become tsetse flies, in other words, they have become the agents of sleeping sickness.

The diarist finds this regrettable, even reprehensible. The story of Creation, as recounted in the novel, eloquently proves her point. According to the myth, the gods had, many times in the past, given mankind Knowledge, but each time man abused it, degraded it, and used it as a destabilizing force. Each time, the gods put the pieces back together, until they had had enough of man's irresponsible behavior and decided to keep it for themselves. But Hilôlômbi, the eldest of the gods, who had himself created mankind and in whom he had much hope, though critical of man's lethargic existence, still perceived what he thought to be an imperfection in his creation. He then decided to send a contingent of Masks on a civilizing mission, to "initiate man into wisdom, i.e., to knowledge and the appropriate use of knowledge" ["initier l'homme à la sagesse c'est-à-dire à la connaissance et à son bon usage"] (*ESJC*, 76). This initiation process, made of "cycles," each comprised a number of "skies" (steps or obstacles) to clear. The initiation went well and Hilôlômbi, confident once again in his creation, cleared the way for him till the sixth sky—the sky of Choice. Man chose to be god and this made the gods very happy. They were grateful they had deferred to their eldest, for man's choice indicated that the path of "Evolution" was open and the people could now take care of themselves without the help of the Masks. This choice also liberated the Masks from their mission as "Masters" of collective consciousness, so they could try their hands at creation as well. Hilôlômbi decided to rest and the gods took a well-deserved vacation. But when the gods woke up, on the eve of a new cycle, they were horrified that men had chosen to glide back into the (idle) animal world of slumber and short-lived pleasures where there was no accountability and no demands were made of them. This time, the gods unanimously condemned these "morons" to vegetate in the animal world, ruminating on their fate.

But some of the Masks had fallen in love with men and were sympathetic to them—specifically *Um*, who on his own, stole a bit of Knowledge, took it with him, and tried to make contact with men. *Um* was unsuccessful because "no male was interested in or would have thought to go to the heart of the earth in search of anything let alone Knowledge" ["aucun male n'avait envie de rien et n'aurait songé à aller chercher quoi que ce soit au coeur de la terre surtout pas la connaissance"] (*ESJC*, 77). Enter Soo, the woman who went to the river to "fish" for love. During her fishing and search, she came into contact not only with love, but with knowledge, wisdom, and the most powerful forces of the universe, which *Um* begged her to bear and regenerate. But she got so scared of herself, of (mothering) such enormous knowledge and power, that these were usurped by the men; the woman was "totally dispossessed" of her powers.

> Mais Soo put garder la sensation de la chaleur de ce premier contact des feux des dieux et des hommes ainsi que le souvenir de cette voix d'Amour et de Connaissance qu'elle avait été la seule à entendre et qu'elle n'oublierait jamais.
> Et à partir de ce jour les femmes eurent le pouvoir de reconnaître la puissance la beauté et la sincérité au premier contact à la nuance de la voix. (*ESJC* 80)
> [But Soo did retain the sensation of the warmth of this first contact with the fires of the gods and of men as well as the memory of this voice of Love and of Knowledge that she had been the only one to hear and that she would never forget.
> And from that day on women had the power to recognize strength beauty and genuineness on contact from the voice's nuances.]

The correlation between this Bassa myth told by Liking and the same type of myth recounted in Beyala's *Soleil* is noteworthy. What is intriguing and worth emphasizing is the fact that both writers show, through the use of myths, that women were originally either the power bearers or just as powerful as men, until men, in their greed and refusal to share power, usurped what was rightfully women's. These writers do not seem to be making a case for matriarchies. I contend that they use these myths as a discursive tool for the purpose of radical consciousness raising. They are reminding women that they had/have a role to play in their loss of power. They are provoking women into taking responsibility and regaining what they have lost. I find the idea that runs through out the novels under discussion—of women taking responsibility, taking action for themselves against oppression—to be valuable feminist politics and practice.

What happened between Soo and *Um* was an initiation rite, out of which Soo emerged empowered. Her contact with the ultimate cosmic force, *Um*, left Soo and women (who never totally gave up that original contact) with the strengths to recognize and define power and sexuality in complex, non-linear ways to which men had no access. But women lost this sense of feeling, of sensuality, and of beauty, according to the diarist, when they became satisfied with being defined as man's other, a definition that limits relations between them to sex: woman as "hole" and man as "meat", as Liking states in the interview. Women, she continues, must cease to let themselves be defined as the other of man, "n'être que la femme de l'autre" (*ESJC* 87), a quote that echoes Simone de Beauvoir's rejection of the male tendency to define woman as Other. Women must reject such definitions because they can only perpetuate the objectification of their bodies by men who only use these bodies as receptacles.

In order to create a new world, women must reclaim the full complexity of their womanhood:

> Je suis femme des hommes et des femmes qui viennent de la femme
> (*ESJC* 93).
> [I am woman of men and of women who come from woman].

They must reclaim that "mot-force," word-force, the power and knowledge that the mask *Um* offers and represents—as spiritual, supernatural embodiment of the powerful forces of divinities that inspire and guide the collective consciousness of a community toward that which is good and valuable. Moreover, they must affirm the erotic in their lives, just as Soo preserved those original energies. It is this reintegration of the erotic into their lives that would give women the power to create and bring new life to Lunaï. They must help Lunaï's people to "wake up" from sleep by refusing to be tsetse flies, refusing to be carriers and transmitters of the (dis)ease.

Throughout the chant-novel, the diarist/misovire weaves her reflections, needs, and desires in and out of the one-dimensional arguments that are (re)presented by both Grozi's Western dogma and Babou's African authenticity. These two men, who are said to be "prisoners of their time," know they are pawns in a game they are losing or have already lost. Her interventions and visions for a rejuvenated Lunaï are laced with the comments of Nuit-Noire, one of the narrative voices in *Elle*, who acts as an alter ego speaking through her, or what the critic Séwano Dabla refers to as her conscience-in-absentia.[32] The body, the diarist maintains, is more than a text of culture, it is the most discursive human asset. The misovire laments:

Vraiment, Lunaï est un village fatidique. . . .

Le pauvre de Lunaï est pauvre de tête de coeur d'esprit de Dieu. *Car le pire des pauvreté n'est-ce pas l'incapacité de voir plusieurs aspects d'une chose d'une vie, de sa propre vie !!!* (*ESJC* 44–45, my emphasis)

[Really, Lunaï is a fateful village. . . .

The poor person of Lunaï is poor in mind in heart in God's spirit. For isn't the worst of impoverishments the inability to see various aspects of a thing a life, one's own life !!!]

These words denote the complex issues that need to be resolved, that underlie the static and tragic way of life in Lunaï. In the same vein, by recapturing the complexity of their identities the people of Lunaï will be subverting the one-sided viewpoints of Grozi and Babou, bridging the gap between (Western) dogma and (African) lived experiences.

This vision earmarks, in one way, what can be read as an essentialist streak in Werewere Liking's writing. She always seems to be speaking to/for women, men, Africa, humanity, the cosmos. Liking has stated in her writing and interviews that personal change must be grounded in the context of collective change. Individual change only has meaning in the context of global change. The chant-novel points out that Lunaï's or Africa's problems are, within (post)colonial discourse, often represented as problems specific to Africans. But Liking believes otherwise; these are problems that pertain to humanity. Although such essentialism can be criticized by feminists, and especially by "Third World" post-colonial women, as too generalizing, what makes Liking's style different and innovative is her belief in specific creative and regenerative Bassa ritual, one that deserves to be highlighted, contextualized and reclaimed. Liking "exploits the dimension of ritual as a means of self-examination and self-regeneration at individual and communal levels" (Dingome 320). Individual change, as part and parcel of collective change, is useful to feminist politics and praxis. I read her positioning in the same light as the Combahee River Collective's effort to posit an identity politics that defines who they are, what their oppressions are, before they can engage in other battles with other women/ feminists. Liking does not totally reject Western ways of thinking in *Elle*. She insists on the fact that Africans via African women must rely on and (re)integrate specific identities, traditions, and positionalities in order to negotiate the links between these personal spaces and complex post-colonial subject positions. Liking seems to be reclaiming some aspects of essentialism only so long as they serve the constructive collective purpose for which they are intended. Women in *Elle* are positioned as speaking/acting subjects whose complex experiences and subject positions prove invaluable to Lunaï society as a whole.

The diarist is herself reclaiming the "cosmic force," the erotic, through her writing, in her style of writing; it is poetic, theatrical, transgressive, exalting, cathartic, because infused with initiation into many participatory and collective cleansing rituals. The diarist is also reclaiming, as a woman, the erotic that empowers her. The erotic thus becomes what Lorde calls "the lens" through which the diarist scrutinizes all aspects of the existence of the people of Lunaï, an existence that ranges from traditional to colonial and post-colonial ways of seeing, thinking, and knowing. The erotic integrates misogynists and misovires, connecting truncated selves and dichotomies that have contributed to the desolation of whole populations. The erotic as creative force is self-actualizing for both men and women, as demonstrated not only by the story but also in the style of writing itself.

Liking refers to *Elle* as a mixture of poetry, prose, drama, in short, a "texte-jeu." If the men and women in this story are seen as spectators of the same "text-play," or as participants in the ritual experience presented by the "texte-jeu," then erotic fulfillment becomes paramount to all participants. The energies acquired from this experience are presented as constructive, creative energies. I will suggest that such innovative and radical ways of writing and inscribing women's voices and experiences are important to post-colonial women who are seeking different ways of writing their texts and voices into the discourses of feminism and postcolonialism.

Lorde has maintained that the use of poetry for women (especially poor, marginalized, black women) is not a luxury:

> It is a vital necessity of our existence. It forms the quality of the light
> within which we predicate our hopes and dreams towards survival and
> change, first made into language, then into idea, then into a more tangi-
> ble action. Poetry is the way we help give name to the nameless so it can
> be thought. . . . Poetry is not only dream and vision; it is the skeleton ar-
> chitecture of our lives. It lays the foundations for a future of change, a
> bridge across our fears of what has never been before. (37–38)

Lorde grounds the transgressive and subversive nature of poetry within the realm of the erotic. The fact that Liking incorporates not only poetry but also prose and drama in her writing puts her work, in my view, at the cutting edge of post-colonial women's radical "intrusion" and subversion of Western literary canons, postcolonial discourses, and women's studies within academia. Liking's chant-novel reads like a dramatized initiation rite through which the participants of the story, the people of Lunaï, must proceed to purify the fragmentation and the passivity that has become their way of life. Knowledge is acquired in the context of play, of ritual, of song, of dance and performance.

This purification process serves a cathartic purpose for the entire community, because it makes the people one again with their universe, with the cosmos. The private and individual nature of this diary is thus circumvented by the community that is invited in (through the participatory nature of ritual) and intrudes into the private space and wealth of knowledge that the diarist is open to share.

In *Elle*, Liking clearly shows how women's sexuality is intrinsically linked to power, to the desolation into which they have let the men of Lunaï drag them. She further shows how through women's questioning of this amnesia and of their own participation in the othering of their bodies and selves, they can define new ways of seeing and knowing and give direction to the creation of a new race of jasper and coral. In her text/diary we are constantly confronted by a questioning from within outward. Again in Lorde's words, "as we begin to recognize our deepest feelings, we begin to give up, of necessity, being satisfied with suffering and self-negation, and with the numbness which so often seems like their only alternative in our society. Our acts against oppression become integral with self, motivated and empowered from within" (Lorde 58).

Liking criticizes throughout the chant-novel the numbness and self-negation that has instilled itself in the people of Lunaï. She expresses the need to revitalize the mind, the body, the language, politics, culture, nature, in short, all that will uplift the people of Lunaï from the status quo of inactivity that shrouds its citizens, male or female. Getting in touch with the power of the erotic, allowing its energies to inform and illuminate our thinking and actions is achieved, in Liking's work, through an inner search that the diarist demands of herself and the people of Lunaï. It involves a descent into the subconscious, to those original values and forces that have been neglected, forgotten or lost, to a recapturing of the powerful creative force of *Um*. The force of *Um*, which I liken here to the erotic as creative power, becomes that which revives not only the feminine repressed but the masculine as well, given that in Liking's *Elle* this repression involves both the masculine and feminine. Grozi and Babou are as "empty" and fragmented as the women who are defined as their Other. Women's liberation is directly and intrinsically linked to men's liberation. These men and women can only be reborn by getting in touch with the erotic in their lives, through a communal participation in the purification process of healing and a (re)acquisition and sharing of knowledge, wisdom and power. For Liking, othering must be rejected and difference subverted in regenerative and positive ways. How difference and otherness affect and shape the lives and identities of post-colonial women, as described by Mariama Bâ, Miriam Tlali, and Bessie Head, will be the focus of discussion in the next chapter.

4 Women Redefining Difference: Mariama Bâ, Miriam Tlali, and Bessie Head

The identities of most African and "Third World" women have been shaped by various inscriptions of difference in their daily lived experiences. Early feminists approached the issue of difference in binary terms of male/female or self/other. This approach had little regard for race, age, class, or ethnic differences. Most of all, these early binarisms also ignored or failed to problematize the fact that African and most post-colonial women had simply been represented as the Other of the West.[1] African women (writers) have, of necessity, sought to (re)construct difference in ways that undermine and transgress binary oppositions. This shift has proven to be appropriate, especially if "the other is [said to be] almost unavoidably either opposed to the self or submitted to the self's dominance. It is always condemned to remain its shadow while attempting at being its equal" (Minh-ha 71).

The process that defines African women as Other can be read at multiple levels. They are the Other of man, the Other of Western women, sometimes the Other of African American and other diaspora women. Finally, there exist other politics of difference within any given African context itself. My goal is to show how different women rely on and use their specific histories, spaces, and locations to (re)define difference and their selfhood. I will show that these issues are constantly shifting and/or interlocking in Mariama Bâ's *Scarlet Song*, Miriam Tlali's *Muriel at Metropolitan*, and Bessie Head's *Maru*.

Mariama Bâ wrote two novels before her untimely death in 1981. The more popular and widely acclaimed *Une si longue lettre* (*So Long a Letter*) was published in 1980. *So Long a Letter* has received most of the critical attention that has been given to Bâ's work. Her second novel, *Un chant écarlate*, published in 1981 and translated by Dorothy Blair as *Scarlet Song*, has been given comparatively little critical attention. Many critics hailed Mariama Bâ as a "true feminist," a "defender of women"[2] because of the enormous success of *So Long a Letter*. For example, Cyril Mokwenye describes Bâ's work as one that lays the ground work for future African women writers because Bâ is a writer who "awakens feminine consciousness."[3] Dorothy Blair has proclaimed that "*Une si longue lettre* is the first truly feminist African novel,"[4] while Katherine Frank maintains that "Bâ alone among contemporary women novelists in Africa resolves [the] crucial problem of feminism in conflict with traditionalism" ("Feminist Criticism" 47). On the other hand, both Elizabeth Wilson (1985) and Susan Stringer (1988) state in their dissertations that *Scarlet Song* is not as successful a work as *So Long a Letter* and is not so openly feminist. The issue, I believe, partially lies in the fact that Bâ has been credited with creating a new literary genre with *So Long a Letter* by writing an "epistolary" novel that does not fit squarely into the parameters of its Western counterpart.[5] I will argue in this chapter that Bâ's feminism comes through as strongly in *Scarlet Song*, even if her subject matter is mixed marriages in post-colonial Africa, a subject that some critics say does not bring out the depth of women—and of their very personal pain—as does *So Long a Letter*.

In a 1980 interview, Barbara Harrell-Bond alluded to the fact that Bâ's second novel (not yet published at the time) was about mixed marriages, and proceeded to ask Bâ whether she included both possibilities, a white husband and a black husband. To this question, the author replied:

> No, not both situations. I have taken the white wife and the African husband as the theme. Here, if it is a black woman married to a white man, we can easily accept that, at least *more* easily accept it. What counts here in Senegal for a girl and for her family is that she gets married to a man who shows himself responsible. There are lots of mulatto children here from the time of the colonialists. The colonialists took black women as wives and it never was a tragedy, you see. If the man shows himself to be understanding with the family. If he does what the family expects him to do on the material level and on the level of understanding, there are not many problems. Because here in Senegal, *it is the woman who is given into marriage and who belongs to the husband's family*. It is not the same thing with a man. The man bears the family name. He is the root of the tree which flourishes to give fruit. The fruits contain the seed which will make the race live again and nourish the ground. *Thus the problem of a white wife is more interesting from the point of view of conflict, from the point of view of shock, from the point of view of the mentality of the man's mother, and from the point of view of society.*[6]

I would like to draw attention here to the assertion that "it is the woman who is given into marriage and who [then] belongs to the husband's family." The acts of "giving" and "belonging" inscribed in women's gender set the stage for a complicated view of gender relations that must define, acknowledge, and "accommodate" gender(ed) differences. These differences become even more problematic when the woman who is "given" (or not given, like Mireille) to the Senegalese husband and his family is a white woman. A white woman married to a black man and living in an African society with a black husband puts into play conflicts on the many levels that Bâ identifies, be they racial, sexual, cultural, or political. I will begin this discussion with Mireille in Mariama Bâ's *Scarlet Song*[7] and the dilemma that Mireille finds herself in, despite and because of (her) difference(s).

Mireille . . . The Outsider

In *Scarlet Song*, in the consciousness of Yaye Khady and the ambitious or scheming women that surround her, "outsider" best describes Yaye's white, French daughter-in-law, Mireille de la Vallée. Mireille is perceived as "the intruder to be eliminated, the rival to be dethroned, in a word, the outsider. . . . " (*SS* 135, Bâ's ellipses). She is a "rival" not only to Ouleymatou, the Senegalese second wife that Ousmane, Mireille's husband, eventually marries, but even more so to Yaye Khady, the mother who sees herself as "dethroned" in the life of her son. This outsider status is conferred on Mireille for a number of reasons. She is white. She is French. She is of aristocratic origins, and her father had served as a French diplomat in Dakar. She is intelligent and intellectual, an equal to her husband in education and insight. She is neither versed in Senegalese traditions nor in the responsibilities of a daughter-in-law towards her in-laws, especially towards her mother-in-law. In stark opposition to Mireille is Ouleymatou. She is African. She is Senegalese. She is of poor origins and ambitious enough to seduce Ousmane and pave her way out of the squalor in which she lives. She is barely educated but exceedingly versed in Senegalese traditions, and she excels in the art of manipulating these traditions to her benefit. The man around whom the whole story revolves is Ousmane. He is African, Senegalese, an intellectual with university degrees in philosophy, and a high school teacher like his white wife. Most of all, he is a staunch upholder of Négritude principles, of radical ideologies that, among other things, rejected French policies of assimilation, demanded solidarity among African intellectuals, and proclaimed a return to and revaluing of African roots, identity, and heritage.

These characteristics that define Mireille and Ousmane would seem to spell doom for a mixed marriage between Mireille, the white woman, and Ousmane, the African. Mireille's father, the French diplomat, in many ways still represents the French colonizer who introduced a politics of "direct rule and assimilation" in French West Africa. He is a man who, in Mireille's words, "made speeches preaching fraternization with indigenous people" (*SS* 28), even though this never happened in practice. And then there is Ousmane, the African intellectual, who grew up and was molded by these very assimilatory French policies that drove Africans to think of themselves as Frenchmen. This process of "whitening of the mind," with the negative discourses embedded in the colonizer/colonized dichotomy and the devastating psychological impact that they have had on colonial and post-colonial subjects, was strongly criticized by Frantz Fanon in *Black Skin, White Masks*. In this book Fanon insists that the colonial encounter is fertile ground for a distinctive psychopathology, one that cannot be explained away by a universal Freudian Oedipus complex.[8]

A good number of African intellectuals such as Ousmane, many of whom had studied in France during the colonial era and after independence, married French women who came to live with them in Africa. Mireille's marriage thus puts her in a situation that was not uncommon in post-colonial French-speaking West Africa. Although there were strong attacks on marriages between black men and white women, most male contemporaries of Bâ's wrote virulent satires of white women married to *white* men, especially to colonial administrators, during the colonial period.[9] They were portrayed either as women with no future in Europe who, through their marriage to white men in Africa, acquired privilege and power which they often abused; or, they were lonely and disappointed housewives who turned themselves into seductive femmes fatales. In *White and Black: Imagination and Cultural Confrontations*, Mineke Schipper summarizes the image of the white women in African novels by male authors as follows:

> Despite her privileged position, she was often depicted as thoroughly discontented and ill-tempered. She rarely had a status of her own, had no occupation and was totally dependent on her husband and his position. Now and then allusions were made to a schoolteacher, barmaid or prostitute, but in general the white woman was only known as Mrs so and so, the wife of Mr so and so. The problem that seemed to occupy much of her time was her appearance: her complexion, her figure, her clothes, her jewelry. In the very restricted circles of colonial society, there was fierce competition among the women, each of them eager to be the most beautiful of all. . . . Another favorite pastime was the exchange of critical comments on Africa and the Africans. It was an obsessive, inexhaustible topic of conversation, providing as it did unending opportunities to make certain people feel superior by putting other people down. (47)

Mireille does not seem to fit this literary profile, given her bourgeois origins, coupled with the fact that she is an intellectual with a professional life of her own. She is also of another/younger generation of white women than those described above. The obstacles that stand in her way, therefore, are to be located elsewhere. E. P. Abanime has argued that Francophone black African novelists were highly critical of interracial/sexual relationships, not only because of the racial segregation that the French openly practiced that ran counter to politics they theoretically advocated, but also because they saw in white male–black female relationships another form of colonial domination of blacks by white. White women in interracial relationships in these novels had (sexual) relations with black men in order to spite their parents or defy the prejudices of their society. Abanime criticizes what he sees as inherent racist bias on the part of some authors in most of these works. He concludes that "African Francophone novelists have at times unwittingly subscribed to racist views by their tendency on the one hand to insist on the incompatibility of blacks and whites, and on the other hand to accept clichés and prejudices in which black comes off second-best in implicit comparisons with white."[10] Blair finds the weakness of *Scarlet Song* in such stereotypical representation. She has suggested that the subject of mixed marriages "is a trap for the writer, with its temptation to fall into stereotypes of characterization and situation" (139).

Blair discusses the working title of the novel, *Le Tetre abandonné* [*The abandoned hillock*], to prove her point. She contends that this title only "highlights the main theme of the novel, the old problem of *déracinement*," that of being torn away from one's roots (139). In other words, by tackling a problem already addressed by many post-independence male authors, Bâ is putting the same old wine in new skins. Blair concludes that the plot and structure of this novel lacks the originality of Bâ's first novel because the protagonists "act out a drama arising from the exigencies of the situation and its message, rather than as a product of their own intrinsic personalities" (140).

There is no doubt that writing about mixed marriages in post-colonial Africa, especially about marriages between African men and white women from the former colonial centers, calls into play and question a number of stereotypes about whiteness and blackness that are not only racial and cultural but ideological as well. However, the most important issue for me, in *Scarlet Song*, does not lie with the stereotypes but with what Mariama Bâ, a woman writer, does with these stereotypes that more often than not were the focus of writing by her male counterparts (Ferdinand Oyono and Mongo Beti from Cameroon, or Sembene Ousmane and Cheikh Hamidou Kane from her native Senegal). As I mentioned in the introduction, the gender and experiences of these women writers are crucial and intrinsic to the portrayals of fictional women in their texts. Of import to me, therefore, is how the women in this novel make these "stereotypes" and what I see as other very intrinsic qualities, work to their advantage or detriment. Reading this novel along the lines of stereotypes alone can be very reductive; it is, to say the least, limiting.

Blair makes two points upon which I will build. The first takes as its point of departure the Wolof proverb that inspired the working title of the novel:

> Kou wathie sa tound'eu boo yeck mou tasse (Ka 134).
> When one abandons one's own hillock, any hillock one climbs will
> crumble. (Blair 139)

According to Blair, Mireille's marriage is a failure because both spouses abandoned their traditions, cultures, and totally different upbringings to indulge in a partnership that could not have worked. This is a narrow reading of the story. Nor do I agree with the idea that these two are only meant to act out a drama with a message at the expense of their own intrinsic personalities and struggles. There are two other mixed-marriage couples in the story, whose marriages do stand the test of (Senegalese) times. I will argue instead that the intrinsic "personalities" of Mireille and Ousmane is what actually drives the story.

Mireille, to me, is not the only "outsider" in this story, as her mother-in-law, her "extended" family, and other people in Dakar describe her or would want her to be. She can only be described as an "outsider" in opposition to those who see themselves as "insiders" who do not want anything to do with that "outsider." Mireille, Ousmane, Yaye Khady—the overbearing mother of Ousmane—are all, each in her or his own way, outsiders, to themselves, and to difference. I agree with Minh-ha that "[d]ifferences do not only exist between outsider and insider—two entities. They are also at work within the outsider herself or the insider, herself—a single entity" ("Not You" 76). Mireille, Ousmane, and Yaye Khady relentlessly look at difference in a one-sided way; they keep a close watch on the outsider outside of themselves, but rarely on the outsider within. They are locked into a dynamic of difference that remains hierarchical and dualistic; one that neither crosses boundaries nor overlaps; one that prefers to preach an ideology of separatism (for their own selfish gratification) instead of shared responsibilities. Audre Lorde has suggested that it is not differences that separate women as much as their "reluctance to recognize those differences and to deal effectively with the distortions which have resulted from the ignoring and misnaming of those differences" (SO 112). Mireille and Yaye Khady are reluctant to deal with the distorted definitions that they have of each other. Both women fail to "see" and deal with difference as that which Minh-ha maintains must both be "beyond and alongside identit[ies]" (WNO 104). They are ultimately consumed by their differences.

Ousmane and Mireille remain "outsiders" to their difference(s), right from the beginning of their "friendship":

> Ousmane never talked of himself or his family. He left Mireille the mo-
> nopoly on self-revelations (*SS* 19). . . .
>
> His pride and self-respect would not allow him to speak of the working-
> class neighbourhood of Usine Niari Talli. He erected a mental barrier be-
> tween the aristocratic Mireille and the red earth walls of his parents'
> hut. He said aloud, 'I will never speak of my family or let you into the se-
> cret garden of my origins until I am ready to ask you to be my wife.'
> (*SS* 20)

Ousmane Gueye is clearly ashamed of his working-class origins in front of this aristocratic French woman and hides all there is to know about himself. But he shrewdly ascertains that Mireille does love him for himself and not as "the one toy missing from [her] collection [of family memorabilia], in [her] world where [her] every wish is gratified" (*SS* 20). It is very ironic that Ousmane does not want to be thought of as a "toy" while Mireille is continuously described in terms that liken her to a toy or, worse still, an illusion, a myth.

Yaye Khady refers to the woman in the photographs as a "film-star," a description that Ousmane never refutes (*SS* 20). The numerous color photographs that Mireille sends to Ousmane after her father separates them by whisking her off to France are said to look like "picture postcards" (*SS* 58). Mireille is said to possess "the beauty of a Jinnee . . . [t]he spell that had bewitched and seduced [Ousmane]" (*SS* 67). This statement only reinforces Ousmane's ancestral ties with similar "invisible creatures" known as *rab*. When his future second wife, Ouleymatou, rejects him in their teenage years because he "sweeps the house, fetches buckets of water and smells of dried fish" like a girl (*SS* 10), Ousmane is deeply hurt but consoles himself with pride in a long lineage that has courted the *rab*:

> What was Ouleymatou, compared with these spirit-brides, who were
> said to be as beautiful as the moonlight, with huge luminous eyes and
> long silky hair that hung right down their backs as far as their knees?
> (*SS* 10)

Likening Mireille to a "Jinnee" only puts her in this mythical category of *rab*, "spirit-brides." Although Ousmane acknowledges and appreciates Mireille's intelligence when they meet at school for the first time, images of him gazing at her "silky golden hair" and "grey-blue eyes," of him staring at her milk-white neck "gilded by the reflections from her hair," seem to predominate (*SS* 16, 19). She is " 'his princess,' " the one whose photographs he spends most of his time purring over, the one who is more of an exotic, sensuous essence than a person in flesh and blood. All these descriptions turn Mireille into a fantasy, a prohibited Otherness that the young black male worships, desires, and molds in his subconscious.

When Mireille gets married and returns to Dakar with her husband, her mother-in-law "showed her off to her women friends as an object of curiosity and did not hesitate to bring them to the house, like a visit to the zoo" (SS 81). In another observer's eyes, however, Mireille is "[t]hat beautiful French flower in the hands of that lout! How can that nigger appreciate her, with that hair, those eyes, that aristocratic air?" (SS 88) Guillaume, the French man who speaks these words, proceeds to nickname the couple "Beauty and the beast," thus reversing the "beast" perception by applying it to Ousmane rather than Mireille. The text, in the same vein, does not offer any descriptions of Ousmane by Mireille. Mireille is said to have chosen one of Ousmane's photographs, the one that is "a really good likeness" and that she carries everywhere with her, between the pages of her books, to the bathroom, to bed, and so on (SS 23). The only other description of Ousmane is that given by Jean de la Vallée, who distastefully refers to the man in this photograph as "that object" (SS 25).

There are many levels at which Mireille's difference is constructed within the text. Because she is treated as a mythical, supernatural figure, exclusive of race, age, class, ethnic difference, she is not only idealized but simultaneously objectified, like a fetish that can be worshipped without fully comprehending the proportions of power and control embedded in such fetishization. It is ironic how such fetishization is quite similar to the glorification of the African woman as Mother Africa by the theorists of the Négritude movement. In the same way that the French assimilated the Africans, so, too, it can be argued that when Ousmane asks Mireille to become a Muslim before their marriage, he can also be accused of reversed assimilation and acculturation. Guillaume likewise objectifies Mireille, but this time *because* of her race, class, and ethnic differences. His reactions betray his own internalized colonialist attitudes. He treats Mireille not as a woman in her own right, but as the white (French) "Woman" who has negated or compromised her place and position on the "pedestal" of the "purity" of her race. By referring to Ousmane with this hurtful word, "nigger," who plucks a "beautiful French flower," Guillaume objectifies Mireille and dehumanizes Ousmane. His language of pedestals and racial purity has a threatening tone through whose correlation I can infer the racist and sexist histories of slavery and oppression in the United States, where black men were lynched for (allegedly) bringing white women down from the pedestal on which they had been placed by white males.

Yaye Khady's objectification of Mireille is, in one way, similar to Guillaume's, in the sense that it is also based on Mireille's race, class, and ethnic differences. But the comparison has an even deeper level of familial specificity. For Yaye Khady, Mireille is rejected as a rival, and not just as a daughter-in-law, but as the "wrong" type of daughter-in-law. She reacts indignantly when she is told that her son has clandestinely married a white woman in Paris:

> A *Toubab* can't be a proper daughter-in-law. She'll only have eyes for her man. We'll mean nothing to her. And I who dreamt of a daughter-in-law who'd live here and relieve me of the domestic work by taking over the management of the house, and now I'm faced with a woman who's going to take my son away from me. I shall die on my feet, in the kitchen. (*SS* 66)

The fear of daughters-in-law "taking away" sons expresses the mother's fear that links with their sons will be cut off or drastically curtailed. Mireille's difference is seen as a problem not only at the racial level but also at the familial, cultural level. Yaye Khady assumes that a Senegalese daughter-in-law would automatically fit into a predetermined sexual division of labor—one that directs another woman to relieve her of her domestic duties, thus rewarding her for her numerous years of motherhood and childrearing. Yaye Khady thinks first of herself and her position, and these selfish feelings blind her from developing any constructive or meaningful relationship with Mireille.

Her conceptions of a white and a black daughter-in-law are diametrically opposed:

> A black woman knows and accepts the mother-in-law's rights. She enters the home with the intention of relieving the older woman. The daughter-in-law cocoons her husband's mother in a nest of respect and repose. Acting according to unspoken and undisputed principles, the mother-in-law gives her orders, supervises, makes her demands. She appropriates the greater part of her son's earnings. She is concerned with the running of his household and has her say in the upbringing of her grandchildren. . . . (*SS* 72, Bâ's ellipsis).
> 'A white woman does not enrich a family. She impoverishes it by undermining its unity. She can't be integrated into the community. She keeps herself apart, dragging her husband after her. Has anyone ever seen a white woman pounding millet or fetching buckets of water? On the contrary, the white woman exploits others who have to do the jobs for her that she's not used to doing! . . . She alone controls her household and all the income is turned to her benefit alone. Nothing goes to her husband's family.' (*SS* 73)

This is clearly not a simple issue of either racial or sexual difference but one of women's power and familial control, a struggle that Mireille's difference(s) only serve to bolster. Mireille becomes an outsider and must remain one because Yaye Khady can no longer control those whom she deems she has a right to control by virtue of her position as a mother and mother-in-law. Yaye Khady makes no effort to teach or integrate Mireille into the circle of "undisputed principles." Her silence does not (un)speak, unravel or (re)name those principles to accommodate Mireille. Instead, her "eloquent" silence becomes fertile ground for confrontation and blatant disruptive behavior. For example, she rudely intrudes on the couple's privacy every Sunday morning by walking straight into their bedroom without knocking and without offering any apologies. There is no written role or unspoken principle that gives mothers-in-law the right to walk into their married son's bedroom. Yaye Khady fast becomes one of those mothers-in-law who "act like veritable rivals to their daughters-in-law. They suck the younger woman dry with their insatiable demands" (SS 72).

Yaye Khady always wins the showdowns between Mireille and herself. She is aided by a son who, after getting married to the "spirit-bride," begins to dance to a different tune. He becomes the nemesis of those African intellectuals who live on the margins of the societies and traditions they claim to be upholding. Ousmane's longtime friends, Ali and Lamine, watch with awe as he becomes more racist and sexist with age. They dismiss his callous actions as insincere, having no bearing whatsoever on the need to embrace a lost African identity and heritage. We are told that Lamine, for example, "had an open mind and was not tormented by ideological complexes. His negritude did not sit heavily on him" (SS 98). The magnitude of Ousmane's racist and sexist behavior makes him exploit cultural differences for his own selfish benefits:

> At Ouleymatou's he was the lord and master. He undressed where he
> liked, sat where he liked, ate where he liked, dirtied anything he liked.
> Any damage was made good without a murmur. In this home his slight-
> est whims were anticipated. . . .
> According to Mireille's strict upbringing, the only place for food was the
> living-room or the kitchen. The war on cockroaches had its rules! It was
> unheard of to nibble a piece of bread in the bedroom. As her husband's
> equal, she would challenge his ideas and decisions when these did not
> suit her. . . . Certainly that did not displease Ousmane. But no man is
> averse to being the leader and having the last word. A man doesn't re-
> fuse the prerogatives he is granted. (SS 148)

Mireille finds herself caught between these so-called "prerogatives." She is at the crossroads of a battle between a domineering mother-in-law and an egotistic husband. One is tempted to see Mireille as the victim in view of Ousmane's self-centered behavior.

In some respects, of course, Mireille is no victim. She does not walk blindly into this marriage, despite Ousmane's reticence about his family origins. It is ironic that she "learns" about Africans only from the media in France after she has been taken away from the narrow, sheltered life that she lived as the diplomat's daughter in Dakar. While in France, one of her letters to Ousmane attests to this "awakening" and her own personal convictions:

> 'I am determined to retain my own identity as far as essentials are concerned—the values that I believe in, the truths that light my path. As I have no wish for you to turn into a puppet for me to manipulate, I am quite prepared for you to reject any of my ideas which your conscience will not let you accept. So I, too, am unable to present you, by way of dowry, with a list of sacrifices I shall be making. I shall not tamely espouse all Africa's causes. For the face of Africa, in this country, is not just the face of the immigrant worker, who endures the hardships of exile so that he can feed his family back home. Africa also assumes the loathsome face of those who sponge unashamedly on women in order to survive. I have heard so many heartrending stories, sobbed out by women with faces contorted with misery. . . . These women warn me to beware when I talk to you.' (SS 41)

Mireille is definitely aware of some of the stakes involved in marrying an African. She recognizes that certain sacrifices will have to be made, but there is a big difference between what she knows and the actual reality of living in Dakar with a man, who, as Lamine notes, "won't make any concessions, while demanding concessions from others" (SS 99). Mireille then finds herself embroiled in a dilemma:

> [T]hat of married life and that of a black man's wife in Africa. Over and above the endless round of normal conflicts, inherent in the life of any couple, she suffered from other attacks. She felt as though they wanted to bury her alive and resurrect her as another woman who would have nothing in common with her except her physical appearance. But she resisted. She was shaken in her most firm and innermost convictions and every day eroded a little more of the courage with which she had armed herself when she left her own country and turned herself into a rebel. (SS 99)

What she deplores as her father's oppressive institutions, along with the racist stereotypes that would define the black race as "the grinning primitive Negro of the 'Banana' adverts; the educationally sub-normal Negro; the pudgy-faced, round-eyed Negro" (*SS* 28–29), are replaced by her husband's equally oppressive institutions. In Dakar, she feels asphyxiated, like a person buried alive, choking under the "new" inflexible rules and regulations that seem to govern her existence and suppress her difference.

Nevertheless, Mireille makes herself the victim of her own difference. She adamantly refuses to participate in any of the traditional events that are part of Senegalese life. She fails to grasp the importance of the endless and demanding negotiation embedded in communal life, which forms the essence, the backbone of any African community. Her impatience leads her to give up too easily when she realizes that her efforts to please her in-laws are not appreciated or reciprocated. She fails to recognize the fact that she needs many years to build and ground her identity and difference within her new family and community. Consequently, she resents Ousmane's friends for coming into her home without being invited, eating up her food without her express permission, thus pitting French etiquette against Senegalese etiquette. She is overwhelmed by the complexity and multiple levels of her struggles. She resorts to making clear-cut distinctions about what is right and wrong, what should be done and what ought not to be done. Ousmane's and Mireille's reluctance to seek compromise forces them to quarrel more often than they negotiate.

> And so the rift that separated them increased. . . . Each of them lived encapsulated within themselves.
> Ousmane was irritated by Mireille's meticulousness, her mania for organising, her insistence on clear-cut distinctions which led to endless classifying and reclassifying. . . .
> Mireille's lack of sympathy got worse. She was inflexible, indignantly condemning behaviour which she qualified as 'lack of breeding', 'impertinence', 'lack of consideration', or 'vulgarity', according to the circumstances. (*SS* 93)

Mireille's biggest mistake comes from the fact that she does not actively seek out and court a women's network that would support and offer other avenues for undermining oppressive institutions. Mireille's rebellion in France takes pragmatic form when she takes part in the historic May 1968 revolt of students and workers. The equivalent form of rebellion open to her in Senegal would have been her adherence to the women's network, a sort of radical "underground movement" that would have shown her the ropes, which strings to pull, and which not to and when. As we see from the story, women like Yaye Khady, her mother-in-law, Ouleymatou, her co-wife, or Rosalie, her friend and Ali's wife, once they pinpoint what they want, know exactly how to go after it.

Unfortunately, Mireille adopts a classist attitude toward these women and loses valuable ground and comfort. She has women like her sister-in-law and friend, Soukeyna, or Rosalie at her disposal, but she does not make ample use of them either. She quickly gives up on the advice given her by Rosalie, such as to visit her parents-in-law without her husband, bringing them something new to wear on special occasions, since "giving solves many problems." She does not take it too seriously when Rosalie advises her: "Don't shut yourself up in your room brooding when your husband is entertaining his friends. A cheerful welcome from you will be your trump card if outsiders try to break up your marriage" (SS 96–97). This is crucial because if "outsiders" did try to break up her marriage, then those to whom she had given a "cheerful welcome" in her home would be the first to rally behind her and beat some sense into her husband or whoever the "outsider" might be.

Mireille oddly enough authenticates the "outsider" status that has been conferred on her. She abhors "the demands of a society that was completely oriented towards outward appearances, in search of status, and in which her husband seemed remarkably at ease" (SS 97–98). This attitude clouds her personal struggles and undoes the gains that she attempts to make. Worst of all, she becomes an "outsider" even within the confines of her most private and political space, her home. In this space, she and her husband seem to be engaged more often than not in ethnocentric, ideological battles, in the absence of the love that once kept them close together.

Mireille gives up the network of women, gives up courting her in-laws, and recoils inward. Her enthusiasm for life wanes with every new day. She sits, lonely, in her unswept home, either feeling sorry for herself, resenting her predicament, or waiting for her husband to return to her. She completely neglects herself while spending endless time reading his letters, reminiscing over what had been their ideal love for each other. She puts all her hopes on the child growing within her, hoping that this child will be a stepping stone to reconciliation, harmony, and rebirth of the love that once was. But the child is born a *Gnouloule Khessoule*, a child who is "Not black! Not white!" (SS 164).

The tragedy of the birth of this child lies, to a certain extent, with the Senegalese family's rejection of a mulatto. Yaye Khady, who welcomed Ouleymatou's son with open arms and with the baptism rituals that reconfirm her own status among her peers, treats her mulatto son with disdain. "Mulattoes" have been called many different names within specific cultural contexts: métis, half-breed, mixed-blood. In Cameroon we also have the term "café au lait," and the list goes on.[11] As Françoise Lionnet maintains in *Autobiographical Voices: Race, Gender, Self-Portraiture,* "these expressions always carry a negative connotation, precisely because they imply biological abnormality and reduce human reproduction to the level of animal breeding."[12] Odile Cazenave contends that when perceptions of these children are limited to a biological economy, they are automatically rejected by the societies into which they are born.[13] Yaye Khady's reaction does not come as a surprise, given that the mother of the child was never integrated into the family. Even Ousmane, in discussions with his friends on what they see as the rebirth of Africa and the evolution of the black woman, states that, "cross-breeding impoverishes and exploits Africa" (*SS* 122). He claims that mulatto children would become "the harshest and most contemptuous racists," except those mulattoes whose mothers had adopted the African lifestyle (*SS* 122). It does not occur to him that these children can only absorb the limited, racist thinking and teaching of people like himself. Of course, he holds no monopoly on such attitudes: Mireille thinks that her parents might tolerate her return home, but not with a child who is "an embarrassing piece of evidence" (*SS* 160).

The tragedy of this colored, mixed-marriage, mixed-blood child lies partly with the families, but even more so with the contradictions embedded in its mother's (racial) identity and experiences. Mireille is justifiably offended by the discriminatory politics inherent in the label "neither white nor black" that is given her son. Unfortunately, she is a woman whose life at this point seems to have been overtaken by the need for clear-cut definitions, who consequently cannot deal with or take advantage of the richness, the plurality of discursive practices embodied in/by her son's *métissage* in positive ways.[14] She fails to grasp the heterogeneous nature of her son's identities and difference(s), as that which is undefinable, completely resisting definition, that which is multiple, shifting, and ungraspable. This heterogeneity is inscribed and succinctly expressed by the Senegalese expression *Gnouloule Khessoule,* irrespective of the pejorative connotations that the expression also embodies. Mireille's inability to place her son in an open or shifting category forces her to hate her child, to adopt an attitude similar to that of a Yaye Khady or a Jean de la Vallée. Gorgui does not bring the joy she expected from his birth; consequently, this child's failure to serve as a bridge to her husband drives her to madness and a desperate act of murder. I see in Mireille's failure to fully comprehend and exploit her son's multiple identities the main reason behind her breakdown and the irrational decision that she makes. She keeps on chanting the words *Gnouloule Khessoule!* over and over, but this chant does not have a purifying, cathartic effect on her thoughts. It triggers instead the tragic (re)action:

'There is no place in this world for the *Gnouloule Khessoule!* A world of filthy bastards! A world of liars! You, my child, you're going to leave this world! *Gnouloule Khessoule!*' . . .

A drowsy Ousmane Gueye was greeted by a dishevelled naked woman screaming, 'Dirty nigger! Liar! Cheat! Adulterer! It's better with your nigger woman, isn't it? Answer me! You love your little Blackie better than your *Gnouloule Khessoule!*' (*SS* 164)

Mireille's screams underline Bâ's virulent critique of polygamy, of some Négritude ideologies, of dualistic thinking, and of the interaction of all of these with or in opposition to difference. Technically speaking, Ousmane is not a cheat. They are both Muslims, and that gives Ousmane the right to marry another wife. Ousmane turns out to be a cheat because of the insincerity and secrecy involved in his second marriage, one that he contracts because he claims "[his] meeting with the white girl was determined by Fate" and because of "his resolve not to 'Be lost' " (*SS* 149). The trappings conferred on this second marriage—at once clandestine and idealistic—vividly point to the fact that, though legal, it has no substance. Why would a Muslim be afraid of his wife's finding out about another wife? Because he has married the second wife for the wrong reasons:

> 'Ouleymatou, the symbol of my double life!' Symbol of the black
> woman, whom he had to emancipate; symbol of Africa, one of whose
> 'enlightened sons' he was.
> In his mind he confused Ouleymatou with Africa, 'an African [sic]
> which had to be restored to its prerogatives, to be helped to evolve!'
> When he was with the African woman, he was prophet of the 'word
> made truth', the messiah with the unstinting hands, providing nourish-
> ment for body and soul. And these roles suited his deep involvement.
> Mireille, armed by centuries of civilisation, could survive, with her iron
> will, her enthusiasm for a confrontation, and with her immense fortune.
> (*SS* 149–50)

Herein lies the strongest feminist statement made in this novel. It takes shots at African men, patriarchal institutions, and essentializing discourses delivered by privileged African intellectuals who have either idealized African women (to suit their own black nationalism) or see them as helpless victims who are just sitting around waiting for the "enlightened sons" to come and either liberate or care for them by nourishing their bodies and souls. Where are the "enlightened daughters," one might ask, and when will they also save the black man? The Other woman, Mireille, the "outsider," does not escape Ousmane's essentialist thinking. She can survive because she is and has all that Ouleymatou is not. If Ouleymatou is that figurative symbol of Africa, what then is Mireille? Fanon's theories suggest the answer: she is most probably the prohibited Otherness desired by the black male from the moment of the colonial encounter.

Ousmane's thinking proves wrong on both counts. Ouleymatou does not confuse her identity or subjectivity with that of an elusive African identity. She plans a way out of poverty and the slums and gets exactly that. And Mireille does not "survive," in spite of her race and class privileges. Indeed, those advantages only serve to compound an already difficult existence with Ousmane in Senegal. His personal or idealistic convictions accentuate their differences instead of bringing them together. They both use their outsider/insider relationship, or what I prefer to call their outsider/outsider relationship, to validate power struggles. Minh-ha suggests that in order for race, class, and ethnic differences to survive and complement each other, they must seek to undermine opposition as well as separatism. Difference must "[n]either [be] a claim for special treatment, nor a return to an authentic core (the 'unspoiled' Real Other), it acknowledges in its moves, the coming together and drifting apart both within and between identities" ("Inappropriate/d Other" 3). Mireille and Ousmane use their differences as essences, and this has proved very limiting and tragic in their relationship. The fact that they often regress to "an authentic core" in their deepest moments of conflict prevents them from coming together and drifting apart within and between identities and differences.

This movement of or between different worlds, worlds that converge and/or conflict, is tackled by Miriama Bâ as well as by Mariam Tlali. But the concept of difference in Tlali's work, written in the context of South Africa, problematizes other complex levels of difference in a society where people are first and foremost categorized by race and treated differently because of their skin color. I will argue that Tlali seeks to transgress the limited barriers of race and gender differences through the character of Muriel in *Muriel at Metropolitan*.[15]

Muriel, in between "Battlefields" of Difference

There are two distinct worlds in *Metropolitan*:

The one, a white world—rich, comfortable, for all practical purposes organised—a world in fear, armed to the teeth. The other, a black world; poor, pathetically neglected and disorganised—voiceless, oppressed, restless, confused and unarmed—a world in transition, irrevocably weaned from all tribal ties. (*MM* 11)

This binary division sets the tone for the challenges, centered around political, racial, and ethnic differences, that are confronted by these very opposing worlds. The salient contrasts, in terms of skin color, white/black (racial difference); rich/poor (class difference); armed/unarmed, organized/neglected (power relations), are all laid out from the word go. The blacks belong to the disadvantaged and dispossessed side of this opposition. They are the laborers, factory workers, garage workers, office workers, helpers, domestics, in short, the "black proletariat" (*MM* 111): voiceless, landless, oppressed, their victimization compounded by their dislocation from tribal ties. Most of them have no cultural or traditional knowledge to fall back on for strength, support, and guidance. Of all these difference(s), skin color is the marker that consciously or unconsciously, overtly or covertly, drives other conflicts grounded in difference. Henry Louis Gates has suggested that, in such circumstances, "race" becomes "a trope of ultimate, irreducible difference between cultures, linguistic groups, or adherents of specific belief systems which—more often than not—also have fundamentally opposed economic interests."[16]

According to the character Muriel, "Blackness" is synonymous with multiple degrading definitions that have been constructed within the South African context as ontological givens. The blacks are either irrational or inherently stupid, they are lazy, they are good objects for amusement, they are born to serve:

> [The white people] picked on me because it was natural to them to do
> so. In the Republic of South Africa, the colour of your skin alone con-
> demns you to a position of eternal servitude from which you can never
> escape. You cannot throw away the shackles no matter how hard you try.
> You are like a doormat. You are a *muntu*; your place is at the bottom of
> the ladder and there you must stay. (*MM* 117)

Many workers speak of themselves as "bilong[ing]" [sic] at one time or another to this or that white master, and are often identified by their Pass numbers, just as convicts would be (*MM* 76). Worst of all, they are "nameless." They are the "so-called shop-girls and shop-boys, tea-boys and tea-girls, flat-girls and flat-boys—in fact, so-called 'boys' and so-called 'girls' of every age and description" (*MM* 95). It is the namelessness of these people that most eloquently speaks of the dehumanizing effect of the apartheid system under which they live. Because they are thus de-humanized, the question of difference cannot be contained in the trope of "race" alone, as this problematic must simultaneously question sexual, ethnic, cultural, and political difference. Muriel suggests that the struggle comprises slices of a war fought on many "battlefields," beginning with re-humanizing the black race by deconstructing the c/overt relations of power and knowledge intrinsic to the South African construction of racial difference. This struggle must begin by naming and putting a human face where there is facelessness, a name where there is no-name.

Muriel's disclaimer at the beginning of the story only goes to emphasize the fight that lies ahead in the novel:

> I am no authority in the study of human behaviour. I do not profess great knowledge. I am not a writer. But I do not have to be any of these to know about Africans, their feelings, hopes, desires and aspirations. I have read a lot of trash by the so-called 'authorities' on the subject of the urban Africans. . . .
>
> The whites, with a few exceptions, are ignorant of Africans' living conditions. This is partly due to their indifference and partly to their misconceptions. The Africans, on the other hand, know more about the whites because they *have* to know them in order to survive. *With even fewer exceptions (in fact a very negligible proportion) their daily bread depends entirely on their going into white homes, factories, garages, offices, or standing at their door-steps looking for work, pleading or even begging. With the Africans it is a matter of life and death.* (*MM* 10–11, emphasis added to last two sentences)

Muriel's task is twofold: to challenge those "so-called authorities" on the subject of urban Africans; and, as an urban African herself, to tell her story and experience(s) of that subject. This critique of who has the authority to say what on urban Africans is pertinent in a South African context where black women, especially, have not been able to write for very personal and political reasons that range from their own work within and outside the home, to not having the time to read and write, to apartheid laws of exclusion, et cetera. Miriam Tlali has stressed in interviews with Sonia Lee[17] and Cherry Clayton that when whites write about them, either they say nothing that they, the blacks, do not already know, or they dismiss the works of blacks outright. She tells Clayton, "I finished writing the first novel, *Muriel*, in 1969, but it was only published in 1975, and even then too, very much expurgated. A lot of material was removed from it to make it acceptable to the white reader."[18] Lockett has stressed the fact that both race and gender are important factors that have accounted for the several stereotypical images of black women by white male and black male authors.[19] I believe Tlali's novel must, therefore, be read both as a challenge to an exclusive male literary canon that has inadequately portrayed the black woman through its own I/eye and an invaluable introduction of the female voice in this South African literary tradition.

Muriel not only rejects their "trash" but legitimizes her own lived experiences, as well as those of other Africans with whom she interacts on a daily basis.[20] This matter of life and death for blacks, inscribed in the fabric of her society's "separate but unequal worlds," is what Muriel sets out to share. This she does by narrating her own struggles to subvert the endemic discrimination at Metropolitan Radio, the installment purchase business where she works, whose clients are mainly Africans like herself. Metropolitan is a microcosmic duplication of the South African situation in which, Tlali maintains, "[s]ocial obstacles are always linked to political and economic obstacles" (interview with Clayton 71).

In the first three pages of the novel, we are introduced to the Africans, who are repeatedly described as standing motionless, bored, tired of waiting and staring blankly in front of them, like zombies. "They just stood there at attention, motionless, staring. The boss shouted, Adam! Just get rid of these boys" (MM 9). There is a clear distinction between who "the boss" is and who the others are. Hierarchies are implied or stated in every act or transaction. Muriel does not get better treatment than any of the "boys." Her blackness determines what kind of work she gets and how her co-workers deal with her. Though the most educated and the most experienced among the women working at Metropolitan Radio, she earns barely a third of what the white women earn. She notes, "Mrs Green and I were therefore both juniors, but because of the colour of my skin, I was the least" (MM 52). The classist/capitalist system of South Africa works for whites. It is a "workers' paradise" that is really a hell for blacks.

Spaces and locations in the shop are literally partitioned along racial lines. There is what Muriel calls a "white side of the 'line' " and a black side (MM 26, 52). She cannot share the toilet with white women. In every instance, her race takes precedence over her gender, so she must suffer the humiliation of using a dirty toilet with (often drunken) men or spend her money to rent clean, hygienic facilities. To Muriel's consternation, the dividing line is even applied to objects of identification like job cards. She comments on the fact that she had never before seen apartheid "applied to ledger or record cards!" even though the Coloureds[21] had the same names as the Europeans (MM 15). Polite warning letters with phrases like " ' . . . We would like to advise you that . . . ', ' . . . Please bring down your arrears . . . ' " (MM 49) are sent out to white customers, while black customers get rude letters such as: " 'This account is simply rotten. Unless it is paid up as soon as possible, we shall definitely repossess our goods!' . . . There was no need to be polite to an African customer" (MM 49). The poorer black clients are always made to wait in line, while "European customers never stood in a queue." Moreover, the former are charged more for their goods and pay higher rates of interest (MM 113).

As she goes to work every day, Muriel notes and reflects on the constant and permanent victimization of blacks at Metropolitan Radio. These lead her to heed the reasoning of her co-worker, William No. 2, about the futility of staging a protest. He tells Muriel:

> 'I've come here to work for my wife and children and I don't want to land in gaol. The white man is the boss in this land, *he* is the one holding the gun. . . . '
> [Muriel] was thinking, 'William No. 2 is right, in a sense. They are crude; their grammar is bad; their spelling is even worse. But what does it matter? *They* have the say anyway, "they are holding the gun".' (*MM* 48–49)

Given the reality of apartheid laws, Muriel tries her best to make her life bearable. It is through her eyes and experiences that one can read the various methods utilized by the black workers in an ever-present uphill struggle to make the life that they have worth living. Their differences become the only weapons at their disposal to subvert that which stifles them in their daily lives; they become a prerequisite to survival.

Although subversion sounds like an impossible task given the conditions of the black workers' lives, Muriel's criticisms, laced with the many expository comments of the author, clearly delineate ways in which such personal and political goals can be achieved. Huma Ibrahim has suggested that "the documentation of black women writer's lives is not simply an accusatory act against imperialism, but rather an attempt by South African women writers to understand their own multitudinous and complex roles in a perpetually embattled state. Ultimately this dialogic documentation, herstorical in nature, forms the foundation of a communicative dialectic between South African women writers and other third-world women writers and readers."[22] Tlali has insisted that even though her writing echoes the cry of all South African women, it must in all instances be political, the politicized nature inherent in the (act of) writing itself. In an interview with Schipper, she explains: "Before *Muriel* was banned I received a lot of letters from so-called white liberals in Pretoria, Bloemfontein and other such places. *They wrote in Afrikaans*: 'Oh, Miriam, we've read your book, but things are not really as bad as that.' Maybe that was their opinion, but they have a different way of looking at things" (62, emphasis added).

This "different way of looking at things" is partly grounded in the privileges of "whiteness" and of class. The politicization of race, of actions, of events, of struggle in general in the bid for black people's survival is, therefore, aptly captured in Tlali's portrayal of Muriel. For example, Muriel constantly shows us how race is an arbitrary construct used by whites and that black people must undermine for survival in the most tragic of circumstances as events unfold at Metropolitan. One such event takes place when Muriel's child gets ill with chicken pox. Mr. Bloch bars Muriel from coming into the shop until he is reassured by his doctor that Muriel does not represent any danger. An African customer (who had to wait for a long time before Muriel could enter the shop and serve him), is so disgusted with the boss's "irrational" behavior that he cannot help but comment on such racist attitudes: " 'And *we* are the ones who do everything for them. Even in their homes *we* cook for them and clean their homes. It is our womenfolk who nurse their babies and give them food' " (*MM* 90). I see in this customer's comment an illustration of the point that black people have to begin their struggle by first recognizing that they are a force, *the* only force to reckon with. If one takes away all the menial labor that they provide in the chain of production that goes from use-value to surplus-value, then the whites cannot reap the fruits of what they "control." This idea is pertinent to issues that have been addressed by feminist-standpoint theorists such as Nancy Hartsock, Sandra Harding, Jane Flax, and Dorothy Smith, who have demonstrated how women's unremunerated, "menial" labor has been very instrumental to the maintenance and progress of capitalist societies and ideologies of domination. Women's work and daily lived experiences, which tend to focus on the transformation of the immediate and concrete world, permits men to abstract from the concrete realities of women's daily work and existence. The analogy that I wish to draw here is with the rich white South Africans who, in the same way, abstract from the concrete realities and work of the black masses.

Muriel describes the multitudes that comprise the "black proletariat" as the key to shifting the balance of power in her society:

> The sunny Republic of South Africa—the white man's paradise—would never tick without them. To their labour the Republic owes her phenomenal industrial development. If they were suddenly to divert their course of movement now, at this moment, to their so-called homelands instead of to the locations on the fringes of the 'white' towns, the white masters would go down on their knees to beg them to remain. As I slowly made my way back to the shop, I thought, our leaders, most of them in exile, others buried alive, and others already dead, were right— a sit-down strike through-out the country lasting only two weeks would bring the whole paradise crumbling down. (*MM* 111–12)

However, it would be suicide for blacks to stop working for whites. First, because these black people are the most dispossessed and working for the whites is their only form of livelihood; and second, because it is "illegal for non-whites to strike" (*MM* 80). Yet, the idea itself is revolutionary, and when Muriel begins to think in terms that would make those who have power bargain with those who have none, her thinking lays the groundwork, at the political level, for negotiation and change.

Muriel regrets what she calls the detribalization of black South Africans, most of whom do not know where they come from because their fathers and grandfathers had no links with their chiefs. Documentation that provides details about the identity of each family member and/or tenants of houses shows on the column under "State Name of Chief," the entry "No Chief" (*MM* 45). The loss of diverse and valuable ethnic points of reference further polarizes the crisis of identity and alienation that Africans face.[23] They have no alternative than to embrace a new way of life that is at best colonizing. Muriel insists that these cultural differences be recorded and preserved for future generations who "may read about them and know them" (*MM* 44).

But for most black people in South Africa, reading is a luxury that lies in excess of the struggle for daily survival against hunger, homelessness, joblessness, death. Tlali often reiterates the fact that blacks do not have the money nor the time to buy and read books, let alone write: "black women do not have time to dream," she laments (interview with Clayton, 71). Even though Tlali can be said to use writing as a means to capture some of her dreams, she still maintains that in addition to the plethora of basic needs of blacks is one simple but vital problem of space. "I write in my kitchen," she says, "not out of choice, but because there is nowhere else where I can write" (77). She has candidly spoken about the many problems that she faced vis-à-vis her own education, which was replete with interruptions. She acknowledges that she had not read much when she wrote *Muriel at Metropolitan* and so, when she quotes other writers (such as Trollope), she is not bragging as much as highlighting the importance of education for black women. We see the character Muriel admonishing herself for not staying home and reading more books when her child was sick: "I could have read all the books I had always wished I could find time to read. Imagine. I felt like kicking myself," she says (*MM* 88).[24]

It is by knowing who one is, by understanding one's own difference, that one can better interact with or confront another person's difference; in other words, knowing the outsider within facilitates facing the outsider without. Knowing who they are and where they come from can enable black South Africans to better confront the white people and the politics that oppress them. This vital point of reference is clearly demonstrated in the story when the blacks speak to one another in their different "vernaculars."

Switching to African languages becomes a subversive act that places the peripheries in defiance of or in response to well-defined centers. The novel shows how the white women often complain that they cannot concentrate on their work, especially when the blacks converse in their own tongues:

> [The blacks] all laughed, and so did Lebitso Pharahlahle, who until
> then had been sitting morosely 'waiting for the master', as patiently as
> only an African can wait.
> But Mrs Kuhn was already complaining about the noise 'on the other
> side'. She called, 'Adam! You'd better go and watch the door.' And turn-
> ing to the other two white women, said, 'The *noise* they can make, I
> can't take it, you know, Mrs Stein, I can't concentrate!' (*MM* 43)

This is an unconscious reaction that belies the anxiety of the whites at being shut out. They are no longer in control. Because they do not understand what the blacks are talking about, Mrs. Kuhn resorts to contemptuously referring to their conversations as "noise," a reaction that only betrays her own shortcomings. Had she understood what they were saying, she would have realized, with awe I might add, that the Africans were talking about the appropriation of their lands by white men; the loss of respect for their traditions and customs; the loss of the powers of their chiefs, who had been replaced by superintendents or city councils controlled by white men.

Speaking these languages therefore gives the blacks some much-needed privacy, empowers them by acting as one of those " 'lines' " that cannot be penetrated by white people or whiteness, in the same way that Mr. Bloch would revert to Yiddish or Mrs. Stein to Afrikaans when they did not want the Africans to listen in on their conversations. Another advantage that only the blacks have is their ability to combine and use the languages of the center and those of the margins. With these combinations, they can shift between the center and the margins at the expense of those who remain locked into the center. For example, Johannes, the tea-boy, understands Yiddish. Daisy, the new (black) clerk and typist, is, in Muriel's judgement, more of a true South African citizen than any of the white people, because Daisy's "marked fluency in both English and Afrikaans made her, besides Mrs Stein and myself, more bilingual than all the white women who had worked at Metropolitan Radio while I was there. She also spoke many African languages" (*MM* 172). The possibilities of using such linguistic knowledge as strengths are endless in a society where one's every move or word is monitored and/or sanctioned.

On more personal levels, individuals like Douglas, Agrippa, and Ben invert the very system that oppresses them and make the system work for them. Douglas devises a devious but easy plan with the postman to steal radios from

Metropolitan and sell them for their profit. Agrippa exploits his position as the "boss-boy" who, with his contingent of "lorry-boys," is the only one who can repossess Mr. Bloch's goods. Repossessing becomes the trump card that Agrippa uses in unscrupulous and abusive ways against Mr. Bloch and the clients.

Ben uses his room to augment his miserly income by renting it out for sexual encounters to couples. The price can skyrocket from twenty-five cents to ten rands per night if the man is white and the woman African or Coloured. The whites have the money and he can "get them black or Coloured women" (*MM* 34). The cruel measures taken against miscegenation in South Africa, coupled with the implementation of the Immorality Act, provide the impetus for this "trade" to flourish and to maintain gender exploitation. Racial segregation no longer obtains when white men want to sleep with (poor) black or Coloured women, those Others who, in their (white men's) thinking and actions, provide them with an overly sexualized/racialized identity that they can consume. In this illegal racket of prostitution, Ben seems to be the one who gains the most, given that he holds the white man's escapades with black/Coloured women as a double insurance policy.

Unfortunately, there are Africans like Adam who have retreated into their own world. They have been so burnt out by the system that they are clothed in a "hard impenetrable mask of indifference" (*MM* 94). On Adam's expressionless face can be seen the direct correlation between economic and political and racial alienation. What Muriel "reads" on Adam's face serves as an impetus to her own critique of any type of oppression that is engineered and reinforced by racial difference:

> It was no use trying to speak to him. The long, painful years of contact
> with the whites had developed within him a hard protective core of in-
> difference to all their constant abusive reprimands. He was dead inside.
> (*MM* 106)

Adam's silence/indifference, though tragic, is a silence that speaks volumes, one that can itself serve as a weapon. It is a silence within which, paradoxically, are embedded the horrible scars endured from being treated all his life at Metropolitan as an underdog, without respect or agency. The protective "skin" generated by these same scars shields his pain and lets him survive the daily insults at Metropolitan.

Of all the things that bother Muriel, the threat of being "dead inside" like Adam scares her the most. Once one feels such internal, psychological emptiness, there seems to be no reason for living. She must reject the death of the subject itself with all her might by constantly interrogating racial, ethnic, gender differences, not letting the mask of indifference cover her like a shroud. She cannot let herself be burnt out by any type of discrimination. She first recognizes that she is "between two fires. [Her] own people on the one hand, and the white staff on the other" (*MM* 81). The white staff, especially the women who think Muriel is there to compete with them, do not hide their resentment toward her education and work experience. Often they ask her who she thinks she is, reminding her that no matter what, she is black and will forever be a "helper," a "girl," inferior to them. Muriel knows that someone like herself will always "be tolerated rather than accepted; because [she is] an indispensable nuisance" (*MM* 62).

With her own people, the battle is on two fronts: she resents their suspicions of anyone in a position like hers, suspicions that make her feel like a traitor, that give her the " 'white-master's-well-fed-dog' feeling" in the pit of her stomach (*MM* 91, 120). She is also troubled by the obvious sexism of the black men who hate giving her their Passes because they cannot stand being subjected to unnecessary scrutiny by a woman. If living in the townships is like "living on shifting sands" (*MM* 169), so, too, is working at Metropolitan. It feels like walking a tightrope with an extremely shaky balance:

> We were all dissatisfied, all trying to get the best out of life, but we were
> struggling on different battlefields. For the whites, the struggle was that
> of human beings trying to better themselves. For the blacks it was the
> under-dogs, voiceless and down-trodden. In addition to making a living, we still had to labour under the effects of a rigid apartheid system
> supported by our own colleagues. Yet we had the same problems. We
> were all under the thumb of a demanding boss, who was unyielding in
> many ways, giving little consideration to the fact that we had private
> lives of our own, homes and dependants to look after. . . . [T]he white
> workers did not want to acknowledge their commonness with their
> black colleagues. As long as the system granted them certain privileges
> that the other racial groups did not enjoy, then they were contented. If
> they were treated the same, they grew resentful. (*MM* 163)

Black South African women writers have been criticized for their deference to men and their wariness, as Margaret Lenta puts it, "to protest against the status quo in relations between the sexes."[25] One example in *Metropolitan* that can validate this critique is seen when Muriel refuses to ask Johannes to bring her anything from the store, even though Johannes makes the offer. "How could I?" she says. "He was a man and I was a woman. According to our custom a woman does not send a man. We reserve a place, an elevated place, for our men" (27). Muriel seems to be condoning these patriarchal customs that endow men with privilege instead of overtly rejecting the status quo. Is she influenced by her nostalgia for traditions that have been lost, by the detribalization of her people, one might ask? Lenta is right in that one does not find many open criticisms of black male attitudes *toward black women* in this first novel by Tlali. By not openly challenging the sexism of these men, even if she is prompted by a false sense of nostalgia, Muriel participates in reinforcing her own oppression. The battles she has to fight must also include a reassessment of her own beliefs.

Waging the war on different battlefields, at Metropolitan and within the black community, becomes inherent in Muriel's own personal and political battles. She takes on "the difficult task of teaching [whites] that the black African is no *gogga* but a human being" (*MM* 175). The resignation that she tenders after she is asked to make tea is concrete proof. Her boss takes her resignation to be a ploy for a salary increase and cannot understand why she keeps insisting she does not want a raise. To Mr. Bloch, Muriel is "healthy and fat," signs that he treats her well and she should not complain. All Muriel wants is for the whites to realize that when they asked her to make tea, "they had gone too far and were treating [her] with contempt" (*MM* 120).

Her husband's response to this treatment is different:

> The answer came spontaneously like a natural reflex action to a painful stimulus. To him I was someone special in spite of being black. He spoke as if he had a goddess for a wife, not a mere black nanny. What right did he think he had to make such a decision, didn't he know that he was only a 'boy', and what right does a mere 'boy' have to be proud of anything—his parents, his wife, his children, what?
> My husband was aware of all the repercussions yet he was willing to make the sacrifice. You don't often come across a type like him these days. (*MM* 118)

This passage underscores the strong feminist statement made against the destruction of the black family in South Africa and the need for a (re)birth of that family unit. The fact that Muriel's husband initiates and supports her resignation emphasizes the need for cooperation between black men and women, in their daily personal lives. Such cooperation complements their participation in struggles that are played out on the political arenas (like the thousands of women and children who used prayer, song, and tears to resist the removal of black families from Sophiatown). Women need their men and vice versa to promote their humanity, to open the eyes of those who only see them as monkeys, baboons, or nannies.

At many points in the story, Muriel laments the breakdown of the black family as the result of apartheid laws. For instance, Muriel needs to be absent from work to acquire a permit for her niece to visit her. If she loses her job because of her absence, her boss has to sign the termination in her pass-book. The employer's signature would cancel her " 'right to be in the magisterial area of Johannesburg for more than seventy-two hours', nor would [she] be 'entitled as of right' to remain with [her] husband for more than seventy-two hours" (*MM* 70). A law that unequivocally separates a woman from her husband simply because she has no job is a law that can be accused of deliberately destroying the family unit/institution, of creating a dysfunctional family situation for the benefit of the law makers who "separate to conquer." As Barbara Loy has noted, "In South Africa the Bantu Consolidation Act of 1945 along with the pass laws of 1952 and since, laws empowering the government to relocate people at will, have effectively divorced men from their wives and children in the townships. Parents have been separated from their children, and people have found themselves without family and home and roots. With these laws, the government has effectively destroyed the traditional Black family in South Africa."[26] In this system, many poor, black, and jobless women, some of whom were mothers, ended up the most victimized.

According to Muriel, this system grounded in cheap labor "undermines all laws of morality and decency, making nonsense of the concept of the family unit. . . . To my mind, it is comparable only with the slave trade" (*MM* 61). It makes togetherness with her husband and children, getting his support when she needs it, sound like a luxury, like utopia; but the closeness and intimacy of the family unit is the best way of getting her humanity and sanity back on track. Although Muriel does not leave Metropolitan after the tea incident, the whites are forced to treat her with respect. Mrs. Kuhn orders in tea and tops her "generosity" with an extra cup for Muriel. What I find most revealing in this incident is the fact that Muriel's action not only questions but also seeks to put an end to the implicit naturalization of black servitude and the racialization of poverty.

The tea incident becomes one of many that Muriel uses to get her points across to her white colleagues. She gradually changes her position from her earlier refusal "to stage a one-woman protest" (*MM* 22) to protesting laws that deny people "the vote" (*MM* 178) or challenging blind attitudes of white people who believe that everything is all right. She gradually unsilences herself, and her acts bit by bit unveil her progress towards a more shifting yet still problematized subjectivity and agency. The heated arguments she exchanges with her colleagues about the successful heart transplant from a Coloured donor to a white recipient only go to confirm her conviction that race, class, and gender difference(s) must not necessarily breed victimization, insecurity, and contempt. It confirms her insight that white South Africans should give up being "segregated in the imaginary oneness" because this oneness does not exist. Nor does "imaginary oneness" obtain in a context where the heart transplant demonstrates "how inextricably the lives of whites and non-whites are interwoven" (MM 174). By using examples pulled out of the daily lived experiences of South Africans, black and white, Tlali presents the strongly historicized and politicized dimensions of race and gender relations.

The differences that separate South Africans—black, white, Coloured—can thus be addressed only through a process that enables individuals to continually question their difference in the light of other differences. Muriel's ability to pinpoint these "battlefields," to negotiate her movement on "shifting sands," both in the townships and at her work place, give her the agency to boldly write her final resignation letter. Even though she does not have an immediate job opening, this decision frees her of the "shackles which had bound not only [her] hands, but also [her] soul" (MM 189). Muriel and Tlali are thus fighting personal and political battles against racial, ethnic, class, and gender difference in a society where racial difference puts other differences in eclipse. As Muriel tells Mrs. Kuhn, "I don't think I'm like you. I don't *want* to be like you. I'm very proud of what I am. You're too small, too full of hatred. You're always preoccupied with issues that don't matter!" (MM 70). In the statement, "I don't *want* to be like you," lies both Muriel's refusal to give up her own difference and a reclaiming of difference as identity. In choosing to be preoccupied by things "that matter," she moves beyond hegemonic concepts of difference as practiced at Metropolitan Radio.

If the lens through which Tlali views and critiques difference is focused on the predicament of black women in the South African context, Bessie Head's look at difference tends to be both specific (to the Botswanan context) and universal (to the African/global context). Head has stressed the global vision that she projects on the problems that she addresses in some of her work. She says of *Maru* in an interview with Adler et al.:

> It is so full of immediate life experience that has to be communicated urgently. There are *huge* urgent messages. What irritates me is that you can't communicate that the production of a book is a full, rich activity— it's got nothing to do with nationalism. But then it's never been a strain for me to *widely* write about life, and then just push onto it a Botswana background. It's simply that I'm living here (10). . . .

There's a *huge* problem like racialism and *Maru* is the long-term view—
it's going to live forever. This *huge* view of life, this is what I'm really
getting at. (13)

In *Maru*, Head shows prejudice is universal, but what is insightful about her
critique is her ability to portray how the ugly face of prejudice is deeply inscribed within African thought processes and behavior. The position of the
Other is here reversed. The African is no longer the Other of the West, of the
white man; rather Africans are treated as other Others, as outsiders within
their clearly defined ethnocentric spaces.

From the beginning to the end of the novel, Head sets up multiple and varying levels of difference that ground her inversion of the Other. She questions
the false pretensions that Africans give of themselves as a people who tolerate
ethnic, class, and gender differences. They are like the people of Dilepe, who
pretend to be incapable of "being exposed to oppression and prejudice. They
always knew it was there but no oppressor believes in his oppression. He always
says he treats his slaves nicely. He never says there ought not to be slaves" (*M*
48). Head's *Maru* gives us an in-depth critique of the dynamic of difference
and oppression from the perspective of an insider-within.

Margaret the Masarwa: An Experiment with/in Difference

Margaret Cadmore is different. She is a Masarwa, a "Bushman! Low
Breed! Bastard!" (*M* 11). To be born a Bushman or a Masarwa is to be "the
equivalent of 'nigger', a term of contempt which means, obliquely, a low, filthy
nation" (*M* 12). Margaret is an educated Masarwa, the adoptive daughter of the
white missionary woman educator working in Botswana after whom she is
named. Though born a Masarwa, she looks like a half-caste, and the fact that
she has a white woman for a mother and "relative" only confirms, in the eyes
of her teacher-training schoolmates, that she is Coloured. The white Margaret
Cadmore not only recognizes Margaret's status as an outcast at birth, but decides to use her daughter as an instrument for experimentation on the complex
issues that circumscribe racial and class difference among the Batswana. She
clearly tells her daughter:

> "They are wrong. You will have to live with your appearance for the rest
> of your life. There is nothing you can do to change it."
>   It never stopped the tin cans rattling, but it kept the victim of the tin
> cans sane. No one by shouting, screaming, or spitting could un-Bush-
> man her. There was only one thing left, to find out how Bushmen were

going to stay alive on the earth because no one wanted them to, except perhaps as the slaves and downtrodden dogs of the Batswana. (*M* 18)

Margaret Cadmore's Masarwa child will have to learn to live with her skin and all the abuse that goes with it, but she does not have to be a slave to illiteracy as well. She gives her daughter the weapon in the form of education that would "enable [her] to gain control over the only part of her life that would be hers, her mind and soul" (*M* 16). The younger Margaret will also have to use her education to help the Bushmen "stay alive on the earth" as both her mothers (biological and adoptive) would have wanted. This child's existence is problematic, and she has to confront multiple obstacles in her cultural context. The text tells us that:

> Of all things that are said of oppressed people, the worst things are said and done to the Bushmen. (*M* 11)
> How universal was the language of oppression! They had said of the Masarwa what every white man had said of every black man: 'They can't think for themselves. They don't know anything.' (*M* 109)

Bessie Head's personal history is in some ways similar to that of Margaret Cadmore. Bits and pieces of Head's biography and other essays were published in 1990, in *A Woman Alone* and *Tales of Tenderness and Power*. She was the daughter of a white woman (whose family was one of the top racehorse-owning strata of South African society) and a black stable boy. When her pregnancy was discovered, Head's mother was locked up in a mental hospital in Pietermaritzburg where Bessie Head was born in 1937. Head's mother insisted on Head getting a good education and left Head enough money at her death. Head was raised by a Coloured foster mother, then sent to a mission orphanage when she was thirteen. Head grew up without any sense or "traces of a family history," with "no frame of reference to anything beyond herself." She suffered so much persecution in South Africa that she exiled herself to Botswana, where, to her consternation, she also found prejudice. *Maru*, she says, "*definitely* tackles the question of racialism because the language used to exploit Basarwa people, the methods used to exploit them, the juxtaposition between white and black in South Africa and black and Masarwa in Botswana is so exact" (interview with Adler et al., 11). Despite the discrimination that Head suffered as a refugee in Botswana, Botswana still offered a less oppressive environment and setting to her literary expression than South Africa ever could.

Margaret Cadmore is born into a world where her people are untouchable, despised, just for being Bushmen. Her adoption by a white woman at birth and her upbringing create "a big hole in the child's mind" because, "unlike other children, she was never able to say: 'I am this or that. My parents are this or that' " (*M* 15). The fact that Margaret could never say, "I am this or that," becomes the focal point on which the story is constructed. It is Margaret's inability to define herself that is relevant to my discussion of the (re)construction of race, class, and ethnic difference among the Masarwa. Margaret becomes the weapon that Head uses to question and subvert the power and privilege of the Totem, who own the Masarwa as slaves. These Totem are a class of people whose paramount chiefs are painted by Head as symbolically representative of the powerful and corrupt African royals and politicians. They are representative of the ruling class that uses its power to oppress, instead of to liberate its people.

That Margaret's identity defies any definition becomes the trump card for her agency and strong subjectivity. Her subjectivity is portrayed as being in constant flux, and her reactions catch the discriminatory Totem people off-guard. We are told that Margaret's heart and mind were composed of a little bit of everything:

> It was hardly African or anything but something new and universal, a
> type of personality that would be unable to fit into a definition of some-
> thing as narrow as tribe or race or nation. (*M* 16)

The ungraspable nature of her identity undermines the foundations on which the biases against her people and herself are built. The inability of those who come into her life to pin her down to any reductive, one-dimensional social definition throws them off balance and leads them to question not only who Margaret "really" is, but who they themselves are. They are forced to rethink the well-established binary oppositions that they have long upheld. Such binarisms, Head maintains, are at the roots of racial hatred. Her research among the Batswana for the writing of *Maru* reinforced her conviction that this re-thinking process is paramount to the existence of the Masarwa people and to human existence. She explains:

> I found out above all that that type of exploitation and evil is depen-
> dent on a lack of communication between the oppressor and the people
> he oppresses. It would horrify an oppressor to know that his victim has
> the same longings, feelings, and sensitivities as he has. Nothing pre-
> vented a communication between me and Botswana people and noth-
> ing prevented me from slipping into the skin of a Mosarwa person.
> (*AWA* 69)

Margaret's open and straightforward declaration of her ethnic origins, "I am a Masarwa," rattles everyone, even the most virtuous, taking them by surprise, invading their scorn for the other. They all take her (want her) to be Coloured. Or else, how can she fit their definition of Bushmen as non-thinking, subhuman illiterates? She must be a Coloured who benefits from the graces of her white parent. They have heard that the new schoolmistress has an academic profile of excellence; how could this person be a Masarwa? They think she is Coloured; and the light complexion of her skin makes it easier for them to tolerate her person, because coupled with her first-class education is the fact that "the new mistress had dignity and respect for everyone" (*M* 51). This reason is enough for them to enroll their children in Margaret's Leseding school. But by boldly stating her tribal and racial background, she antagonizes those people whose only means of self-gratification is treating other "lesser-humans" with contempt. The following word of "advice" from Mistress Dikeledi to Margaret foreshadows the reactions of the people of Dilepe:

> "Don't mention this to anyone else," she said, shock making her utter strange words. "If you keep silent about the matter, people will simply assume you are a Coloured. I mistook you for a Coloured *until you brought up the other matter*." (By 'Coloured' Dikeledi meant children of mixed marriages who also could look half Chinese, etc.)
> "But I am not ashamed of being a Masarwa," the young girl said seriously. (*M* 24, my emphasis)

As soon as Pete, the principal of the school, learns about "the other matter," he reverts to calling Margaret " 'it' " (*M* 40). He wonders whether Mistress Dikeledi knows she is talking to "it?" In no time, her identity has shifted from "the other matter" to "it." Pete is so dumbfounded by Margaret's candor that he cannot hide his own confusion. He finds Margaret to be "a mystery" and this bothers him, even though as an intellectual, he prides himself on impressing others with his knowledge. Pete finds himself in a contemptible position of ignorance and can only snort, " 'They don't look you in the face and say, 'I am a Masarwa.' It was like a slap in the face. I had given her a loophole. Coloureds are just trash, but at least she could have passed as one" (*M* 44). Pete does not realize that by accepting his so-called loophole, Margaret would, by the same token, be "killing" her-self. Her refusal to take on an-other identity, a Coloured's identity, to ease her situation and avoid hostility, puts everything in disarray. The people's reactions towards Margaret are no longer simple, exclusionary counteractions based on tribe and race distinctions, but those of caged animals with their backs to the walls, of people who, for the first time, find symbolic and physical confrontation where formerly there was none. She remains a mystery, an enigma, that they all try to unravel.

Two men, Maru and Moleka, find themselves entangled with this enigmatic

Masarwa woman. Maru (the future paramount chief) and Moleka (his rival and closest friend) are the two Totem men who run the affairs of the Dilepe tribe. They find themselves enmeshed in this ungraspable "it" that is Margaret. Both men are described in these terms:

> The clue to Moleka and Maru lay in their relationships with women. They were notorious in Dilepe village for their love affairs, and the opposing nature of their temperaments was clearly revealed in the way they conducted these affairs. The result was the same: their victims exploded like bombs, for differing reasons. . . . Moleka and women were like a volcanic explosion in a dark tunnel. Moleka was the only one to emerge, on each occasion, unhurt, smiling. . . .
> It was different with Maru. . . . Maru always fell in love with his women. He'd choose them with great care and patience. There was always some outstanding quality; a special tenderness in the smile, a beautiful voice or something in the eyes which suggested mystery and hidden dreams. He associated these things with the beauty in his own heart, only to find that a tender smile and a scheming mind went hand in hand, a beautiful voice turned into a dominating viper who confused the inner Maru, who was a king in heaven, with the outer Maru and his earthly position of future paramount chief of a tribe. (M 34–35)

Moleka, the womanizer, whose sexuality is both attractive and destructive to women, falls in love, for the first time in his life, with Margaret. No one, not even Dikeledi, Maru's sister who loves Moleka herself, knew "where he had hidden his heart" (M 27). Margaret is the only woman he treats differently. Her "quiet and repressed heart" comes alive when she meets him and vice versa (M 21). Moleka is said to make her "feel as though she was the most important person on earth, when no one had ever really cared whether she was dead or alive" (M 30).

Margaret meets the all-powerful Maru for the first time when she goes to see him about a bed that Moleka had lent her upon her arrival at Dilepe. Maru wants the bed returned, and she matter-of-factly agrees to comply with his order. Margaret is said to have, "looked down at him, indifferently, from a great height, where she was more than his equal. It had nothing to do with the little bit of education she had acquired from a missionary" (M 64). It had everything to do with who/what she was, that complex subject who quickly understands that Maru has complete authority and cannot be opposed by anyone.

Margaret, the Masarwa, the despised subject, becomes the object of desire of the two most powerful men in Dilepe. Before Margaret's arrival, their different personalities seemed to mutually complement each other, facilitating their love for each other and their personal goals. Suddenly, this love triangle becomes of dramatic import, as it ultimately exposes their ambitions, laying bare who Maru and Moleka really are. Moleka keeps on silently loving and being silently loved by Margaret, while coveting the powerful administrative position of paramount chief. Maru engineers and promotes a union between his sister, Dikeledi, and Moleka while secretly planning "to snatch" Margaret away. When Dikeledi gets pregnant, Moleka marries her, earning his right to the position of paramount chief, leaving Margaret for Maru. Maru resents losing Moleka's "creativity" and covets Margaret to "replace" Moleka. The selfishness of these two men is clearly stated in the text:

> [Maru] needed a puppet of goodness and perfection to achieve certain things he felt himself incapable of achieving. He could project the kind of creative ferment that could change a world, but he was not a living dynamo. [Dikeledi] was. So was Moleka. All he wanted was the freedom to dream the true dreams, untainted by the clamour of the world. Moleka and Dikeledi were the future kings and queens of the African continent, those of stature in character and goodness. He, Maru, was a dreamer of this future greatness. (*M* 70)

Maru and Moleka scheme and struggle to achieve their respective goals. Margaret becomes the one trophy that they each want to win, her "quiet," probing attitude bringing out the good and the evil in them. I agree with Lloyd Brown, who has suggested that the underdeveloped narrative of Margaret and Moleka's mutual attraction "is consistent with Head's presentation of sexual roles as modes of power" (172). Head uses Margaret's intermediary position between these two men to question and revise how the two view each other; but she also questions the larger context of African politics, and the use of power by the men who hold it and wield it. Women's position in this arena of power politics is most revealing. They are used as pawns by men for personal and political fulfillment. Dikeledi gets the man she loves, not because he feels the same strong emotions for her, but because this marriage gives him the chance to "dethrone" Maru. Margaret silently marries Maru, against her will, to "save" her people.

Margaret's silence, coupled with her painting and drawing, act as the most subversive and the most revealing elements of her subjectivity and agency. As a Bushman, Margaret "had no weapons of words or personality, only a permanent silence and a face which revealed no emotion, except that now and then an abrupt tear would splash down out of one eye" (*M* 17). Her silence and the mask that is her face are as (un)revealing as they are intriguing. Once in a while this silence is broken, not by words, but by a single tear. The use of the verb "splash" in reference to *one* tear aptly and figuratively conveys how much *is said* by that one tear. It is a tear that trails behind it a whole history of being spit on, screamed and laughed at; of rejection, victimization, and dispossession. That tear bears not only Margaret's mind and her soul but also entire herstories.

For Margaret, both silence and painting become weapons against race and gender discrimination. The paintings vividly bring to the surface that which is burgeoning underneath, but which remains concealed by verbal silence. They are an expression of her yearnings to be free and her refusal to be locked into predetermined race and gender hierarchies. But, ironically, they also communicate her "willingness to be incarcerated" to Maru, who "reads" her silence as his right to possess her.

Margaret's friend Dikeledi gradually discovers the "oddities" that are embedded in Margaret's silence after an incident in the classroom. Margaret handles the children's racist uproar with quiet rage (she visualizes herself breaking their necks) and dignity. Her tribe and race become inconsequential to the richness of who she is, and her ability to move in and out of subject positions. As Coco Fusco has suggested, one's otherness can be used as a measure of resistance that does not necessarily "imply one sole position of otherness—it can also mean being able to do a lot of code switching to survive" (82–83). Margaret engages in a great deal of code switching to accommodate the different types of discrimination directed towards her. We are told that

> She was a shadow behind which lived another personality of great vig-
> our and vitality. . . . [T]he two constantly tripped up each other.
> Dikeledi had seen that morning also that she was very violent and domi-
> nant but seemingly unable to project that hidden power. You were never
> sure whether she was greater than you, or inferior, because of this con-
> stant flux and inter-change between her two images. (*M* 71)

Margaret's character makes the crucial points that Bessie Head wants carried, having herself seen the ugly face of racial prejudice, victimization, and alienation. Head would agree with Lorde, who says that if we have no patterns for relating across our human differences as equals, those differences will remain "misnamed and misused" (*SO* 115). The most powerful man of the Dilepe tribe, Maru, gives up his throne to the next most powerful man, Moleka, in order to marry Margaret, the untouchable Masarwa. He is convinced that she can learn to love him because they are kindred spirits, who "dream the same dreams" (*M* 124). He is persuaded by the paintings that she has made of the places he has seen in his dreams but never spoken about:

[He thought] of her as a symbol of her tribe and through her he sought to gain an understanding of the eventual liberation of an oppressed people. There was this striking vitality and vigour in her work and yet, for who knew how long, people like her had lived faceless, voiceless, almost nameless in the country. That they had a life or soul to project had never been considered. At first they had been a conquered tribe, but the conquered were often absorbed through marriage. Who could absorb the Masarwa, who hardly looked African, but Chinese? (*M* 108)

Margaret remains "conquered" and is "absorbed" through marriage to Maru. Many critics have questioned this marriage arrangement and Maru's orchestration of his sister's marriage to Moleka (who then becomes paramount chief) in terms of what it says to women. Some believe that this marriage only serves to undermine Margaret's identity and subjectivity, as if she were waiting for the prince charming to come along and relieve her of her misery. Cecil Abrahams, for example, describes the novel's plot as "a rather weak, vapoury study on the theme of racial prejudice" whose ending "seems somewhat contrived,"[27] and maintains in another essay that the novel, "unfortunately, has a fairytale ending."[28] Charlotte Bruner has stated that "Margaret's story is inconclusive. She has achieved the education and the prestige of a teaching position. But she cannot maintain these in an alien setting."[29] Yakini Kemp contends that "Head wanted to see the Masarwa freed while leaving intact the elitist and patriarchal social relations that continue to suppress her Masarwa protagonist."[30] But critics also agree that Head's greatest strength is her portrayal of strong individual women and their relentless search for self-definition and regeneration.[31]

The fact that Margaret gets married as if in a game in which women are exchanged to appease men, and then is carried off to live in a distant land, raises many questions about Margaret's own liberation. Her marriage shatters boundaries and pervasive practices of discrimination with symbolic political implications for the Masarwa. It reshapes the faces of ethnic, race, and class differences that have taken root in the discursive practices of Dilepe. But, ironically, the liberation and freedom of the Masarwa is potentially gained by making Margaret the victim of Maru's power.

Bessie Head has spoken lovingly of her reasons for writing *Maru*. Not only did she want to write a story on the hideousness of racial prejudice, but she wanted "the book to be so beautiful and so magical that [she], as the writer would long to read and re-read it" (*AWA* 68). Head has addressed the fact that she was raised by *different* mothers, and how each individual child "needs" a mother, no matter what. One also needs and deserves an acceptable, peaceful environment to grow up and live in. She found such a place in Botswana. In the Introduction to *Tales of Tenderness and Power*, Eilersen writes about the author:

> Bessie Head always maintained her individualism. Though feeling strongly about racism and sexual discrimination—and having gained by the bitterest experience a considerable knowledge of both problems—she never allowed herself to be totally identified with either African nationalism or feminism. Her vision included whites and blacks, men and women. What she feared was the misuse of power, what she strove towards was human goodness and love. The idea of the basic goodness and decency of the ordinary person never left her. Though she became increasingly susceptible to the evil around her as she grew older, including the constant misuse of power at local, national and international levels, she clung bravely to her ideals. This often made her feel isolated. Her quiet village life became a retreat. (14–5)

Head's beliefs and wishes for a better humanity that must learn to balance "the good and the evil" lead me to contend that the ending of this fairytale is not contrived. Furthermore, I can see Margaret choosing to be Moleka's wife, in the spirit of true love, only if he *is not* a paramount chief because she knows that becoming a royal wife would only serve to put her on public display. That would have meant switching one form of "display" for another. A life with Maru, away from public display, provides her with the peace of mind to explore her creativity.

Arthur Ravenscroft notes that when one reads Head's novels, "[i]t is as if one were observing a process that involves simultaneously progression, introgression, and circumgression."[32] The character of Margaret is constantly in flux, refusing to be hemmed in by any one person or discourse. The first ten pages of the story, which in fact narrate the story's resolution, illustrate this point. Despite her marriage to Maru, one can read within the text that the process of Margaret's personal fight for freedom and self-determination is only beginning. Maru is haunted by the demons of his actions and his fears that Margaret would abandon him:

> It was only over the matter of Moleka that he was completely undone, not the way one would expect a wrong-doer to be undone. He was thrown off-balance by the haunting fear that he would one day be forced to kill Moleka, one way or another.
>
> There were two rooms. In one his wife totally loved him; in another, she totally loved Moleka. He watched over this other room, fearfully, in his dreams at night. It was always the same dream. Moleka would ap-

pear trailing a broken leg with blood streaming from a wound in his mouth and his heart. No one ever cried with such deep, heart-rending sobs as his wife did on those occasions. Often he would start awake to find those hot tears streaming on his arm from her closed eyes. "Why are you crying?" he'd ask, pretending not to know. (*M* 8–9)

Maru had always needed Moleka's help in making decisions at Dilepe and getting them carried out, but Moleka is capable of ruling the kingdom without Maru's help. Maru has recognized his flawed potential as a ruler and has decided to give up kingship at Dilepe because he has found another "kingdom," a single Masarwa woman, a subject of low caste that he believes himself capable of dominating. Nevertheless, he realizes that he is still unable to dominate this woman even after kidnapping and taking her away from the watchful, reproachful eyes of the people of Dilepe. They may be connected by their ability to dream the same dreams, but she continues to maintain a loving connection to Moleka.

In her interview with Adler et al., Head maintained that Margaret is "an emotionally *passive* character because she is communicating a message. She's not emotionally drained" (18). She is so constructed because the "essences of racial prejudice are communicated against her, through her. She holds herself together through creativity" (20). Margaret marries Maru, but she can still maintain and sustain her love for Moleka. Maru laments this edge that Margaret holds, possessing the best of both men within her self, since he wants *all* of Margaret for himself. The multidimensional aspects of her strong subjectivity underline her refusal to be "possessed" and undermine the hierarchies and structures of power and domination that are represented by Maru and Moleka. Both Maru and Moleka have parts of Margaret's selfhood, which are imprinted in her paintings about them. But the paintings are also a reminder of their sexual relations and the meanings of power, race, ethnicity that have infused and groomed their lives of feudal privilege.

Head demonstrates how limited and limiting one's understanding of difference can be when it is engendered by something as arbitrary as skin color. In *Maru*, she moves beyond race and gender, problematizing skin color as social, ethical, and aesthetic sign, to use Linberg-Seyersted's words.[33] The "message" in Margaret's pictures raises an ethical issue in Maru's heart:

> [The Batwsana] were still laughing with such horror in their midst,
> finding it more inconceivable than the white man to consider the
> Masarwa a human being. Thus the message of the pictures went even
> deeper to [Maru's] heart: 'You see, it is I and my tribe who possess the
> true vitality of this country. You lost it when you sat down and let us

clean your floors and rear your children and cattle. Now we want to be
free of you and be busy with our own affairs.' (*M* 109)

The message confirms the fact that the Bushmen, though looked down upon,
are in a better position to be knowers; they are not as ignorant as the Totem
since they have an all-encompassing view of both worlds, of *different* worlds.
Maru sees his marriage not as an end "but a beginning" (*M* 126). It is a beginning not only for the Masarwa on whose enslavement his wealth and privilege
has depended, but a beginning for himself as well. He realizes that the Totem
will have to reconstruct their lives, and the Masarwa will have to reject their
lives of dispossession at a time when everything is in constant renewal:

> When people of the Masarwa tribe heard about Maru's marriage to one
> of their own, a door silently opened on the small, dark airless room in
> which their souls had been shut for a long time. The wind of freedom,
> which was blowing throughout the world for all people, turned and
> flowed into the room. As they breathed in the fresh, clear air their hu-
> manity awakened. They examined their condition (*M* 126). . . .
> People like the Batswana, who did not know that the wind of freedom
> had also reached people of the Masarwa tribe, were in for an unpleasant
> surprise because it would be no longer possible to treat Masarwa people
> in an inhuman way without getting killed yourself. (*M* 127)

One wonders whether Maru is not actually haunted by the (recurrent
dreams and) fears of "getting killed himself" for not freeing Margaret along
with her people. Nevertheless, there are positive signs in the text showing that
change and acceptance of freedom for the oppressed can occur. When Moleka
meets Margaret for the first time, he radically decides to "sit and eat" with his
Masarwa slaves, an act that causes an uproar. When he becomes paramount
chief, it is clear that more radical changes will take place. Craig Mackenzie has
observed that with *Maru*, Bessie Head "further establishes her uniqueness in
Africa by its incisive probing into the racism that exists in traditional African
societies and by its dramatic inversion of the social pyramid in Botswana."[34]
She not only infuses her personal and political struggles with a philosophical
dimension, as Katrak suggests,[35] but she also shows that if dispossessed people
are said to be insane because of their skin color or because of the complexity
that lies embedded in ethnic, class, or gender differences, then, as Ojo-Ade
notes, "the insane may be saner than you and I could ever be."[36] They possess
a complex understanding of issues that those who refer to them as mad, different, or deviant cannot fully grasp. Bessie Head sets up multiple and varying
levels of difference from the beginning to the end of the story that do facilitate

such an inversion. It is the constant shifting in and out of these differences, comparable to Margaret Cadmore's constantly shifting identity and agency, that give *Maru* its depth, richness, and strengths. The world would be a much better place, in Bessie Head's idealistic view, if humans could shift in and out of difference(s) like Margaret Cadmore, combining their silence(s) and other forms of (artistic) expression anchored in difference(s) as weapons for daily communication and survival.

Conclusion: African Women's Writing as a Weapon

> We cannot go forward without culture, without saying what we believe, without communicating with others, without making people think about things. Books are a weapon, a peaceful weapon perhaps, but they *are a weapon*. (interview with Harrell-Bond, 214)

Mariama Bâ said these words not long before her death. She wanted African women writers to paint a realistic picture of the African woman's condition—and predicament—within their cultures. Bâ insisted on women taking charge of their destiny in order to disrupt the patriarchal establishment's predetermined hierarchies. She urged women to use their writing as a weapon that (re)inscribes African women in such ways that transgress and shatter hegemonic (male) representations while infusing these same discourses with more realistic representations. Little did she know that many women, whether they had heard her cry or not, would take up the challenge and delve into the African woman question, broadly, vigorously, and on their own terms.

African women writers have not just openly lamented, questioned, and criticized the neglect of their work; they have also attacked this neglect through their ongoing exercise of the act of writing. They have slowly but surely used their writings as weapons to invade the battlefields that had hitherto been occupied and dominated by male writers, making tangible gains along the way. These women writers have beaten and are still beating their drums and are letting their war-cries be heard side by side with those of their counterparts at home and abroad. In the same way that they have responded to/ challenged their African male counterparts, so too have they challenged their counterparts in the global enterprise of "sisterhood" and feminism. African women writers have reclaimed and reaffirmed the anteriority of an African feminism, one that their maternal ancestors have relied on for millennia, a feminism that has grounded and continues to ground their daily lived experiences, one that is open to learning from the new global agenda of feminism(s) but one that can also share with and teach a (Eurocentric) feminist movement a few things as well. In this way they demand their place at the pulpit, they demand that their voices continue to be heard, given that their contributions to feminism(s) can no longer be blatantly ignored, erased, or forgotten.

Hearing their (gendered) voices is precisely what this book has been about. Hearing their voices, taking seriously what they have to say, means that we must hear what their voices/texts are inherently telling/teaching us. We the critics do not only have the privilege of interrogating these texts, but we also must let ourselves be questioned by the texts themselves. As we pay more critical attention, we realize that these women writers are not necessarily "reflecting," "duplicating," or "writing back" to (radical) feminism or the so-called imperial center, nor are they seeking to fit their texts into Western theoretical parameters and/or conventional literary forms. On the contrary, these women writers seek to create spaces for themselves. They do so by rewriting conventional literary forms, by questioning a combination of the multiple oppressive conditions both traditional and specific to their post-colonial heritage in a constantly changing post-colonial context, a context that therefore positions their challenges sometimes alongside, but mostly beyond the limits of Western feminism and within postcolonial theoretical practice.

I see in the act of reclaiming and the recovery of African women's texts a practice of writing and theory not common to feminist politics and praxis. Recovering this fiction belongs in the realm of recovering some forms of African indigenous theory (that were hitherto exclusive to and grounded in orature), those forms of theory that sometimes rewrite or redefine conventional theory, with their theoretical practice existing in unconventional places such as women's fiction. Consequently, these texts can be read as "fictionalized theory" or as "theorized fiction." We have seen in the works of these women writers "indigenous" theory that is autonomous and self-determining, the theory often being embedded in the polymorphous and heterogenous nature of the texts themselves. These texts have as such been able to provide us with the weapons to critique feminist theories of gender and post-colonial theories that too often have been grounded in Eurocentric biases and have neglected to problematize the position of post-colonial-women-as-subjects in most theoretical renderings on "the postcolonial condition." Consequently, these texts can be said to effectively rewrite existent feminist and post-colonial theories.

For instance, while acknowledging the multiple ways in which patriarchal institutions do oppress women, these writers also often reject allegations of absolute male power and control, of which women's networking is seen as a concrete refutation. These women writers portray women's identities and subjectivities as not only shaped by male control but by women as well who take part in the control/oppression of other women and, consequently, in the contextual inscription of these identities. Such women, in these writers' worldview, must be made accountable for their participation in the writing of the cultural script, rather than proclaimed as perpetual victims. They criticize such binary oppositions as either/or, mind/body, men, education/women, home, et cetera, that naturalize women's oppression. They argue for a sexual politics that does not view African womanhood as necessarily linked to motherhood, and they show how women's bodies and sexualities are not necessarily static areas of oppression but are/can be contested terrains where battles for control are played out. As participants (even if, sometimes, unequal) in these power struggles, women can effectively reshape gender relations.

Women's marginal positions are reclaimed and often shown as spaces of strength within and between which they fluctuate, the position of the Other being reversed and sometimes inverted through the perspectives of those same women who are no longer just outsiders-within, but who also become and act as insiders-within. This is often clearly seen, for instance, when this fiction is informed by historical actuality or when the writers explicitly claim their roles as spokespersons for other (wo)men. They repossess and maintain a tradition that speaks directly to women's roles as custodians of (oral) histories and indigenous forms of knowledge. This tradition of remembering and retelling, which is culturally defined and acknowledged as women's work, is reclaimed by women in ways that are empowering and sometimes subversive. If this custodianship is empowering to women in oral cultures, then the act of writing, the act of accepting the task of spokesperson, becomes a subversive act that is empowering not only for the writers, but also for the community (of women) for and about whom they write.

By speaking for other African women, these women writers do not convey an "un-self-conscious appropriation" of women's experiences, but do speak with and for others, "out of a concrete analysis of the particular power relations and discursive effects involved."[1] This study has demonstrated that the novels create and redefine new spaces, not only in their internal margins but also in the margins of feminist and hegemonic discourses. Although women in these novels are portrayed as experiencing oppression in multiple ways, they are also shown to develop and/or hand down strategies and subject positions that further what Sandra Harding has described as "situated politics." Such politics emphasize and ground what they share with "situated knowledge" gleaned from theirs and other women's lives.[2]

When women writers, as knowers, speak from the position of women's lives, identities of fictional characters are infused with various and varying positional perspectives. These characters do not present an essential, unified identity, but rather multiple and contradictory identities and subjectivities that are constantly changing, within specific social locations. We see how most of the characters have to strive for agency within each social location or gender relation in their bid to construct subjectivity. The characters who choose to restrict themselves to specific gender(ed) roles are shown to live very limiting, sometimes tragic lives, while those who simultaneously juggle the multiple and sometimes contradictory roles that are conferred on them are shown to live self-determining lives. They are harbingers of change who do not necessarily let their identities be dictated by some of the gender ideologies and hierarchies that oppress them. Similarly, they also use some of the flexible gender ideologies to their advantage.

Female characters in these women's writing, therefore, are portrayed not in stereotypical subservient, unchanging roles, or in roles that are deliberately limiting. Instead, they come alive as speaking subjects and agents for change. The ability of these characters to reclaim the power of speech, sometimes usurping it, sometimes alternately silencing and unsilencing themselves, has made it possible to read these novels as theoretical texts. As such, they are not "responding to" or "writing back" to Western feminist theories; rather, they are engaging with other feminist discourses as they seek to question gender relations from and within their specific cultural spaces and social locations. Most of the female characters in these texts are portrayed as having substantially moved beyond "consciousness-raising." These characters therefore seek to occupy shifting subjects positions that do/would enable them to (re)construct subjectivity through multiple intersecting discourses of identity, sexuality, and difference.

Sexuality, like identity, is not a static site of oppression. The women characters in these novels are seen to refuse and contest the exploitation of their bodies as reproductive receptacles or as instruments of sexual pleasure for men. They contest and reject the subjugation and commodification of women's bodies by men—and, sometimes, by other women. The novels show how women's bodies can be written into the cultural text for mass consumption, and bring out how women's bodies and sexuality then become sites of power struggles where multiple discourses of pleasure, domination, and exploitation can/do converge.

These characters often have to redefine difference, given that multiple inscriptions of race, class, ethnic, or gender differences do come to bear on constructions of identity and sexuality. Although some of these African women are also shown as other Others—within their specific social locations that sometimes do have other internal centers and margins—the characters show that no single type of difference, be it racial, class, age, gender, or ethnic difference, should take primacy or be more stifling than the other. They subvert these differences by switching codes as needs arise. Identity, sexuality, and difference are not experienced as separate entities. On the contrary, the multiple ways of simultaneously experiencing identity, sexuality, and difference in the construction of subjectivity are shown to ground their strengths, not weaknesses.

The ability of these women writers to reinscribe postcolonial women, as speaking subjects whose identities, sexualities, and subjectivities are constructed as valuable sites of difference within feminist discourses, makes their texts invaluable testimonies to herstories and the politics of feminism. From my standpoint, these texts are, within African literature and the context of post-colonial women's writing, not only doing what radical feminists did for feminism, but in fact are theoretically anterior to some Western feminist theorizing. They are also opening an invaluable window in the ongoing debates in the field of post-colonial theory that has so far failed to adequately problematize the position of these women. As such, they offer us reconstructive insights to the future of feminist and postcolonial theories.

Notes

Introduction

1.   17. 2 (1986).

2.   For instance, Toni Cade, ed., *The Black Woman: An Anthology* (New York: Signet, 1970); Joyce Lardner, *Tomorrow's Tomorrow: The Black Woman* (Garden City, NY: Doubleday, 1972); Angela Davis, *Women, Race and Class* (New York: Vintage, 1981); bell hooks, *Ain't I a Woman: Black Women and Feminism* (Boston: South End Press, 1981); doris davenport, "The Pathology of Racism: A Conversation with Third World Wimmin," in *This Bridge Called My Back: Writings by Radical Women of Color*, ed. Cherrie Moraga and Gloria Anzaldua (New York: Kitchen Table/Women of Color Press, 1983), 85–90; Audre Lorde, "The Master's Tools Will Never Dismantle the Master's House," *Sister Outsider* (Freedom, CA: The Crossing Press, 1984), 110–13.

3.   Valerie Smith, "Gender and Afro-Americanist Literary Theory and Criticism," *Speaking of Gender*, ed. Elaine Showalter (New York: Routledge, 1989), 56–70; Henry Louis Gates, ed., introduction to *Reading Black, Reading Feminist: A Critical Anthology* (New York: Meridian, 1990), 1–17.

4.   Frances Beal, "Double Jeopardy: To Be Black and Female," in *Sisterhood Is Powerful*, ed. Robin Morgan (New York: Random House, 1970), 340–53.

5.   Deborah King, "Multiple Jeopardy, Multiple Consciousness: The Context of a Black Feminist Ideology," in *Feminist Theory in Practice and Process*, ed. Micheline Malson et al. (Chicago: U of Chicago P, 1989), 75–105.

6.   Cheryl A. Wall, ed., *Changing Our Own Words: Essays on Criticism, Theory, and Writing by Black Women* (New Brunswick, NJ: Rutgers UP, 1989).

7.   Mari Evans, ed., *Black Women Writers (1950–1980): A Critical Evaluation* (New York: Anchor/Doubleday, 1984); Barbara Christian, *Black Feminist Criticism: Perspectives on Black Women Writers* (New York: Pergamon, 1985); Barbara Smith, "Towards a Black Feminist Criticism," in *The New Feminist Criticism: Essays on Women, Literature, and Theory*, ed. Elaine Showalter (London: Virago, 1986), 168–85; Deborah McDowell, "New Directions for Black Feminist Criticism," in Showalter, 186–99.

8.   See Roseann Bell, "The Absence of the African Woman Writer," *College Language Association Journal* 21. 4 (1978): 491–98; Arlette Chemain-Degrange, *Emancipation féminine et roman africain* (Dakar: Nouvelles Editions Africaines, 1980).

9.   Oladele Taiwo, *Female Novelists of Modern Africa* (London: Macmillan, 1984); Mineke Schipper, "Women and Literature in Africa," in *Unheard Words: Women and Literature in Africa, the Arab World, Asia, the Caribbean and Latin America*, ed. Mineke Schipper (London: Allison and Busby, 1985), 22–68; Kembe Milolo,

L'Image de la femme chez les romanciers de l'afrique noire francophone (Fribourg: Editions Universitaires, 1986); Jean-Marie Volet, *La parole aux africaines ou l'idée du pouvoir chez les romancières d'expression française de l'Afrique sub-Saharienne* (Amsterdam: Rodopi, 1993); Beverley Ormerod and Jean-Marie Volet, *Romancières africaines d'expression française: Le sud du Sahara* (Paris: Editions l'Harmattan, 1994).

10. See Femi Ojo-Ade, "Female Writers, Male Critics," *African Literature Today* 13 (1983):158–79; Jean-Marie Volet, "Romancières francophones d'Afrique noire: vingt ans d'activité littéraire à découvrir," *French Review* 65.5 (April 1992):765–73.

11. In *Criticism and Ideology,* ed. Kirsten H. Petersen (Uppsala: Nordiska afrikainstitutet, 1988), 155–72.

12. For example, the fifteenth volume of *African Literature Today* on women in African literature, published in 1987.

13. It is interesting to note that the African Literature Association dedicated (for the first time) an annual conference, their seventeenth, in 1991, *exclusively* to African women writers, titled " 'Nwayibu': Woman being . . . "

14. For some of the reasons why the teaching of African literature in Africa has not gained as much ground as would be expected since 1963, see Chidi Ikonné, "African Literature in Africa Twenty-Five Years after the Dakar and Freetown Conferences," in *African Literature (1988) New Masks,* ed. Hal Wylie et al. (Washington, DC: Three Continents, 1990), 97–105.

15. Esther Smith, "Images of Women in African Literature: Some Examples of Inequality in the Colonial Period," in *Ngambika: Studies of Women in African Literature,* ed. Carole Boyce Davies and Anne Adams Graves (Trenton, NJ: Africa World Press, 1986), 27–44.

16. "Women in African Literature," in *African Women South of the Sahara,* ed. Margaret Hay and Sharon Stichter (London: Longman, 1984), 102.

17. Marie Linton-Umeh, "The African Heroine," in *Sturdy Black Bridges: Visions of Black Women in Literature,* ed. Roseann P. Bell et al. (Garden City, NY: Anchor Books, 1979), 39–51.

18. Carroll Yoder, *White Shadows: A Dialectical View of the French African Novel* (Washington, DC: Three Continents, 1991).

19. Mineke Schipper, "Mother Africa on a Pedestal: The Male Heritage in African Literature and Criticism," *Women in African Literature Today,* ed. Eldred Jones et al. (London: James Currey, 1987), 35–54.

20. Quoted in Lloyd Brown, "The African Woman as Writer," *Canadian Journal of African Studies* 9.3 (1975): 493.

21. " 'Periodic Embodiments': A Ubiquitous Trope in African Men's Writing," *Research in African Literatures* 20.1 (1990): 120.

22. "Senegalese Women Writers, Silence, and Letters: Before the Canon's Roar," *Theories of Africans: Francophone Literature and Anthropology in Africa* (Chicago: U of Chicago P, 1990) 259.

23. Filomina Steady, "The Black Woman Cross-Culturally: An Overview," in *The Black Woman Cross-Culturally*, ed. Filomina Steady (Cambridge, MA: Schenkman, 1981), 7–41; Carole B. Davies, "Introduction: Feminist Criticism and African Literary Criticism," in Davies and Graves, 1–23.

24. Susheila Nasta, introduction to *Motherlands: Black Women's Writing from Africa, the Caribbean, and South Asia*, ed. Susheila Nasta (New Brunswick, NJ: Rutgers UP, 1992), xv.

25. Abena P. B. Busia, "Words Whispered over Voids: A Context for Black Women's Rebellious Voices in the Novel of the African Diaspora," in *Black Feminist Criticism and Critical Theory*, ed. Joe Weixlmann and Houston A. Baker (Greenwood, FL: Penkevill, 1988), 5.

26. Gay Wilentz, *Binding Cultures: Black Women Writers in Africa and the Diaspora* (Bloomington: Indiana UP, 1992), xiv.

27. See Femi Ojo-Ade, "Still a Victim? Mariama Bâ's *Une si Longue Lettre*," *African Literature Today* 12 (1982):71–87.

28. "Weight of Custom, Signs of Change: Feminism in the Literature of African Women," *World Literature Written in English* 25.2 (1985):183.

29. Interview with Flora Veit-Wild in *Black Women's Writing: Crossing the Boundaries*, ed. Carole Boyce Davies (Frankfurt a.M.: Ehling, 1989), 106.

30. *Manushi* 61 (Nov.-Dec. 1990):3. See also Maivân Clech Lâm, "Feeling Foreign in Feminism," *Signs: Journal of Women in Culture and Society* 19.4 (Summer 1994):865–93; Sara Suleri, "Woman Skin Deep: Feminism and the Postcolonial Condition," *Critical Inquiry* 18 (Summer 1992):756–69.

31. "Colonialism and Modernity: Feminist Re-presentations of Women in Non-Western Societies," *Inscriptions* 3/4 (1988): 80.

32. "Women without Men: The Feminist Novel in Africa," in Jones et al., 24–34.

33. I have discussed this issue elsewhere, "African Women and Feminism: The Context of an-Other Black Woman's Voice," at the conference on "African and African American Women: The Ties That Bind" (Baton Rouge: Southern University, 1992).

34. In Davies and Graves, 10. See also Kirsten Petersen, "First Things First: Problems of a Feminist Approach to African Literature," *Kunapipi* 6.3 (1984): 35–47, and Amy Kaminsky, "Issues for an International Feminist Literary Criticism," *Signs* 19.1 (Autumn 1993): 213–27.

35. For example, Katherine Frank, "Feminist Criticism and the African Novel," *African Literature Today* 14 (1984):34–48; Filomina Steady, "African Feminism: A Worldwide Perspective," in *Women in Africa and the African Diaspora*, ed. Rosalyn Terborg-Penn et al. (Washington, DC: Howard UP, 1987), 3–24; Rotimi Johnson, "Womanism and Feminism in African Letters," *Literary Criterion* 25.2 (1990): 25–35; Cecily Lockett, "Feminism(s) and Writing in English in South Africa," *Current Writing* 2 (1990): 1–21; Cheryl Johnson-Odim, "Common Themes, Different Contexts: Third World Women and Feminism," in *Third World Women and the Politics of Feminism*, ed. Chandra Mohanty et al. (Bloomington: Indiana

UP, 1991) 314–27; Irène d'Almeida, "Femme? Féministe? Misovire? Les roman-cières africaines face au féminisme," *Notre Librairie* 117 (Avril-Juin 1994): 48–51; and *Francophone African Women Writers: Destroying the Emptiness of Silence* (Gainesville, FL: University Press of Florida, 1994) 1–31.

36. *In Search of Our Mothers' Gardens* (San Diego: Harcourt Brace Jovanovich, 1983), xi–xii.

37. "Womanism: The Dynamics of the Contemporary Black Female Novel in En-glish," *Signs* 11.1 (1985): 72.

38. "Misovire" literally means "manhater," analogous to mysogynist, a word that she coined out of Latin, Greek, and her African experience. See chapter 3.

39. "Stiwa" is an acronym for Social Transformation Including Women in Africa, in *Re-Creating Ourselves: African Women and Critical Transformations* (Trenton, NJ: Africa World Press, 1994), 229.

40. "La fonction politique des littératures africaines écrites," *Ecriture française dans le monde* 5.3 (1981): 6–7, my emphasis.

41. Unless otherwise indicated, this and all other translations within the text are mine.

42. "The Technology of Gender," in *Technologies of Gender: Essays on Theory, Film, and Fiction* (Bloomington: Indiana UP, 1987) 1–30.

1. Gender, Feminist Theory, and Post-Colonial (Women's) Writing

1. " 'Gender' for a Marxist Dictionary: The Sexual Politics of a Word," in *Simians, Cyborgs, and Women: The Reinvention of Nature* (New York: Routledge, 1991), 131.

2. "Introduction: The Rise of Gender," in *Speaking of Gender*, ed. Elaine Showalter (New York: Routledge, 1989), 2.

3. "Why has the Sex/Gender System Become Visible Only Now?" in *Discovering Reality*, ed. Sandra Harding and Merrill Hintikka (Dordrecht: D. Reidel, 1983), 314.

4. Simone de Beauvoir, *The Second Sex*, trans. H. M. Parshley (New York: Vintage, 1974); Hilary Lips, *Sex and Gender: An Introduction* (California: Mayfield, 1988); Linda Lindsey, *Gender Roles: A Sociological Perspective* (New Jersey: Prentice Hall, 1990); Judith Lorber and Susan Farrell, eds., *The Social Construction of Gender* (Newbury Park, CA: Sage, 1991).

5. Ann Oakley, *Sex, Gender and Society* (New York: Harper Colophon, 1972); Suzanne Kessler and Wendy McKenna, *Gender: An Ethnomethodological Approach* (New York: John Wiley and Sons, 1978); Ivan Illich, *Gender* (London: Marion Boyars, 1983); Robert Stroller, *Presentations of Gender* (New Haven: Yale UP, 1985).

6. For example, Nancy Chodorow, *The Reproduction of Mothering: Psychoanalysis and the Sociology of Gender* (Berkeley: U of California P, 1978); Linda Nicholson, *Gender and History: The Limits of Social Theory in the Age of the Family* (New York: Columbia UP, 1986); Linda Lindsey, *Gender Roles*; Kessler and McKenna, *Gender*.

7. Michelle Rosaldo and Louise Lamphere, eds., *Women, Culture, and Society* (Stanford: Stanford UP, 1974); Gayle Rubin, "The Traffic in Women: Notes on the 'Political Economy' of Sex," in *Toward an Anthropology of Women*, ed. Rayna Rapp (New York: Monthly Review Press, 1975), 157–210; Sherry Ortner and Harriet Whitehead, eds., *Sexual Meanings: The Cultural Construction of Gender and Sexuality* (Cambridge: Cambridge UP, 1981); Adrienne Rich, "Compulsory Heterosexuality and Lesbian Existence," in *The Signs Reader*, ed. Elizabeth Abel and Emily Abel (Chicago: U of Chicago P, 1983), 139–67; *Of Woman Born: Womanhood as Experience and Institution* (New York: W. W. Norton, 1986); Pat Caplan, ed., *The Cultural Construction of Sexuality* (London: Routledge, 1989).

8. For instance, the French feminists presented in *New French Feminisms: An Anthology*, ed. Elaine Marks and I. de Courtivron (New York: Schocken, 1981); Monique Wittig, *The Straight Mind and Other Essays* (Boston: Beacon, 1992); Nancy Fraser and Sandra Bartky, eds., *Revaluing French Feminism: Critical Essays on Difference, Agency, and Culture* (Bloomington: Indiana UP, 1992).

9. Chodorow, *The Reproduction of Mothering*, and *Feminism and Psychoanalytical Theory* (New Haven: Yale UP, 1989).

10. Alison Jaggar, *Feminist Politics and Human Nature* (Sussex: Harvester, 1983); Nancy Hartsock, "The Feminist Standpoint: Developing the Ground for a Specifically Feminist Historical Materialism," in *Feminism and Methodology*, ed. Sandra Harding (Bloomington: Indiana UP, 1985), 157–80; Dorothy Smith, *The Everyday World as Problematic: A Feminist Sociology* (Toronto: U of Toronto P, 1987).

11. Jane Flax, "Postmodernism and Gender Relations in Feminist Theory," in Malson et al., 51–73; Trinh Minh-ha, *Woman, Native, Other: Writing Postcoloniality and Feminism* (Bloomington: Indiana UP, 1989); bell hooks, *Yearning: Race, Gender, and Cultural politics* (Toronto: Between the Lines, 1990); Chandra Mohanty et al., eds., *Third World Women*.

12. Audre Lorde, *Sister Outsider* (Freedom, CA: Crossing Press, 1984); Elly Bulkin et al., *Yours in Struggle: Three Feminist Perspectives on Anti-Semitism and Racism* (Ithaca, NY: Firebrand, 1988); Trinh Minh-ha, "Not You/Like You: Post-Colonial Women and the Interlocking Questions of Identity and Difference," *Inscriptions* 3/4 (1988): 71–77.

13. Jean F. O'Barr, "Feminist Issues in the Fiction of Kenya's Women Writers," in Jones et al., 55.

14. Frederic Jameson, "Third-World Literature in the Era of Multinational Capitalism," *Social Text* 15 (1986): 69; Homi Bhabha, "Of Mimicry and Man: The Ambivalence of Colonial Discourse," *October* 28 (Spring 1984): 126. (For a critique of Jameson, see Aijaz Ahmad, "Jameson's Rhetoric of Otherness and the 'National Allegory,' " *Social Text* 17 [1987]: 3–25.)

15. "Whose Post-Colonialism and Whose Postmodernism?" *World Literature Written in English* 30.2 (1990): 1–2.

16. See, for instance, Anne McClintock, "The Angel of Progress: Pitfalls of the Term 'Post-Colonialism,' " *Social Text* 31–32 (1992): 84–98; Ella Shohat, "Notes on the

'Post-Colonial,' " *Social Text* 31–32 (1992): 99–113; Kwame Anthony Appiah, "Is the Post- in Postmodernism the Post- in Postcolonial?" *Critical Inquiry* 17 (Winter 1991): 336–57.

17. Vijah Mishra and Bob Hodge, "What is Post(-)Colonialism?" *Textual Practice* 5.3 (1991): 401.

18. "Unsettling the Empire: Resistance Theory for the Second World," *World Literature Written in English* 30.2 (1990): 35.

19. See also Frank Schulze-Engler, "Beyond Post-Colonialism: Multiple Identities in East African Literature," in *US/THEM: Translation, Transcription and Identity in Post-Colonial Literary Cultures*, ed. Gordon Collier (Amsterdam: Rodopi, 1992), 319–28.

20. Mishra and Hodge, 408. See also Suleri 155n30, and Spivak, "Imperialism and Sexual Difference," *Oxford Literary Review* 8:1–2 (1986): 225–40.

21. Bloomington: Indiana UP, 1992, 18. See also Eileen Julien's *African Novels and the Question of Orality* (Bloomington: Indiana UP, 1992), 7.

22. I am here borrowing the words of one of the reviewers of my manuscript, who characterizes this act as "a truly *liberating* force."

23. "African Literature as Restoration of Celebration," *New African* (March 1990): 40–43.

24. "The Race for Theory," *Feminist Studies* 14.1 (1988): 67–79.

25. Henry Louis Gates, *Figures in Black* (New York: Oxford UP, 1987), xxi, my emphasis.

26. "Those Left Out in the Rain: African Literary Theory and the Re-Invention of the African Woman," *African Studies Review* 37.2 (Sept. 1994): 77–95. See also Chinua Achebe, "Colonialist Criticism," in *Hopes and Impediments: Selected Essays* (New York: Anchor Books, 1989), 68–90.

27. *Thresholds of Change in African Literature: The Emergence of a Tradition* (Portsmouth, NH: Heinemann, 1993) 4.

28. "Decolonizing Culture: Toward a Theory for Postcolonial Women's Texts," *Modern Fiction Studies* 35.1 (1989): 158.

29. "Notes toward a Politics of Location (1984)" in *Blood, Bread, Poetry: Selected Prose* 1979–1985 (New York: W. W. Norton, 1986), 213–14.

30. Rich, "Compulsory Heterosexuality"; Kate Millett, *Sexual Politics* (New York: Ballantine Books, 1970); Rosemarie Tong, *Feminist Thought* (Boulder: Westview, 1989), 95–138; Gayatri Spivak, *In Other Worlds* (New York: Routledge, 1987), 80.

31. "Feminism, Marxism, Method, and the State: An Agenda for Theory," in *The Signs Reader*, ed. Abel and Abel (Chicago: U of Chicago P, 1983), 227.

32. Cixous and Irigaray in Marks and de Courtivron, eds., *New French Feminisms*; Wittig, *The Straight Mind*. Also, Hartsock "The Feminist Standpoint," and Smith, *The Everyday World as Problematic.*

33. Review of *Male Daughters, Female Husbands* in *Signs* 16.3 (1991): 611.

34. "Stories of Women and Mothers: Gender and Nationalism in the Early Fiction of Flora Nwapa," in Nasta, 14. It is worth noting that Amadiume's study also provides data that points to the fact that this flexible gender system exists in many parts of Africa.

35. I have been asked a number of times, at conferences, by total strangers, "how it feels to be circumcised." The obvious assumption itself that I am, or must be, is mind-boggling. See Nfah-Abbenyi, "Reflections of an African Woman," in the special issue on racism and gender of *Canadian Woman Studies* 14.2 (Spring 1994): 25–28; and "Why (What) Am I (Doing) Here: A Cameroonian Woman?" in *Our Own Agendas: Autobiographical Essays by Woman Associated with McGill University*, ed. Margaret Gillett and Ann Beer (Montreal: McGill-Queen's University Press, 1995), 250–61; and "Bridging North and South . . . Notes Towards Dialogue and Transformation," in the special issue on "Bridging North/South: Patterns of Transformation" of *Canadian Woman Studies* 17.2 (Spring 1997): 145–48.

36. See, for instance, Fran Hosken, *Genital and Sexual Mutilation of Females* (Lexington, MA: Women's International Network, 1979).

37. *La parole aux négresses* (Paris: Denoël/Gonthier, 1978), trans. by Dorothy S. Blair as *Speak Out, Black Sisters: Feminism and Oppression in Black Africa* (London: Pluto Press, 1986), 87.

38. Boston: Beacon Press, 1980.

39. *Columbia Human Rights Law Review* 23 (1991–92): 191.

40. *Research in African Literatures* 20.3 (Fall 1989): 422–48. See also Daniel Vignal, "L'homophilie dans le roman négro-africain d'expression anglaise et française," *Peuples Noirs, Peuples Africains* 33 (May-June 1983): 63–81.

41. In *The History of Sexuality, Vol. 1: An Introduction*, trans. Robert Hurley (New York: Vintage Books, 1978), 33. Diamond and Quinby have suggested in "The Feminist Sexuality Debates" that Foucault "does not particularly illuminate the effects of the deployment of sexuality on the lives of women," *Signs* 10.1 (1984): 120. For a gendered view of some uses of Foucault to feminist readings on sexuality, see Susan Hekman, *Gender and Knowledge: Elements of a Postmodern Feminism* (Boston: Northeastern UP, 1990); Susan Bordo, "The Body and the Reproduction of Femininity: A Feminist Appropriation of Foucault," in Jaggar and Bordo, 13.

42. Trinh Minh-ha, "She: The Inappropriate/d Other," *Discourse* 8 (Fall-Winter 1986–87): 3.

43. Gayatri Spivak, "Can the Subaltern Speak?" in *Marxism and the Interpretation of Culture*, ed. Cary Nelson and Lawrence Grossberg (Urbana: U of Illinois P, 1988), 295.

44. For an example, see Benita Parry's reading of what she describes as Spivak's "deliberated deafness to the native voice where it is to be heard," in "Problems in Current Theories of Colonial Discourse," *Oxford Literary Review* 9:1–2 (1987): 34–39.

45. Patricia Hill Collins, "Learning from the Outsider Within," *Social Problems* 33.6 (1986): 14–32.

46. "U.S. Third World Feminism: The Theory and Method of Oppositional Consciousness in the Postmodern World," *Genders* 10 (Spring 1991): 1–24.

47. "Cultural Feminism versus Post-Structuralism: The Identity Crisis in Feminist
Theory," in Malson et al., 324.

48. For the concept of identity politics, see The Combahee River Collective, "A Black
Feminist Statement," in Moraga and Anzaldua, 212.

49. See also de Lauretis, "Feminist Studies/Critical Studies: Issues, Terms and Contexts," and Mohanty and Martin, "Feminist Politics: What's Home Got to Do
with It," in *Feminist Studies/Critical Studies*, ed. Teresa de Lauretis (Bloomington:
Indiana UP, 1986).

50. Also, Coco Fusco, "Managing the Other," *Lusitania* 3.3 (1990): 77.

2. (Re)Constructing Identity and Subjectivity:
Buchi Emecheta, Ama Ata Aidoo, Tsitsi Dangarembga

1. Davies, "Motherhood in the Works of Male and Female Igbo Writers: Achebe,
Emecheta, Nwapa, and Nzekwu," in Carole Boyce Davies and Anne Adams
Graves, ed., *Ngambika: Studies of Women in African Literature* (Trenton, NJ: Af-
rica World Press, 1986), 247.

2. "The Female Writer and Her Commitment," in Jones et al., 6.

3. Jane Bryce-Okunlola, "Motherhood as a Metaphor for Creativity in Three African Women's Novels: Flora Nwapa, Rebeka Njau and Bessie Head," in Nasta, 201.

4. *The Joys of Motherhood* (New York: George Braziller, 1979), henceforth cited
within the text as *Joys*. *Changes—A Love Story* (London: The Women's Press, 1991)
will be cited within the text as *Changes*. *Nervous Conditions* 1988 (Seattle: The
Seal Press, 1989) will be cited using its full title. All references in the text will be
made to these editions.

5. Chikwenye Ogunyemi, "Buchi Emecheta: The Shaping of a Self," *Komparatistische Hefte* 8 (1983): 75.

6. See Naana Banyiwa-Horne, "African Womanhood: The Contrasting Perspectives
of Flora Nwapa's *Efuru* and Elechi Amadi's *The Concubine*," in Davies and
Graves, 129.

7. Kirsten Petersen, "Unpopular Opinions: Some African Women Writers," in *A
Double Colonization: Colonial and Post-Colonial Women's Writing*, ed. Kirsten
Petersen and Anna Rutherford (Mundelstrup: Dangaroo, 1986), 111.

8. "The Black Woman Cross-Culturally: An Overview," in *The Black Woman Cross-
Culturally*, ed. F. Steady (Cambridge, MA: Schenkman, 1981), 29. See also Barbara
Christian, "An Angle of Seeing: Motherhood in Buchi Emecheta's *Joys of Mother-
hood* and Alice Walker's *Meridian*," in *Black Feminist Criticism*, 211–52.

9. Mugambi has described the situation in which women find themselves as one of
"conformity and marginality" in "The Wounded Psyche and Beyond," (doctoral
dissertation: Indiana U, 1988). I will add that it is often more complex than occu-
pying one position or the other.

10. Interview in Charlotte Bruner, ed., *Unwinding Threads: Writing by Women in Africa* (London: Heinemann, 1983): 49.

11. *In Their Own Voices: African Women Writers Talk* (London: James Currey, 1990), 42.

12. See Raoul Granqvist and John Stotesbury, *African Voices: Interviews with Thirteen African Writers* (Sidney: Dangaroo Press, 1989): 17; Davidson Umeh and Marie Umeh, "Interview: Buchi Emecheta," *Ba Shiru* 12.2 (1985): 22.

13. "The Shallow Grave: Archetypes of Female Experience in African Fiction," *Research in African Literatures* 19.2 (1988): 150.

14. "Weight of Custom, Signs of Change: Feminism in the Literature of African Women," *WLWE* 25.2 1985): 186.

15. See Eustace Palmer, "The Feminine Point of View: Buchi Emecheta's *The Joys of Motherhood*," *African Literature Today* 13 (1983): 42; Ogunyemi, "Buchi Emecheta," 75.

16. "The Woman of Black Africa, Buchi Emecheta: The Woman's Voice in the New Nigerian Novel," *English Studies* 64.3 (1983): 260.

17. "What They Told Buchi Emecheta: Oral Subjectivity and the Joys of 'Otherhood,' " *Publications of the Modern Language Association* 105.1 (1990): 92.

18. "Assertiveness vs. Submissiveness in Selected Works by African Woman Writers," *Ba Shiru* 12.2 (1985): 8.

19. Stratton, "The Shallow Grave," 158.

20. "Rethinking Modernism: Minority vs. Majority Theories," *Cultural Critique* 7 (1987): 196.

21. *Sisterhood Is Global*, ed. Robin Morgan (New York: Anchor Books, 1984), 259.

22. See Janice Radway, *Reading the Romance: Women, Patriarchy, and Popular Literature* (Chapel Hill: U of North Carolina P, 1984).

23. Virginia Woolf in *A Room of One's Own* and Alice Walker in *In Search of Our Mothers' Gardens* have shown how women (Walker rewrites Woolf to include black women) develop "contrary instincts" because their ingenuity and creativity has been stifled by patriarchal ideologies that reject or refuse to recognize women's freedom of expression by either branding them as witches or pushing them to (the brink of) madness and/or suicide.

24. For example, Charlotte Bruner, "Been-to or Has-been: A Dilemma for Today's African Woman," *Ba Shiru* 8.2 (1977): 23-31; Lloyd Brown, "Ama Ata Aidoo," in Brown, *Women Writers in Black Africa*, 84-121; Brenda Berrian, "African Women as Seen in the Works of Flora Nwapa and Ama Ata Aidoo," *College Language Association Journal* 25.3 (1982): 331-39; Chimalum Nwankwo, "The Feminist Impulse and Social Realism in Ama Ata Aidoo's *No Sweetness Here* and *Our Sister Killjoy*," in Davies and Graves, eds., *Ngambika*, 151-59; Caroline Rooney, "Are We in the Company of Feminists? A Preface for Bessie Head and Ama Ata Aidoo," *Diverse Voices*, ed. Harriet Jump (New York: Harvester Wheatsheaf, 1991), 214-46; and Gay Wilentz, "Ama Ata Aidoo, *The Dilemma of a Ghost*," in Wilentz, *Binding Cultures*, 38-57.

25. For a discussion on how language assimilates and distorts the realities of colonized subjects, see Ngugi wa Thiong'o, "The Language of African Literature," *Decolonising the Mind: The Politics of Language in African Literature* (London: James Currey, 1986), 4–33, and "Freeing Culture from Eurocentrism," *Moving the Centre: The Struggle for Cultural Freedoms* (London: James Currey, 1993), 2–57.

26. "Killing the Hysteric in the Colonized's House: Tsitsi Dangarembga's *Nervous Conditions*," *Journal of Commonwealth Literature* 27.1 (1992): 28.

27. Oraliterature is a neologism used by Gay Wilentz that "refers to the written creative works which retain elements of the orature that informed them" (*Binding Cultures*, xvii).

28. "A Correspondence without Theory: Tsitsi Dangarembga's *Nervous Conditions*," *Current Writing* 2 (1990): 92.

29. See *A Room of One's Own* and *To the Lighthouse*.

30. "Embodying Subjectivity: A Literary Genealogy of Anorexic Discourse," M.A. Thesis, McGill U (1993), 88.

31. "Tsitsi Dangarembga's *Nervous Conditions*: At the Crossroads of Feminism and Post-Colonialism," *World Literature Written in English* 31.1 (1991): 111.

32. *Talking with African Writers*, ed. Jane Wilkinson (London: James Currey, 1992), 193.

33. "Discussion" with Gayatri Spivak and Catharine MacKinnon on MacKinnon's paper, "Desire and Power: A Feminist Perspective," in Nelson and Golberg, 118.

3. Sexuality in Cameroonian Women Writers:
Delphine Zanga Tsongo, Calixthe Beyala, Werewere Liking

1. The three women that I am looking at in this chapter are all Francophone. The paucity of Cameroonian Anglophone writing, and, even more, of Anglophone women's writing has been a cause for concern to critics. Although some Anglophone Cameroonian women have published poetry, short stories, and short plays, the novel is a genre that Anglophone women writers need to work on. In her essay on this topic, Nalova Lyonga mentions two texts: Azanwi Nchami's historical novel *Footprints of Destiny* (1985) and Asheri Jedida's short novel *Promise* (1969). Both texts are not even available on the market. See "La littérature féminine anglophone au Cameroun," in *Notre Librairie* 118 (Juillet-Septembre 1994): 35. The same is true of Kate Ngowo Williams' (privately) published *The Love Seat* (1978), subtitled by the author as "Short Story Series No. 1" and designated by Karen Keim as "a sentimental novelette" in her essay on "Popular Fiction Publishing in Cameroon," *The African Book Publishing Record* 9.1 (1983): 8. I published some poetry and short stories in the creative writer's journal, *The Mould*. These are mentioned in Bole Butake's essay, "Cameroon Literature in English," *Notre Librairie* 99 (Oct.-Dec. 1989): 105, but are unfortunately not cited in Brenda Berrian's *Bibliography of African Women Writers and Journalists [Ancient Egypt—1984]* (Washington, DC: Three Continents Press, 1985). Berrian does cite Gladys Anyangwe's "folklore" that appeared in the same creative writer's journal. However, some of my short stories have been published here in North America. See

"The Healer," in *Callaloo* 19.3 (Summer 1996): 771–76; "Your Madness, Not Mine," in *Crab Orchard Review* 2.2 (Spring/Summer 1997): 186–194 and "Market Scene," in *The Toronto Review* 15.3 (Summer 1997): 41–49. My fiction is published under the pen name MAKUCHI.

2.   Similarly, Ibrahim Tala analyzes only the writings of male authors, in his "Images of Women in Cameroon Fiction," *New Horizons* 3.1 (1983): 1–14.

3.   *Vies de femmes* (Yaounde: Editions Clé, 1983); *C'est le soleil qui m'a brûlée* (Paris: Editions Stock, 1987); *Tu t'appelleras Tanga* (Paris: Editions Stock, 1988); *Elle sera de jaspe et de corail* (Paris: Editions l'Harmattan, 1983).

4.   Interview with David Ndachi Tagne in *Cameroon Tribune* No. 2843 (Dec. 2, 1983): 2. When Zanga Tsogo gave this interview, she was in the Ministry of Social Affairs, now known as the "Ministère de la Condition Féminine." For at least the last ten years, we have been relegated to "owning" one ministry, that of "la condition féminine," whatever that woman condition is. Nowadays in Cameroon, when a woman complains about problems—whether social, cultural, economic, and/or political—it is not uncommon to hear men wryly tell her to go to "their" Ministry. For after all, they say, do women not have a ministry all their own? It is a "joke" that is no longer funny, for it eloquently bespeaks their contempt and trivializes women's issues.

5.   "Peasants, Workers, and Capital: The Political Economy of Labor and Incomes in Cameroon" (Diss.: Harvard U, 1978), 272–73.

6.   "Desire and Power: A Feminist Perspective," in Nelson and Grossberg, 114.

7.   Estelle Freedman and Barrie Thorne, "Introduction to 'The Feminist Sexuality Debates,' " *Signs* 10.1 (1984): 102.

8.   Paris: l'Harmattan, 1986.

9.   "Women in the Rural Economy: Past, Present, and Future," Hay and Stichter, 12.

10. Joyce Ashuntantang comments on the inequalities that are "more hardened" and blatantly discriminatory in favor of men within the context of marriage that have been written into Cameroon law, as opposed to the principle of equality proclaimed by the Constitution. "Women in Cameroon: Equality Before the Law?" in *The Herald* No. 20 (Dec. 30, 1992): 11. See also Marie-Louise Eteki-Otabela, "Dix ans de luttes du Collectif des femmes pour le renouveau (CFR): quelques réflexions sur le mouvement féministe camerounais," *Recherches féministes* 5.1 (1992): 129.

11. In her review of *Vies de femmes* in *Notre Librairie* 100 (Janvier-Mars 1990): 125.

12. See Ann Snitow et al. in their introduction to *Powers of Desire: The Politics of Sexuality* (New York: Monthly Review Press, 1983): 9–47; the contributors to "The Feminist Sexuality Debates," *Signs* 10.1 (1984): 102–35; and Cheryl H. Cohen, "The Feminist Sexuality Debate: Ethics and Politics," *Hypatia* 1.2 (1986): 71–86.

13. Henceforth cited in the text as *Tanga*.

14. Henceforth cited in the text as *Soleil*.

15. I will draw an analogy here with Senghor's poem, "Elegy of the Circumcised," in which the poet celebrates male circumcision and the Phallus as the gateway to

fatherhood, patrilineality, and communal consciousness. In *Poems of Black Africa* (New York: Hill and Wang, 1975), 160.

16. Julia Kristeva, "From One Identity to an Other," in *Desire in Language: A Semiotic Approach to Literature and Art*, ed. Leon Roudiez (New York: Columbia UP, 1980), 136.

17. Calixthe Beyala has been known to adamantly reject the word "lesbian" used in reference to her work by critics on the grounds that this word does not exist in African languages. Granted, but this lack of terminology in no way erases those strong homoerotic feelings that Ateba has for Irène. It seems to me that Beyala wants to distance the limited sexual meanings by which "lesbianism" is often defined for possible cultural, political, or other personal reasons. (I am grateful here to Eloïse Brière for letting me read the manuscript of an interview with Beyala that she co-conducted with Béatrice Gallimore in Paris).

18. See Daniel Atchebro, "Beyala: trop 'brûlante' pour les mecs!" *Regards Africains* 8 (1988): 29; Joseph Ndinda, "Écriture et discours féminin au Cameroun: Trois générations de romancières," *Notre Librairie* 118 (Juillet-Septembre 1994): 12; Doumbi-Fakoly's review of *Tanga* in *Présence Africaine* 148 (1988): 148; Ndache Tagne's review of *Soleil* in *Notre Librairie* 100 (Janvier-Mars 1990): 97.

19. "Calixthe Beyala, or The Literary Success of a Cameroonian Woman Living in Paris," *World Literature Today* 67.2 (Spring 1993): 309.

20. "Sous le signe de l'amour au féminin," *Jeune Afrique* No. 1423 (13 avril, 1988): 55. See also Arlette Chemain, "L'écriture de Calixthe Beyala: Provocation ou révolte généreuse," *Notre Librairie* 99 (Oct.-Déc. 1989): 162–63, and Anny-Claire Jaccard's "Des textes novateurs: La littérature féminine," *Notre Librairie* (Oct.-Déc. 1989): 160.

21. "Le corps: de l'alienation à la réappropriation, chez les romancières d'Afrique noire francophone," *Notre Librairie* 117 (Avril-Juin 1994): 60.

22. The working title of this novel before publication, as quoted extensively by Marie-José Hourantier in *Du rituel au théâtre rituel: Contribution à une esthétique négro-africaine* (Paris: l'Harmattan, 1984), was simply *Le Journal d'une misovire*.

23. "Ritual and Modern Dramatic Expression in Cameroon: The Plays of Werewere-Liking," in *Semper Aliquid Novi: Littérature Comparée et Littératures d'Afrique* (Tübingen: Gunter Narr Verlag, 1990) 318.

24. See Hourantier, 22–23.

25. *Notre Librairie* 79 (Avril-Juin, 1985): 18. Ellipses in the original.

26. See, for instance, Thécla Midiohouan, "La parole des femmes," *Figures et fantasmes de la violence dans les Littératures francophones de l'Afrique subsaharienne et des Antilles* (Bologna: Cooperativa Libraria Universitaria Editrice Bologna, 1991): 150-52; Madeleine Borgomano, "Les femmes et l'écriture-parole," *Notre Librairie* 117 (Avril-Juin 1994): 88–90; and also in the same issue, see Athleen Ellington, "L'interdépendance, un discours d'avenir: Calixthe Beyala, Werewere Liking et Simone Schwarz-Bart," 103–105.

27. Henceforth cited in the text as *Elle*.

28. "La femme par qui le scandale arrive," *Jeune Afrique* 1172 (22 juin, 1983): 69.

29. See Hourantier, 60.

30. According to Dingome, the "powers of *Um*" refer to "a secret society that held su-
     preme justice in Bassaland. Its select few adepts reached the highest degrees of
     esotericism very late in life. They were the figures of divine authority and justice
     on earth" (in "Ritual and Modern Dramatic Expression").

31. Amos Sam-Abbenyi has described in "Assessment of Two Gambian Trypanosomi-
     asis Screening Programmes in the Focus of Fontem [Cameroon]," (M. Sc. thesis:
     U of Montreal, 1989), the epidemiological impact that the tsetse fly—the agent/
     transmitter of trypanosomiasis, commonly known as sleeping sickness, that is
     prevalent in some parts of Africa—has had in some communities in Cameroon.
     Cameroon has endemic foci where thousands of people since the birth of this
     century have died or have been diagnosed and treated for this disease.

32. *Nouvelles Ecritures Africaines: Romanciers de la Seconde Génération* (Paris: Edi-
     tions l'Harmattan, 1986) 194.

4. Women Redefining Difference: Mariama Bâ, Miriam Tlali, and Bessie Head

1. I say "most" here because I am excluding white post-colonial women of settler
    colonies whose literatures, Slemon has argued, should be studied as "Second
    World" literature (158n18).

2. Aminata Maïga Ka, "Ramatoulaye, Aïssatou, Mireille et . . . Mariama Bâ," *Notre
    Librairie* 81 (Oct.-Dec. 1985): 134.

3. "La polygamie et la révolte de la femme africaine moderne: Une lecture d'*Une si
    longue lettre* de Mariama Bâ," *L'Afrique Littéraire* No. 65–66 (1982): 64.

4. *Senegalese Literature: A Critical History* (Boston: Twayne, 1984) 139.

5. See Miller, "Senegalese Women Writers," 246–93.

6. "Mariama Bâ: Winner of the First Noma Award for Publishing in Africa," in *The
    African Book Publishing Record* 6.3/4 (1980): 213–14, my emphasis.

7. Mariama Bâ, *Un chant écarlate* (Dakar: Nouvelles Editions Africaines, 1981), trans-
    lated by Dorothy S. Blair, *Scarlet Song* (Essex: Longman, 1986). All references
    within the text will be made to this English edition.

8. For a discussion of various influences of French colonial politics on writers and
    their writing, see also Janos Riesz, "Mariama Bâ's *Une si longue lettre*: An Erzie-
    hungsroman," *Research in African Literatures* 22.1 (1991): 27–42; Karen Wallace,
    "Women and Identity: A Black Francophone Female Perspective," *Sage* 2.1 (1985):
    19–23.

9. For a good example, see Ferdinand Oyono's *Une Vie de Boy* (1956), translated as
    Houseboy (London: Heinemann, 1966).

10. "Ideologies of Race and Sex in Literature: Racism and Antiracism in the African
    Francophone Novel," *College Language Association Journal* 30.2 (1985): 143. In her
    dissertation on the white woman and interracial relationships in the West African

novel of French expression (1988), Odile Cazenave notes that problems arising in these relationships are rooted in cultural rather than racial differences.

11. See Thérèse Kuoh-Moukouri, *Les couples dominos* (Paris: l'Harmattan, 1973), 174.

12. Ithaca: Cornell UP, 1989, 13.

13. "Marginalisation et identité des personnages dans la littérature negro-africaine des années 80: l'image du Métis," *Présence Francophone* 38 (1991): 111–32.

14. See Lionnet's concept of *métissage* as *bricolage* (in *Autobiographical Voices*, 8).

15. (London: Longman, 1979), cited within the text as *Metropolitan*.

16. "Writing 'Race' and the Difference It Makes," in *"Race," Writing, and Difference*, ed. Henry L. Gates (Chicago: U of Chicago P, 1986), 5.

17. "Conversation with Miriam Tlali," *ALA Bulletin* 17.3 (1991): 40–42.

18. In *Between the Lines* (Grahamstown, South Africa: National English Literary Museum Interviews 4, 1989), 71. See also Lockett, "Feminism(s) and Writing in English in South Africa," (155n35) 19.

19. "The Black Woman in South African English Literature," *Journal of Literary Studies* 4.1 (1988): 21–37.

20. In the interview with Clayton, Tlali states that, although there are autobiographical elements in her writings, a lot of her work also incorporates experiences of other (black) South Africans (78).

21. For a definition of the term "Coloured" in the South African context, see Mohamed Adhikari, "Between Black and White: The History of Coloured Politics in South Africa," *Canadian Journal of African Studies* 25.1 (1991): 110.

22. "The Autobiographical Content in the Works of South African Women Writers: The Personal and the Political," in *Biography East and West*, ed. Carol Ramelb (Honolulu: U of Hawaii P, 1989), 122.

23. For a discussion on the sexual division of labor in Southern Africa and how it adversely affects the lives of black women, see Cherryl Walker, in *Women and Gender in Southern Africa to 1945* (London: James Currey, 1990).

24. In an interview with Granqvist and Stotesbury, Tlali explains that the Bantu education system and the lack of proper libraries has been detrimental to blacks, especially to black women.

25. "The Need for a Feminism: Black Township Writing," *Journal of Literary Studies* 4.1 (1988): 61.

26. "The Destruction of the South African Family by Apartheid Laws as Revealed in Select works of Tlali and Ngcobo," in *African Literature—1988—New Masks*, ed. Hal Wylie et al. (Washington, DC: Three Continents Press, 1990), 23.

27. "The Tyranny of Place: The Context of Bessie Head's Fiction," *World Literature Written in English* 17.1 (1978): 23.

28. "The Tragic Life of Bessie Head," in *The Tragic Life*, ed. Cecil Abrahams (Trenton, NJ: Africa World Press, 1990) 7.

29. "Bessie Head: Restless in a Distant Land," in *When the Drumbeat Changes*, ed. Parker et al. (Washington, DC: Three Continents, 1981) 265.

30. "Romantic Love and the Individual in Novels by Mariama Bâ, Buchi Emecheta, and Bessie Head," Wylie et al., 20.

31. See, for example, Virginia Ola, "Women's Role in Bessie Head's Ideal World," *Ariel* 17.4 (Oct. 1986): 39.

32. "The Novels of Bessie Head," in *Aspects of South African Literature*, ed. Christopher Heywood (London: Heinemann, 1976) 175.

33. "The Color Black: Skin Color as Social, Ethical, and Esthetic Sign in Writings by Black American Women," *English Studies* 73.1 (1992): 55.

34. "Alienation, Breakdown, and Renewal," in *International Literature in English: Essays on the Major Writers*, ed. Robert Ross (New York: Garland Publishing, 1991), 558.

35. "From Pauline to Dikeledi: The Philosophical and Political Vision of Bessie Head's Protagonists," *Ba Shiru* 12.2 (1985): 26–35.

36. "Bessie Head's Alienated Heroine: Victim or Villain?" *Ba Shiru* 8.2 (1977): 21.

Conclusion

1. Linda Alcoff, "The Problem of Speaking for Others," *Cultural Critique* 20 (Winter 1991–92): 24.

2. "Reinventing Ourselves as Other: More New Agents of History and Knowledge," in *Whose Science? Whose Knowledge? Thinking from Women's Lives* (Ithaca, NY: Cornell UP, 1991), 273.

Bibliography

Primary Sources

Aidoo, Ama Ata. *Changes—A Love Story.* London: Women's Press, 1991.
Bâ, Mariama. *Un chant écarlate.* Dakar: Nouvelles Éditions Africaines, 1981.
——. *Scarlet Song.* Trans. Dorothy S. Blair, Essex: Longman, 1986.
Beyala, Calixthe. *C'est le soleil qui m'a brûlé.* Paris: Editions Stock, 1987.
——. *Tu t'appelleras Tanga.* Paris: Editions Stock, 1988.
Dangarembga, Tsitsi. *Nervous Conditions.* (1988) Seattle: Seal Press, 1989.
Emecheta, Buchi. *The Joys of Motherhood.* New York: George Braziller, 1979.
Head, Bessie. *Maru.* London: Heinemann, 1971.
Liking, Werewere. *Elle sera de jaspe et de corail (journal d'une misovire . . .).* Paris: l'Har-
    mattan, 1983.
Tlali, Miriam. *Muriel at Metropolitan.* London: Raven Press, 1979.
Zanga Tsogo, Delphine. *Vies de femmes.* Yaounde: Éditions CLE, 1983.

Secondary Sources

Abanime, E. P. "Ideologies of Race and Sex in Literature: Racism and Antiracism in the
    African Francophone Novel." *College Language Association Journal* 30.2 (1986):
    125–43.
Abel, Elizabeth, and Emily K. Abel, eds. *The Signs Reader: Women, Gender, and Scholar-
    ship.* Chicago: U of Chicago P, 1983.
Abrahams, Cecil. "The Context of Black South African Literature." *World Literature Writ-
    ten in English* 18.1 (1979): 8–19.
——. "The Tragic Life of Bessie Head." Abrahams. 3–10.
——. "The Tyranny of Place: The Context of Bessie Head's Fiction." *World Literature
    Written in English* 17.1 (1978): 22–29.
Abrahams, Cecil, ed. *The Tragic Life: Bessie Head and Literature in Southern Africa.* Tren-
    ton, NJ: Africa World Press, 1990.
Achebe, Chinua. "African Literature as Restoration of Celebration." *New African* (March
    1990): 40–43.
——. *Hopes and Impediments: Selected Essays.* New York: Anchor Books, 1989.
——. *Things Fall Apart.* London: Heinemann, 1969.
Ackad, Josette. *Le roman camerounais et la critique.* Paris: Silex, 1985.
Adam, Ian, and Helen Tiffin, eds. *Past the Last Post: Theorizing Post-Colonialism and Post-
    Modernism.* Calgary: U of Calgary P, 1990.
Adhikari, Mohamed. "Between Black and White: The History of Coloured Politics in
    South Africa." *Canadian Journal of African Studies* 25.1 (1991): 106–10.
Ahmad, Aijaz. "Jameson's Rhetoric of Otherness and the 'National Allegory.'" *Social Text*
    17 (1987): 3–25.

Aidoo, Ama Ata. "Ghana: To Be a Woman." Morgan. 1984. 258–265.

——. "Interview." James. 8–27.

——. "Interview: African Women's Writing." Granqvist and Stotesbury. 12–15.

——. "To Be an Africa Woman Writer—An Overview and a Detail." *Criticism and Ideology: Second African Writers' Conference, Stockholm 1986.* Ed. Kirsten H. Petersen. Uppsala: Nordiska afrikainstitutet, 1988.

Alcoff, Linda. "Cultural Feminism versus Post-Structuralism: The Identity Crisis in Feminist Theory." Malson et al. 295–326.

——. "The Problem of Speaking for Others." *Cultural Critique* 20 (Winter 1991–92): 5–32.

Amadi, Elechi. *The Concubine.* London: Heinemann, 1966.

Amadiume, Ifi. *Male Daughters, Female Husbands: Gender and Sex in an African Society.* London: Zed Books, 1987.

Andriamirado, Sennen. "La femme par qui le scandale arrive." *Jeune Afrique* 1172 (22 juin, 1983): 68–70.

Appiah, Kwame Anthony. "Is the Post- in Postmodernism the Post- in Postcolonial?" *Critical Inquiry* 17 (Winter 1991): 336–57.

Ashcroft, Bill, Gareth Griffiths, and Helen Tiffin. *The Empire Writes Back: Theory and Practice in Post-Colonial Literatures.* London: Routledge, 1989.

Ashuntantang, Joyce. "Women in Cameroon: Equality Before the Law?" *The Herald* No. 20 (Wednesday Dec. 30, 1992): 11.

Atchebro, Daniel. "Beyala: trop 'brûlante' pour les mecs!" *Regards Africains* 8 (1988): 29.

Bâ, Mariama. "La fonction politique des littératures africaines écrites." *Écriture française dans le monde* 5.3 (1981): 3–7.

——. "Interview," with Harrell-Bond. 209–14.

Banyiwa-Horne, Naana. "African Womanhood: The Contrasting Perspectives of Flora Nwapa's *Efuru* and Elechi Amadi's *The Concubine.*" Davies and Graves. 119–29.

Bazin, Nancy T. "Venturing Into Feminist Consciousness: Bessie Head and Buchi Emecheta." Abrahams. 45–58.

——. "Weight of Custom, Signs of Change: Feminism in the Literature of African Women." *World Literature Written in English* 25.2 (1985): 183–97.

Beal, Frances M. "Double Jeopardy: To Be Black and Female." Morgan. 1970. 340–53.

Belenky, Mary F., Blythe M. Clinchy, Nancy R. Goldberger, and Jill M. Tarule. *Women's Ways of Knowing: The Development of Self, Voice, and Mind.* New York: Basic Books, 1986.

Bell, Roseann P. "The Absence of the African Woman Writer." *College Language Association Journal* 21.4 (1978): 491–98.

——, Bettye J. Parker, and Beverly Guy-Sheftall, eds. *Sturdy Black Bridges: Visions of Black Women in Literature.* Garden City, NY: Anchor Books, 1979.

Berrian, Brenda F. "African Women as Seen in the Works of Flora Nwapa and Ama Ata Aidoo." *College Language Association Journal* 25.3 (1982): 331–39.

——. *Bibliography of African Women Writers and Journalists (Ancient Egypt—1984).* Washington, DC: Three Continents, 1985.

Bhabha, Homi K. "Interrogating Identity: The Postcolonial Prerogative." *Anatomy of Racism.* Ed. David Theo Goldberg. Minneapolis: U of Minnesota P, 1990. 183–209.

——. "The Other Question: Difference, Discrimination and the Discourse of Colonialism." Ferguson et al. 71–87.

———. "Of Mimicry and Man: The Ambivalence of Colonial Discourse." *October* 28 (Spring 1984): 125–33.

Blair, Dorothy S. *Senegalese Literature: A Critical History.* Boston: Twayne Publishers, 1984.

Bjornson, Richard. *The African Quest for Freedom and Identity: Cameroonian Writing and the National Experience.* Bloomington: Indiana UP, 1991.

Boehmer, Elleke. "Stories of Women and Mothers: Gender and Nationalism in the Early Fiction of Flora Nwapa." Nasta. 3–23.

Bordo, Susan. "The Body and the Reproduction of Femininity: A Feminist Appropriation of Foucault." Jaggar and Bordo. 13–33.

Borgomano, Madeleine. "Les femmes et l'écriture-parole." *Notre Librairie* 117 (Avril-Juin 1994): 87–94.

Bosman, Brenda. "A Correspondence without Theory: Tsitsi Dangarembga's *Nervous Conditions.*" *Current Writing* 2 (1990): 91–100.

Brière, Eloïse. "Le retour des mères dévorantes." *Notre Librairie* 117 (Avril-Juin 1994): 66–71.

———. *Le roman camerounais et ses discours.* Ivry: Editions Nouvelles du Sud, 1993.

Brown, Lloyd. "The African Woman as Writer." *Canadian Journal of African Studies* 9.3 (1975): 493–501.

———. *Women Writers in Black Africa.* Westport, CT: Greenwood Press, 1981.

Bruner, Charlotte H. "Been-to or Has-been: A Dilemma for Today's African Woman." *Ba Shiru* 8.2 (1977): 23–31.

———. "Bessie Head: Restless in a Distant Land." *When the Drumbeat Changes.* Ed. Carolyn A. Parker and Stephen Arnold. Washington, DC: Three Continents, 1981. 261–77.

———, ed. *Unwinding Threads: Writing by Women in Africa.* London: Heinemann, 1983.

Bryce-Okunlola, Jane. "Motherhood as a Metaphor for Creativity in Three African Women's Novels: Flora Nwapa, Rebeka Njau, and Bessie Head." Nasta. 200–18.

Bulkin, Elly, Minnie Bruce Pratt, and Barbara Smith. *Yours in Struggle: Three Feminist Perspectives on Anti-Semitism and Racism.* Ithaca, NY: Firebrand, 1988.

Busia, Abena P. B. "Words Whispered over Voids: A Context for Black Women's Rebellious Voices in the Novel of the African Diaspora." *Black Feminist Criticism and Critical Theory.* Ed. Joe Weixlmann and Houston A. Baker Jr. Greenwood, FL: Penkevill, 1988. 1–41.

Butake, Bole. "Cameroon Literature in English/Littérature camerounaise anglophone." *Notre Librairie* 99 (Oct.-Déc. 1989): 102–105.

Cade, Toni, ed. *The Black Woman: An Anthology.* New York: Signet, 1970.

Caplan, Pat, ed. Introduction. *The Cultural Construction of Sexuality.* London: Routledge, 1989. 1–30.

Cazenave, Odile. "Blanche Othello: La femme blanche dans le couple interracial à travers le roman ouest-africain d'expression française." Diss. Pennsylvania State U, 1988. Ann Arbor: UMI, 1989. 8826719.

———. "Marginalisation et identité des personnages dans la littérature négro-africaine des années 80: l'image du Métis." *Présence Francophone* 38 (1991): 111–32.

Cévaër, Françoise. "Interview de Calixthe Beyala." *Revue de Littérature Comparée* 67.1 (Janvier-Mars 1993): 161–64.

Chemain-Degrange, Arlette. "L'écriture de Calixthe Beyala: Provocation ou révolte généreuse." *Notre Librairie* 99 (Oct.-Déc. 1989): 162–63.

———. *Emancipation féminine et roman africain*. Dakar: Nouvelles Éditions Africaines, 1980.

Chodorow, Nancy. *Feminism and Psychoanalytical Theory*. New Haven: Yale UP, 1989.

———. *The Reproduction of Mothering: Psychoanalysis and the Sociology of Gender*. Berkeley: U of California P, 1978.

Christian, Barbara. "An Angle of Seeing: Motherhood in Buchi Emecheta's *Joys of Mother-hood* and Alice Walker's *Meridian*." *Black Feminist Criticism: Perspectives on Black Women Writers*. New York: Pergamon, 1985. 211–52.

———. "The Race for Theory." *Feminist Studies* 14.1 (1988): 67–79.

Clignet, Remi. "Women, Education, and Labor Force Participation: Social Change and Sexual Differentiaton in the Cameroun and the Ivory Coast." *Signs* 3 (1977): 244–60.

Cohen, Cheryl H. "The Feminist Sexuality Debates: Ethics and Politics." *Hypatia* 1.2 (1986): 71–86.

Collins, Patricia H. *Black Feminist Thought: Knowledge, Consciousness and the Politics of Empowerment*. Boston: Unwin Hyman, 1990.

———. "Learning From the Outsider Within: The Sociological Significance of Black Feminist Thought." *Social Problems* 33.6 (1986): 14–32.

Combahee River Collective. "A Black Feminist Statement." Moraga and Anzaldua. 211–18.

Dabla, Séwanou. *Nouvelles Ecritures Africaines: Romanciers de la Seconde Génération*. Paris: l'Harmattan, 1986.

Dallery, Arleen B. "The Politics of Writing (the) Body: Écriture Féminine." Jaggar and Bordo. 52–67.

d'Almeida, Irène A. "The Concept of Choice in Mariama Bâ's Fiction." Davies and Graves. 161–71.

———. "Femme ? Feministe ? Misovire ? Les romancières africaines." *Notre Librairie* 117 (Avril-Juin 1994): 48–51.

———. *Francophone African Women Writers: Destroying the Emptiness of Silence*. Gaines-ville, FL: UP of Florida, 1994.

Dangarembga, Tsitsi. "Interview." Wilkinson. 188–98.

———. "Interview." Davies. 101–108.

davenport, doris. "The Pathology of Racism: A Conversation with Third World Wim-min." Moraga and Anzaldua. 85–90.

Davies, Carole B. "Introduction: Feminist Consciousness and African Literary Criticism." Davies and Graves. 1–23.

———. "Motherhood in the Works of Male and Female Igbo Writers: Achebe, Emecheta, Nwapa, and Nzekwu." Davies and Graves. 241–56.

———, ed. *Black Women's Writing: Crossing the Boundaries*. Frankfurt a.M.: Ehling, 1989.

———, and Anne Adams Graves, eds. *Ngambika: Studies of Women in African Literature*. Trenton, NJ: Africa World Press, 1986.

Davis, Angela. *Women, Race and Class*. New York: Vintage, 1981.

de Beauvoir, Simone. *The Second Sex*. Trans. H. M. Parshley. New York: Vintage, 1974.

de Jager, Marjolijn. "To Speak or Be Spoken: Some Women in African Literature." *To Speak or Be Spoken: The Paradox of Disobedience in the Lives of Women*. Ed. Lena B. Ross. Wilmette, IL: Chiron Publications, 1993. 75–84.

de Lauretis, Teresa, ed. *Feminist Studies/Critical Studies*. Bloomington: Indiana UP, 1986.

———. "Feminist Studies/Critical Studies: Issues, Terms, and Contexts." de Lauretis. 1–19.

———. "The Technology of Gender." *Technologies of Gender: Essays on Theory, Film, and Fiction.* Bloomington: Indiana UP, 1987. 1–30.

Dehon, Claire. *Le roman camerounais d'expression française.* Birmingham, AL: Summa Publications, 1989.

Diallo, Assiatou B. "Un nouveau roman de Calixthe Beyala." *Amina* 223 (Novembre 1988): 85.

Dill, Bonnie T. "Race, Class, and Gender: Prospects for an All-Inclusive Sisterhood." *Feminist Studies* 9.1 (1983): 131–50.

Dingome, Jeanne N. "Ritual and Modern Dramatic Expression in Cameroon: The Plays of Werewere Liking." *Semper Aliquid Novi: Littérature Comparée et Littératures d'Afrique.* Ed. Janos Riesz and Alain Ricard. Tübingen: Gunter Narr Verlag, 1990. 317–25.

Doumbi-Fakoly. "Rev. of *Tu t'appelleras Tanga.*" *Présence Africaine* 148 (1988): 147–48.

Dunton, Chris. " 'Wheyting Be Dat?' The Treatment of Homosexuality in African Literature." *Research in African Literatures* 20.3 (Fall 1989): 422–48.

Ekoto Etonde, Grace. "La femme et la libération de l'Afrique: Quelques figures culturelles." *Présence africaine* 140 (1986): 140–53.

Ekwensi, Cyprian. *Jagua Nana.* London: Panther Books, 1961.

El Saadawi, Nawal. *The Hidden Face of Eve: Women in the Arab World.* Trans. and ed. Sherif Hetata. Boston: Beacon, 1980.

Ellington, Athleen. "L'interdépendence, un discours d'avenir: Calixthe Beyala, Werewere Liking et Simone Schwarz-Bart." *Notre Librairie* 117 (Avril-Juin 1994): 102–106.

Emecheta, Buchi. "Interview." James. 34–45.

———. "Interview." Umeh and Umeh. 19–25.

———. "Interview: The Dilemma of Being in between Two Cultures." Granqvist and Stotesbury. 16–20.

Eteki-Otabela, Marie-Louise. "Dix ans de luttes du Collectif des femmes pour le renouveau (CFR): quelques réflexions sur le mouvement féministe camerounais." *Recherches féministes* 5.1 (1992): 125–34.

Evans, Mari, ed. *Black Women Writers (1950–1980): A Critical Evaluation.* New York: Anchor Books/Doubleday, 1984.

Fanon, Frantz. *Black Skin, White Masks.* Trans. Charles L. Markmann. New York: Grove Weidenfeld, 1967.

———. *The Wretched of the Earth.* Trans. Constance Farrington. New York: Grove Press, 1963.

Ferguson, Russell. "Introduction: Invisible Center." Ferguson et al. 9–14.

———, Martha Gever, Trinh Minh-ha, and Cornell West, eds. *Out There: Marginalization and Contemporary Cultures.* New York: The New Museum of Contemporary Art and MIT P, 1990.

Ferguson, Ann, et al. "Forum: The Feminist Sexuality Debates." *Signs* 10.1 (1984): 106–35.

Flax, Jane. "Postmodernism and Gender Relations in Feminist Theory." Malson et al. 51–73.

Flewellen, Elinor C. "Assertiveness vs. Submissiveness in Selected Works by African Women Writers." *Ba Shiru* 12.2 (1985): 3–18.

Flockemann, Miki. " 'Not-Quite Insiders and Not-Quite Outsiders': The 'Process of Womanhood' in *Beka Lamb, Nervous Conditions* and *Daughters of the Twilight.*" *Journal of Commonwealth Literature* 27.1 (1992): 37–47.

Foucault, Michel. *The History of Sexuality. Vol. I. An Introduction.* Trans. Robert Hurley. New York: Vintage, 1978.

Fradkin, Betty M. "Conversation with Bessie." *World Literature Written in English* 17.2 (1978): 427–34.

Frank, Katherine. "Feminist Criticism and the African Novel." *African Literature Today* 14 (1984): 34–48.

———. "Women Without Men: The Feminist Novel in Africa." Jones et al. 24–34.

Fraser, Nancy, and Sandra L. Bartky, eds. *Revaluing French Feminism: Critical Essays on Difference, Agency, and Culture.* Bloomington: Indiana UP, 1992.

Freedman, Estelle B., and Barrie Thorne. "Introduction to 'The Feminist Sexuality Debates.' " *Signs* 10.1 (1984): 102–105.

Freud, Sigmund. "The Dissolution of the Oedipus Complex." *The Complete Standard Edition*, vol. 19. Trans. James Strachey. London: Hogarth, 1964. 173–79.

———. "Femininity." *New Introductory Lectures on Psychoanalysis*, vol. 2. Ed. James Strachey and Angela Richards, trans. James Strachey. Harmondsworth: Penguin, 1973. 144–69.

Fusco, Coco. "Managing the Other." *Lusitania* 3.3 (1990): 77–85.

Gallimore, Rangira B. "Le corps: de l'aliénation à la réappropriation, chez les romancières d'Afrique noire francophone." *Notre Librairie* 117 (Avril-Juin 1994): 54–60.

Gates, Henry Louis Jr. *Figures in Black.* New York: Oxford UP, 1987.

———. Introduction. *Reading Feminist, Reading Black: A Critical Anthology.* Ed. H. L. Gates Jr. New York: Meridian, 1990. 1–17.

———. "Introduction: Writing 'Race' and the Difference It Makes." *"Race," Writing, and Difference.* Ed. H. L. Gates Jr. Chicago: U of Chicago P, 1986. 1–20.

Genevoix, Sylvie. "Portrait: Calixthe Beyala." *Madame Figaro* (24 juillet 1993): 18.

Granqvist, Raoul, and John Stotesbury. *African Voices: Interviews with Thirteen African Writers.* Sidney, Australia: Dangaroo, 1989.

Gunning, Isabelle R. "Arrogant Perception, World-Travelling and Multicultural Feminism: The Case of Female Genital Surgeries." *Columbia Human Rights Law Review* 23 (1991–92): 189–248.

Gupta, Nila, and Makeda Silvera, eds. *The Issue is 'Ism: Women of Colour Speak Out.* Toronto: Sister Vision Press, 1989.

Haraway, Donna. " 'Gender' for a Marxist Dictionary: The Sexual Politics of a Word." *Simians, Cyborgs, and Women: The Reinvention of Nature.* New York: Routledge, 1991. 127–48.

———. "Reading Buchi Emecheta: Contests for 'Women's Experience' in Women's Studies." 109–24.

Harding, Sandra. "Why Has the Sex/Gender System become Visible Only Now?" *Discovering Reality: Feminist Perspectives on Epistemology, Metaphysics, Methodology, and Philosophy of Science.* Ed. Sandra Harding and Merrill B. Hintikka. Dordrecht: D. Reidel, 1983. 311–24.

———. "Reinventing Ourselves as Other: More New Agents of History and Knowledge." *Whose Science? Whose Knowledge? Thinking from Women's Lives.* Ithaca, NY: Cornell UP, 1991. 268–95.

———, ed. *Feminism and Methodology.* Bloomington: Indiana UP, 1985.

Harrell-Bond, Barbara. "Interview: Mariama Bâ, Winner of the First Noma Award for Publishing in Africa." *The African Book Publishing Record* 6.3/4 (1980): 209–14.

Harrow, Kenneth W. *Thresholds of Change in African Literature: The Emergence of a Tradition*. Portsmouth, NH: Heinemann, 1993.

Hartsock, Nancy. "The Feminist Standpoint: Developing the Ground for a Specifically Feminist Historical Materialism." Harding. 157–80.

———. "Rethinking Modernism: Minority vs. Majority Theories." *Cultural Critique* 7 (1987): 187–206.

Hay, Margaret J. and Sharon Stichter, eds. *African Women South of the Sahara*. London: Longman, 1984.

Head, Bessie. *A Woman Alone: Autobiographical Writings*. Ed. Craig MacKenzie. London: Heinemann, 1990.

———. "Interview," with Adler et al. *Between the Lines*. Ed. Craig MacKenzie and Cherry Clayton. Grahamstown, South Africa: NELM Interviews Series No. 4, 1989. 5–29.

———. "Interview," with Fradkin. 427–34.

———. *Tales of Tenderness and Power*. London: Heinemann, 1990.

Hekman, Susan J. *Gender and Knowledge: Elements of a Postmodern Feminism*. Boston: Northeastern UP, 1990.

Henn, Jeanne K. "Peasants, Workers, and Capital: Economy of Labor and Incomes in Cameroon." Diss. Harvard U, 1978. Ann Arbor: UMI, 1979. 7925675.

———. "Women in the Rural Economy: Past, Present, and Future." Hay and Stichter. 1–18.

hooks, bell. *Ain't I A Woman? Black Women and Feminism*. Boston: South End Press, 1981.

———. *Feminist Theory: From Margin to Center*. Boston: South End Press, 1984.

———. *Talking Back: Thinking Feminist, Thinking Black*. Boston: South End Press, 1989.

———. *Yearning: Race, Gender, and Cultural Politics*. Toronto: Between the Lines, 1990.

Hosken, Fran. *Genital and Sexual Mutilation of Females*. Lexington, MA: Women's International Network, 1979.

Hourantier, Marie-José. *Du rituel au théâtre rituel: contribution à une esthétique négro-africaine*. Paris: l'Harmattan, 1984.

Hull, Gloria T. "Black Women Writers and the Diaspora." *The Black Scholar* 17.2 (1986).

Ibrahim, Huma. "The Autobiographical Content in the Works of South African Women Writers: The Personal and the Political." *Biography East and West*. Ed. Carol Ramelb. Honolulu: U of Hawaii P, 1989. 122–26.

Ikonné, Chidi. "African Literature in Africa Twenty-Five Years after the Dakar and Freetown Conferences." Wylie et al. 97–105.

Illich, Ivan. *Gender*. London: Marion Boyars, 1983.

Jaccard, Anny-Claire. "Des textes novateurs: la littérature féminine." *Notre Librairie* 99 (Oct.-Déc. 1989): 155–61.

———. Rev. of *Vies de femmes* by Delphine Z. Tsogo. *Notre Librairie* 100 (Jan.-Mars 1990): 124–25.

Jaggar, Alison. *Feminist Politics and Human Nature*. Sussex: Harvester, 1983.

———, and Susan Bordo, eds. *Gender/Body/Knowledge: Feminist Reconstructions of Being and Knowing*. New Brunswick, NJ: Rutgers UP, 1989.

James, Adeola. *In Their Own Voices: African Women Writers Talk*. London: James Currey, 1990.

James, Stanlie M., and Abena P. A. Busia, eds. *Theorizing Black Feminisms: The Visionary Pragmatism of Black Women*. London: Routledge, 1993.

Jameson, Fredric. "Third-World Literature in the Era of Multinational Capitalism." *Social Text* 15 (1986): 65–88.

Johnson, Rotimi. "Womanism and Feminism in African Letters." *Literary Criterion* 25.2 (1990): 25–35.

Johnson-Odim, Cheryl. "Common Themes, Different Contexts: Third World Women and Feminism." Mohanty et al. 314–27.

Jones, Ann R. "Writing the Body: L'Écriture Féminine." Showalter. 1986. 361–77.

Jones, Eldred D., Eustace Palmer, and Majorie Jones, eds. *Women in African Literature Today*. London: James Currey, 1987.

Julien, Eileen. *African Novels and the Question of Orality*. Bloomington: Indiana UP, 1992.

Ka, Aminata M. "Ramatoulaye, Aïssatou, Mireille et . . . Mariama Bâ." *Notre Librairie* 81 (Oct.-Déc. 1985): 129–34.

Kalu, Anthonia C. "Those Left Out in the Rain: African Literary Theory and the Re-invention of the African Woman." *African Studies Review* 37.2 (September 1994): 77–95.

Kaminsky, Amy. "Issues for an International Feminist Literary Criticism." *Signs* 19.1 (Autumn 1993): 213–27.

Katrak, Ketu H. "Decolonizing Culture: Toward a Theory for Postcolonial Women's Texts." *Modern Fiction Studies* 35.1 (1989): 157–79.

———. "From Pauline to Dikeledi: The Philosophical and Political Vision of Bessie Head's Protagonists." *Ba Shiru* 12.2 (1985): 26–35.

Keim, Karen R. "Popular Fiction Publishing in Cameroon." *The African Book Publishing Record* 9.1 (1983): 7–11.

Kemp, Yakini. "Romantic Love and the Individual in Novels by Mariama Bâ, Buchi Emecheta and Bessie Head." Wylie et al. 11–21.

Kessler, Suzanne J., and Wendy Mckenna. *Gender: An Ethnomethodological Approach*. New York: John Wiley and Sons, 1978.

King, Deborah. "Multiple Jeopardy, Multiple Consciousness: The Context of a Black Feminist Ideology." Malson et al. 75–105.

Kishwar, Madhu. "Why I Do Not Call Myself a Feminist." *Manushi* 61 (Nov.-Dec. 1990): 2–8.

Kom, Ambroise. *Dictionnaire des oeuvres littéraires négro-africaines de langue française: des origines à nos jours*. Sherbrooke, PQ: Editions Naaman, 1983.

Koulibaly, Isaie B. "Werewere Liking: Une femme mystérieuse." *Amina* No. 211 (Déc. 1987): 9–10.

Kristeva, Julia. *Desire in Language: A Semiotic Approach to Literature and Art*. Ed. Leon S. Roudiez. Trans. Thomas Gora, Alice Jardine, and Leon S. Roudiez. New York: Columbia UP, 1980.

Kuhn, Annette. "Introduction to Hélène Cixous's 'Castration or Decapitation?' " *Signs* 7.1 (1981): 36–59.

Kuoh-Moukouri, Thérèse. *Les couples dominos*. (1973) Paris: Harmattan, 1983.

———. *Rencontres essentielles*. Paris: Edgar, 1969.

Lacan, Jacques. *Ecrits: A Selection*. Trans. Alan Sheridan. New York: W. W. Norton, 1977.

———, et al. *Feminine Sexuality: Jacques Lacan and the École Freudienne*. Ed. Juliet Mitchell and Jacqueline Rose. New York: W. W. Norton, 1982.

Lâm, Maivân Clech. "Feeling Foreign in Feminism." *Signs* 19.4 (Summer 1994): 865–93.

LaPin, Deirdre. "Women in African Literature." Hay and Stichter. 102–18.

Lardner, Joyce. *Tomorrow's Tomorrow: The Black Woman*. Garden City, NY: Doubleday, 1972.

Lee, Sonia. "Conversation with Miriam Tlali." *African Literature Association Bulletin* 17.3 (1991): 40–42.

Lenta, Margaret. "The Need for a Feminism: Black Township Writing." *Journal of Literary Studies* 4.1 (1988): 49–63.

Liking, Werewere. "Interview," with Koulibaly. 9–10.

———. "Interview," with Magnier. 17–21.

———. "Interview," with Ndjicki. 18–21.

———. "Interview: Je vois l'Afrique à l'envers," with Andriamirado. 69–70.

Lindberg-Seyersted, Brita. "The Color Black: Skin Color as Social, Ethical, and Esthetic Sign in Writings by Black American Women." *English Studies* 73.1 (1992): 51–67.

Lindsey, Linda L. *Gender Roles: A Sociological Perspective*. New Jersey: Prentice Hall, 1990.

Linton-Umeh, Marie. "The African Heroine." Bell et al. 39–51.

Lionnet, Françoise. *Autobiographical Voices: Race, Gender, Self-Portraiture*. Ithaca: Cornell UP, 1989.

Lips, Hilary. *Sex and Gender: An Introduction*. California: Mayfield, 1988.

Lockett, Cecily. "The Black Woman in South African English Literature." *Journal of Literary Studies* 4.1 (1988): 21–37.

———. "Feminism(s) and Writing in English in South Africa." *Current Writing* 2 (1990): 1–21.

Lorber, Judith and Susan A. Farrell, eds. *The Social Construction of Gender*. Newbury Park, CA: Sage Publications, 1991.

Lorde, Audre. *Sister Outsider*. Freedom, CA: The Crossing Press, 1984.

Loy, Barbara. "The Destruction of the South African Family by Apartheid Laws as Revealed in Select Works of Tlali and Ngcobo." Wylie et al. 23–28.

Lyonga, Nalova. "La littérature féminine anglophone au Cameroun." *Notre Librairie* 118 (Juillet-Septembre 1994): 29–35.

———. "Uhamiri or a Feminist Approach to African Literature: An Analysis of Selected Texts by Women in Oral and Written Literature." Diss. University of Michigan, 1985. Ann Arbor: UMI, 1986. 8520936.

MacKenzie, Craig. "Bessie Head: Alienation, Breakdown and Renewal." *International Literature in English*. Ed. Robert R. Ross. New York and London: Garland Publishing, 1991. 557–69.

———, and Cherry Clayton, eds. *Between the Lines*. Grahamstown, South Africa: NELM, Interviews Series Four, 1989.

MacKinnon, Catharine A. "Desire and Power: A Feminist Perspective." Nelson and Grossberg. 105–16.

———. "Feminism, Marxism, Method, and the State: An Agenda for Theory." Abel and Abel. 227–56.

———, Gayatri Spivak, and Ellen Willis. Discussion on "Desire and Power: A Feminist Perspective," by MacKinnon. Nelson and Grossberg. 117–21.

Magnier, Bernard. "A la rencontre de . . . Werewere Liking." *Notre Librairie* 79 (Avril-Juin 1985): 17–21.

Malson, Micheline, J. F. O'Barr, S. Westphal-Wihl, and M. Wyer, eds. *Feminist Theory in Practice and Process*. Chicago: U of Chicago P, 1989.

Marks, Elaine, and Isabelle de Courtivron, eds. *New French Feminisms: An Anthology.* New York: Schocken, 1981.

McClintock, Anne. "The Angel of Progress: Pitfalls of the Term 'Post-Colonialism.' " *Social Text* 31-32 (1992): 84-98.

McDowell, Deborah E. "New Directions for Black Feminist Criticism." Showalter. 1986. 186-99.

McWilliams, Sally. "Tsitsi Dangarembga's *Nervous Conditions*: At the Crossroads of Feminism and Post-Colonialism." *World Literature Written in English* 31.1 (1991): 103-12.

Midohouan, Thécla M. "La parole des femmes." *Figures et fantasmes de la violence dans les Littératures francophones de l'Afrique subsaharienne et des Antilles.* Ed. Franca Marcato Falzoni. Bologna: Cooperativa Libraria Universitaria Editrice Bologna, 1991. 149-62.

Miller, Christopher. *Theories of Africans: Francophone Literature and Anthropology in Africa.* Chicago: U of Chicago P, 1990.

Millett, Kate. *Sexual Politics.* New York: Ballantine, 1970.

Milolo, Kembe. *L'Image de la femme chez les romanciers de l'afrique noire francophone.* Fribourg: Éditions Universitaires, 1986.

Minyono-Nkodo, Mathieu François. Rev. of *Elle sera de jaspe et de corail* by Werewere Liking. *Notre Librairie* 100 (Jan.-Mars 1990): 112-13.

Mishra, Vijay, and Bob Hodge. "What is post(-)colonialism?" *Textual Practice* 5.3 (1991): 399-414.

Mohanty, Chandra T., Ann Russo, and Lourdes Torres, eds. *Third World Women and the Politics of Feminism.* Bloomington: Indiana UP, 1991.

Mohanty, Chandra T. "Under Western Eyes: Feminist Scholarship and Colonial Discourses." Mohanty et al. 51-80.

———, and Biddy Martin. "Feminist Politics: What's Home Got to Do with It?" de Lauretis. 191-212.

Mokwenye, Cyril. "La Polygamie et la révolte de la femme africaine moderne: Une lecture d' *Une si longue lettre* de Mariama Bâ." *L'Afrique Littéraire* 65-66 (1982): 59-64.

Moraga, Cherríe, and Gloria Anzaldua, eds. *This Bridge Called My Back: Writings by Radical Women of Color.* New York: Kitchen Table/Women of Color Press, 1983.

Morgan, Robin, ed. *Sisterhood is Global.* New York: Anchor Books/Doubleday, 1984.

———, ed. *Sisterhood is Powerful.* New York: Random House, 1970.

Mouellé Kombi II, Narcisse. "Calixthe Beyala et son petit prince de Belleville." *Amina* 268 (Août 1992): 10-12.

Mugambi, Helen N. "The Wounded Psyche and Beyond: Conformity and Marginality in Selected African and Afro-American Novels." Diss. Indiana U, 1988. Ann Arbor: UMI, 1989. 8914826.

Mukherjee, Arun P. "Whose Post-Colonialism and Whose Postmodernism?" *World Literature Written in English* 30.2 (1990): 1-9.

Nacef, Armelle. Rev. of *C'est le soleil qui m'a brûlé* by Calixthe Beyala. *Jeune Afrique* 1423 (13 Avril 1988): 55.

Narayan, Uma. "The Project of Feminist Epistemology: Perspectives from a Nonwestern Feminist." Jaggar and Bordo. 259-69.

Nasta, Susheila, ed. Introduction to *Motherlands.* Nasta. xiii-xxx.

──. *Motherlands: Black Women's Writing from Africa, Caribbean and South Asia*. New Brunswick, NJ: Rutgers UP, 1992.

Ndachi Tagne, David. Rev. of *C'est le soleil qui m'a brûlé* by Calixthe Beyala. *Notre Librairie* 100 (Jan.-Mars 1990): 96–97.

──. *Roman et réalités camerounaises*. Paris: L'Harmattan, 1986.

Ndinda, Joseph. "Écriture et discours féminin au Cameroun: trois générations de romancières." *Notre Librairie* 118 (Juillet-Septembre 1994): 6–12.

Ndjicki, Florent. "Interview: Werewere Liking." *Sista* 2 (Juil. 1992): 18–21.

Nelson, Cary, and Lawrence Grossberg, eds. *Marxism and the Interpretation of Culture*. Urbana: U of Illinois P, 1988.

Nfah-Abbenyi, Juliana M. "African Women and Feminism: The Context of an-Other Black Woman's Voice." Paper presented at the conference "African and African-American Women: The Ties that Bind." Baton Rouge: Southern University, March 28, 1992.

──. "Bridging North and South . . . Notes Towards True Dialogue and Transformation." *Bridging North/South: Patterns of Transformation*, Special issue of *Canadian Women's Studies* 17.2 (Spring 1997): 145–48.

──. "Calixthe Beyala: 1961– ." *Postcolonial African Writers: A Bio-Bibliographical Sourcebook*. Ed. Pushpa Parekh. Forthcoming from Greenwood Press, 1997.

──. "Calixthe Beyala's 'femme-fillette': Womanhood and the Politics of (M)Othering." *The Politics of (M)Othering in African Literature: Womanhood, Identity, and Resistance in African Literature*. Ed. Obioma Nnaemeka. London: Routledge, 1996. 101–13.

──. "Ecological Postcolonialism in African Women's Literature." *The Nature Book of Garland Literature*. Ed. Patrick Murphy. Forthcoming from Garland, 1997.

──. "The Image of the Woman in Beba Folktales." Maîtrise: University of Yaounde, 1980.

──. Linda Alcoff and 'Positionality': Rethinking the Identity Crisis in Feminist Theory." *Comparative Literature in Canada/Littérature Comparée au Canada* 23.2 (Fall 1992): 93–100.

──. "A Literary Analysis of the Folktale among the Beba." Diss.: University of Yaounde, 1987.

──. "Reflections of an African Woman." *Racism and Gender*. Special issue of *Canadian Woman Studies* 14.2 (Spring 1994): 91–103.

──. "Rev. of *Le petit prince de belleville* and *Maman a un amant*." In the two-part special issue on "nouvelles écritures féminines" of *Notre Librairie* 118 (Juillet-Septembre 1994): 183.

──. "Why (What) Am I (Doing) Here: A Cameroonian Woman?" *Our Own Agendas: Autobiographical Essays by Women Associated with McGill University*. Ed. Margaret Gillett and Ann Beer. Montreal: McGill Queen's UP, 1995. 250–61.

──. "Women's Sexuality and the Use of the Erotic in Calixthe Beyala." 1993. African Literature Association Selected Conference Papers, 21pp. (*ALA Bulletin* 20.2 [Spring 1994]). Forthcoming from Africa World Press.

Nicholson, Linda. "Toward a Method for Understanding Gender." *Gender and History: The Limits of a Social Theory in the Age of the Family*. New York: Columbia UP, 1986. 69–104.

Nnaemeka, Obioma. "Mariama Bâ: Parallels, Convergence, and Interior Space." *Feminist Issues* (Spring 1990): 13–35.

———. Rev. of *Male Daughters, Female Husbands* by Ifi Amadiume. *Signs* 16.3 (1991): 610–13.

Nwankwo, Chimalum. "The Feminist Impulse and Social Realism in Ama Ata Aidoo's *No Sweetness Here* and *Our Sister Killjoy*." Davies and Graves. 151–59.

Nwapa, Flora. *Efuru*. London: Heinemann, 1966.

Oakley, Ann. *Sex, Gender and Society*. New York: Harper Colophon, 1972.

O'Barr, Jean F. "Feminist Issues in the Fiction of Kenya's Women Writers." Jones et al. 55–70.

Ogundipe-Leslie, Molara. "The Female Writer and Her Commitment." Jones et al. 5–13.

———. *Re-Creating Ourselves: African Women and Critical Transformations*. Trenton, NJ: Africa World Press, 1994.

Ogunyemi, Chikwenye O. "Buchi Emecheta: The Shaping of a Self." *Komparatistische Hefte* 8 (1983): 65–77.

———. "Womanism: The Dynamics of the Contemporary Black Female Novel in English." *Signs* 11.1 (1985): 63–80.

Ojo-Ade, Femi. "Female Writers, Male Critics." *African Literature Today* 13 (1983): 158–79.

———. "Still a Victim? Mariama Bâ's *Une si longue lettre*." *African Literature Today* 12 (1982): 71–87.

Okpewho, Isidore. *African Oral Literature: Backgrounds, Character, and Continuity*. Bloomington: Indiana UP, 1992.

Ola, Virginia U. "Women's Role in Bessie Head's Ideal World." *Ariel: A Review of International English Literature* 17.4 (Oct. 1986): 39–47.

Ombolo, Jean-Pierre. *Sexe et société en Afrique noire. L'anthropologie sexuelle beti: essai analytique, critique et comparatif*. Paris: l'Harmattan, 1990.

Ormerod, Beverley, and Jean-Marie Volet. *Romancières africaines d'expression française: le sud du Sahara*. Paris: l'Harmattan, 1994.

Ong, Aihwa. "Colonialism and Modernity: Feminist Re-presentations of Women in Non-Western Societies." *Inscriptions* 3/4 (1988): 79–93.

Ortner, Sherry B. "Is Female to Male as Nature Is to Culture?" Rosaldo and Lamphere. 67–87.

———, and Harriet Whitehead, eds. *Sexual Meanings: The Cultural Construction of Gender and Sexuality*. Cambridge: Cambridge UP, 1981.

Oyono, Ferdinand. *Houseboy*. Trans. John Reed. London: Heinemann, 1966.

Palmer, Eustace. "The Feminine Point of View: Buchi Emecheta's *The Joys of Motherhood*." *African Literature Today* 13 (1983): 38–55.

Parmar, Pratibha. "Woman, Native, Other: Interview with Minh-ha." *Feminist Review* 36 (Autumn 1990): 65–74.

Parry, Benita. "Problems in Current Theories of Colonial Discourse." *Oxford Literary Review* 9.1–2 (1987): 27–58.

p'Bitek, Okot. *Song of Lawino*. (1966). London: Heinemann, 1984.

Percy, Marina. "Embodying Subjectivity: A Literary Genealogy of Anorexic Discourse." Montreal: M. A. Thesis, McGill U, 1993.

Petersen, Kirsten H. "First Things First: Problems of a Feminist Approach to African Literature." *Kunapipi* 6.3 (1984): 35–47.

———. "Unpopular Opinions: Some African Women Writers." *A Double Colonization: Co-*

lonial and Post-Colonial Women's Writing. Ed. Kirsten H. Petersen and Anna
Rutherford. Mundelstrup, Denmark: Dangaroo Press, 1986. 107–20.

——, ed., *Criticism and Ideology: Second African Writers' Conference, Stockholm 1986.*
Uppsala: Nordiska afrikainstitutet, 1988.

Radway, Janice A. *Reading the Romance: Women, Patriarchy, and Popular Literature.*
Chapel Hill: U of North Carolina P, 1984.

Ravenscroft, Arthur. "The Novels of Bessie Head." *Aspects of South African Literature.* Ed.
Christopher Heywood. London: Heinemann, 1976. 174–86.

Rich, Adrienne. "Compulsory Heterosexuality and Lesbian Existence." Abel and Abel.
139–67.

——. "Notes toward a Politics of Location (1984)." *Blood, Bread, Poetry: Selected Prose
1979–1985.* New York: W. W. Norton, 1986. 210–31.

——. *Of Woman Born: Motherhood as Experience and Institution.* New York: W. W.
Norton, 1986.

Riesz, Janos. "Mariama Bâ's *Une si longue lettre:* An Erziehungsroman." *Research in African Literatures* 22.1 (1991): 27–42.

Rooney, Caroline. "Are We in the Company of Feminists? A Preface for Bessie Head and
Ama Ata Aidoo." *Diverse Voices: Essays on Twentieth-Century Women Writers in
English.* Ed. Harriet D. Jump. New York: Harvester Wheatsheaf, 1991. 214–46.

——. " 'Dangerous Knowledge' and the Poetics of Survival: A Reading of *Our Sister
Killjoy* and *A Question of Power.*" Nasta. 99–126.

Rosaldo, Michelle Z. "Women, Culture, and Society: A Theoretical Overview." Rosaldo
and Lamphere. 17–42.

——, and Louise Lamphere, eds. Introduction to *Women, Culture, and Society.* Stanford: Stanford UP, 1974. 1–15.

Rubin, Gayle. "The Traffic in Women: Notes on the 'Political Economy' of Sex." *Toward
an Anthropology of Women.* Ed. Rayna R. Rapp. New York: Monthly Review Press,
1975. 157–210.

Sam-Abbenyi, Amos. "Assessment of Two Gambian Trypanosomiasis Screening Programmes in the Focus of Fontem (Cameroon)." Montreal: M.Sc. Thesis, Université de Montréal, 1989.

Sandoval, Chela. "U.S. Third World Feminism: The Theory and Method of Oppositional
Consciousness in the Postmodern World." *Genders* 10 (Spring 1991): 1–24.

Schipper, Mineke, ed. "Mother Africa on a Pedestal: The Male Heritage in African Literature and Criticism." Jones et al. 35–54.

——. *White and Black: Imagination and Cultural Confrontations.* Amsterdam: Royal
Tropical Institute, 1990.

——. "Women and Literature in Africa." Schipper. 22–68.

——. *Unheard Words: Women and Literature in Africa, the Arab World, Asia, the Caribbean and Latin America.* Trans. Barbara P. Fasting. London: Allison and Busby,
1985.

Schulze-Engler, Frank. "Beyond Post-Colonialism: Multiple Identities in East African Literature." *US/THEM: Translation, Transcription and Identity in Post-Colonial Literary Cultures.* Ed. Gordon Collier. Amsterdam: Rodopi, 1992. 319–34.

Senghor, Léopald S. "Elegy of the Circumcised." *Poems of Black Africa.* Ed. Wole Soyinka.
New York: Hill and Wang, 1975. 159–61.

Shohat, Ella. "Notes on the 'Post-Colonial.' " *Social Text* 31–32 (1992): 99–113.

Showalter, Elaine. "Introduction: The Rise of Gender." *Speaking of Gender*. Ed. Elaine
    Showalter. New York: Routledge, 1989. 1–13.
——, ed. *The New Feminist Criticism: Essays on Women, Literature, and Theory*. London:
    Virago, 1986.
Singleton, Carrie J. "Race and Gender in Feminist Theory." Sage 6.1 (1989): 12–17.
Slemon, Stephen. "Unsettling the Empire: Resistance Theory for the Second World."
    World Literature Written in English 30.2 (1990): 30–41.
Smith, Barbara. "Towards a Black Feminist Criticism." Showalter. 1986. 168–85.
Smith, Dorothy. *The Everyday World as Problematic: A Feminist Sociology*. Toronto: U of
    Toronto P, 1987.
Smith, Esther Y. "Images of Women in African Literature: Some Examples of Inequality
    in the Colonial Period." Davies and Graves. 27–44.
Smith, Valerie. "Gender and Afro-Americanist Literary Theory and Criticism." Showalter.
    1989. 56–70.
Snitow, Ann, Christine Stansell, and Sharon Thompson, eds. Introduction. *Powers of De-
    sire: The Politics of Sexuality*. New York: Monthly Review Press, 1983. 9–47.
Solberg, Rolf. "The Woman of Black Africa, Buchi Emecheta: The Woman's Voice in the
    New Nigerian novel." *English Studies* 64.3 (1983): 247–62.
Songue, Paulette. *Prostitution en Afrique: l'exemple de Yaoundé*. Paris: l'Harmattan, 1986.
Spelman, Elizabeth V. "Theories of Race and Gender: The Erasure of Black Women."
    Quest 5.4 (1980): 36–62.
Spivak, Gayatri C. "Can the Subaltern Speak?" Nelson and Grossberg. 271–313.
——. "Imperialism and Sexual Difference." *Oxford Literary Review* 8.1–2 (1986): 225–40.
——. *In Other Worlds: Essays in Cultural Politics*. New York: Routledge, 1987.
——. *The Post-Colonial Critic: Interviews, Strategies, Dialogues*. Ed. Sarah Harasym. New
    York: Routledge, 1990.
Staunton, Cheryl A. "Three Senegalese Women Novelists: A Study of Temporal/Spatial
    Structures." Diss. George Washington U, 1986. Ann Arbor: UMI, 1986. 8608366.
Steady, Filomina C. "African Feminism: A Worldwide Perspective." Terborg-Penn et al.
    3–24.
——. "The Black Woman Cross-Culturally: An Overview." *The Black Woman Cross-
    Culturally*. Ed. Filomina Steady. Cambridge, MA: Schenkman Publishing, 1981.
    7–41.
Stratton, Florence. *Contemporary African Literature and the Politics of Gender*. London:
    Routledge, 1994.
——. " 'Periodic Embodiments': a Ubiquitous Trope in African Men's Writing." *Re-
    search in African Literatures* 20.1 (1990): 111–26.
——. "The Shallow Grave: Archetypes of Female Experience in African Fiction." *Re-
    search in African Literatures* 19.2 (1988): 143–69.
Stringer, Susan. "Through Their Own Eyes: The Beginnings of the Senegalese Novel by
    Women." Diss. U of Colorado, 1988. Ann Arbor: UMI, 1989. 8819707.
Stroller, Robert. *Presentations of Gender*. New Haven: Yale UP, 1985.
Suleri, Sara. "Woman Skin Deep: Feminism and the Postcolonial Condition." *Critical In-
    quiry* 18 (Summer 1992): 756–69.
Taiwo, Oladele. *Female Novelists of Modern Africa*. London: MacMillan, 1984.
Tala, Ibrahim K. "Some Images of Women in Cameroon Fiction." *New Horizons* 3.1
    (1983): 1–14.

Terborg-Penn, Rosalyn, Sharon Harley, and Andrea Rushing, eds. *Women in Africa and the African Diaspora*. Washington, DC: Howard UP, 1987.

Thiam, Awa. *La parole aux négresses*. Paris: Editions Denoël/Gonthier, 1978.

———. *Speak Out, Black Sisters: Feminism and Oppression in Black Africa*. Trans. Dorothy S. Blair. London: Pluto Press, 1986.

Thomas, Sue. "Killing the Hysteric in the Colonized's House: Tsitsi Dangarembga's *Nervous Conditions*." *Journal of Commonwealth Literature* 27.1 (1992): 26–36.

Tlali, Miriam. "Interview," with Lee. 40–42.

———. "Interview." MacKenzie and Clayton. 69–85.

———. "Interview." Schipper. 59–68.

———. "Interview: Starting from Scratch." Granqvist and Stotesbury. 74–79.

Tong, Rosemarie. *Feminist Thought: A Comprehensive Introduction*. Boulder: Westview, 1989.

Trinh T. Minh-ha, "Interview," with Parmar. 65–74.

———. "Not You/Like You: Post-Colonial Women and the Interlocking Questions of Identity and Difference." *Inscriptions* 3/4 (1988): 71–77.

———. "She: The Inappropriate/d Other." *Discourse* 8 (Fall-Winter 1986–87): 3–9.

———. *Woman, Native, Other: Writing Postcoloniality and Feminism*. Bloomington: Indiana UP, 1989.

Umeh, Davidson, and Marie Umeh. "Interview: Buchi Emecheta." *Ba Shiru* 12.2 (1985): 19–25.

Vignal, Daniel. "L'Homophilie dans le roman négro-africain d'expression anglaise et française." *Peuples Noirs/Peuples Africains* 33 (Mai-Juin 1983): 63–81.

Volet, Jean-Marie. "Calixthe Beyala, or The Literary Success of a Cameroonian Woman Living in Paris." *World Literature Today* 67.2 (Spring 1993): 309–14.

———. *La parole aux africaines ou l'idée du pouvoir chez les romancières d'expression française de l'Afrique sub-Saharienne*. Amsterdam: Rodopi, 1993.

———. "Romancières francophones d'Afrique noire: vingt ans d'activité littéraire à découvrir." *French Review* 65.5 (April 1992): 765–73.

wa Thiong'o, Ngugi. *Decolonising the Mind: The Politics of Language in African Literature*. London: James Currey, 1986.

———. *Moving the Centre: The Struggle for Cultural Freedoms*. London: James Currey, 1993.

Walker, Alice. *In Search of Our Mothers' Gardens: Womanist Prose*. San Diego: Harcourt Brace Jovanovich, 1983.

Walker, Cherryl. "Women and Gender in Southern Africa to 1945: An Overview." *Women and Gender in Southern Africa to 1945*. Ed. Cherryl Walker. London: James Currey, 1990. 1–32.

Wall, Cheryl A., ed. *Changing Our Own Words: Essays on Criticism, Theory, and Writing by Black Women*. New Brunswick, NJ: Rutgers UP, 1989.

Wallace, Karen S. "Women and Identity: A Black Francophone Female Perspective." *Sage* 2.1 (Spring 1985): 19–23.

Ward, Cynthia. "What They Told Buchi Emecheta: Oral Subjectivity and the Joys of 'Otherhood.'" *Publications of the Modern Language Association* 105.1 (1990): 83–97.

Waters, Harold A. "Black French Theatre Update." *World Literature Today* 57 (1983): 43–48.

Wilentz, Gay. *Binding Cultures: Black Women Writers in Africa and the Diaspora*. Bloomington: Indiana UP, 1992.

Wilkinson, Jane, ed. *Talking with African Writers*. London: James Currey, 1992.

Williams, Sally. "Tsisti Dangarembga's *Nervous Conditions*: At the Crossroads of Feminism and Post-Colonialism." *World Literature Written in English* 31.1 (1991): 103–12.

Wilson, Elizabeth. "The Portayal of Women in the Works of Francophone Women Writers from West Africa and the Caribbean." Diss. Michigan State U, 1985. Ann Arbor: UMI, 1986. 8607148.

Wittig, Monique. *Les Guérillères*. Trans. David Le Vay. Boston: Beacon Press, 1985.

———. *The Straight Mind and Other Essays*. Boston: Beacon Press, 1992.

Woolf, Virginia. *A Room of One's Own*. London: Hogarth Press, 1929.

———. *To the Lighthouse*. London: Hogarth Press, 1927.

Wylie, Hal, Dennis Brutus, and Juris Silenieks, eds. *African Literature (1988) New Masks*. Washington, DC: Three Continents Press, 1990.

Yoder, Carroll. *White Shadows: A Dialectical View of the French African Novel*. Washington, DC: Three Continents Press, 1991.

Young, Iris. "Is Male Gender Identity the Cause of Male Domination?" *Mothering: Essays in Feminist Theory*. Ed. Joyce Trebilcot. New Jersey: Rowman and Allanheld, 1983. 129–46.

Zabus, Chantal. "Criticism of African Literatures in English: Towards a Horizon of Expectation." *Revue de Littérature Comparée* 67.1 (Janvier-Mars 1993): 129–47.

Zanga Tsogo, Delphine. Interview. *Cameroon Tribune*, No. 2843 (Dec. 2, 1983): 2.

Index

feminist standpoint, 17, 157*n*10; on sex and women's pleasure, 25–28 *passim;* theory and practice, 32, 159*n*35; challenge of global sisterhood, 148
—African: criticism of male critics, 3, 6, 10; feminist consciousness, 6; anteriority of African indigenous, 10, 148; flexible gender ideologies, 23, 30
—French: the feminine and writing the body, 17, 157*n*8
—Radical: on sexual asymmetry, 22–23; and absolute male power, 45
—Third World: African women disapprove of, 9, 50–51; labeling at issue, 10–11, 12; different terminologies (misovire, Stiwanism, womanism), 12
Freud, Sigmund: phallic symbolization, 22–23

Generations of fictional women: group one at the end of colonialism, 36–37; group two and Western education, 51; group three, of educated parentage, 61

Heterosexuality: compulsory, 17, 157*n*7; and motherhood, 24; the marginalization of lesbian women, 24; *vs.* homosexuality in Africa, 29; rejection seen as separatist, 30. *See also* Homosexuality
Hilôlômbi: Bassa god and myth of creation, 102
Homosexuality: repression in Africa, 28, 29; silence of African critics, 28–29; silence in African literature, 29
—lesbian: on lesbian continuum, 90; continuum in Beyala, revised, 92; rejection of terminology, 164*n*17
—lesbianism: stereotyped and silenced, 29, 93; repression of women's homoerotic bonding, 31

Idemili: Igbo goddess, 23
Idu (Nwapa), 36

Jagua Nana (Ekwensi), 35

Kane, Cheikh Hamidou, 112

Lacan, Jacques: phallic symbolization, 23

Madness: women's contrary instincts and suicide, 70, 161*n*23; collective amnesia, 101. *See also* Motherhood

Makuchi: fiction writing (Cameroon anglophone), 162–63*n*1
Mandela, Winnie, 12
Manhater: in context, 95–97 *passim*
May 1968 revolts: in France and Senegal, 119
Métissage: defined in context, 120–22; crossbreeding, 121
—*gnouloule khessoule:* mulatto, 109; not white! not black!, métis, half-breed, mixed blood, café au lait, 120–21; half-caste, 136. *See also* Racism
Misogynist: in context, 96, 97, 99
Misovire: instead of feminist, 12; defined in context, 96–98, 100–101; literal meaning, 156*n*38. *See also* Feminism
Motherhood: criticism of, 24; and African nationalism, 34; and concepts of masculinity and femininity, 39; and madness, 37–40 *passim,* 55; and suicide, 41, 77; rebuttal of the joys of, 49; childlessness *vs.* woman-as-witch, 54; revolt against patriarchy, 92–93
The Mould: Magazine of Creative Writing, 162*n*1
Mvet: instrument/epic poem, 20

Naming: subversion of the Father's Law, 50; hyphenated identities, 85; namelessness as dehumanization, 124
Ndoto': Beba men's dance, 24
Ndzang: Beba women's dance, 24
Négritude: images of African women, 4–6; Mother Africa trope, 5–6; movement, 73, 110; and racism, 117; and black nationalism, 122
Ngugi wa Thiong'o: in context, ix; on language and colonized subjects, 162*n*25
Nsaa: defined in context, 57
Nwapa, Flora: woman of the lake, 35, 50

Oedipus complex, 38, 45, 111. *See also* the Phallus
OFUNC: Organisation des femmes de l'Union nationale camerounaise, 74
Oral traditions: women in Beba folktales, ix; oral artists, 2; oral literature and performance, 20–21 *passim;* deterrent of violence against women, 28; and naming, 50; oraliterature, 66; African literary aesthetic, 95–96; effects of detribalization on South African blacks, 133
—Bassa rituals: purification, 20, 98, 101, 105; initiation rites, 95; *meneur de rite,* 98
—oral histories: women as custodians of, 150
—storytelling: transmission of collective cul-

Juliana M. N. Abbenyi, Assistant Professor of English and Post-Colonial Literature in the Department of English at the University of Southern Mississippi, has contributed chapters to such books as *The Garland Book of Nature Literature, Postcolonial African Writers: A Bio-Bibliographical Sourcebook, Oral Literature in Africa Today,* and *The Politics of (M)Othering: Womanhood, Identity, and Resistance in African Literature.* She also writes fiction under the pen name Makuchi.